# EXORCISM AND DELIVERANCE

# EXORCISM AND DELIVERANCE

## Multi-Disciplinary Studies

edited by
William K. Kay and
Robin Parry

**British Library Cataloguing in Publication Data**

A catalogue record for this book is available from the
British Library

ISBN-13: 978-1-84227-764-5

Cover design by Paul Airy at DesignLeft (www.designleft.co.uk)

# Contents

# Studies in Pentecostal and Charismatic Issues

*Consultant Editors*: Max Turner, Andrew Walker
*Series Editors*: Mark J. Cartledge, Neil Hudson and Keith Warrington

*Studies in Charismatic and Pentecostal Issues* is a new series of academic monographs, which explore issues of interest to charismatic and Pentecostal scholars, students and leaders. The books will be multi-disciplinary covering:

- **Biblical** studies on the Spirit and spiritual gifts.
- **Historical** studioes on Pentecostal-charismatic Christianity.
- Pentecostal-charismatic **theological** studies.
- **Empirical** analysis of contemporary Pentecostal-charismatic Christianity.

# Contributors

**Allan Anderson** is Professor of Global Pentecostal Studies at the University of Birmingham, UK.

**Mark Cartledge** is Senior Lecturer in Pentecostal and Charismatic Theology at the University of Birmingham, UK.

**James Collins** is Pastor of Redhill Baptist Church in Surrey, UK.

**Andrew Daunton-Fear** is Lecturer in Church History at St. Andrew's Theological Seminary, Manila, Philippines.

**Kabiro Wa Gatumu** is Senior Lecturer in New Testament Studies, New Testament Greek, and African Biblical Hermeneutics at St. Paul's University, Limuru, Kenya.

**Lucy Huskinson** is Lecturer in Philosophy and Psychology of Religion at the School of Theology and Religious Studies at the University of Bangor, North Wales.

**William K. Kay** is Professor of Theology at Glyndwr University, Wrexham, North Wales.

**Wonsuk Ma** is the Executive Director of the Oxford Centre for Mission Studies, Oxford, UK.

**Robin Parry** is an Editor at the US-based publisher, Wipf and Stock. He works out of the city of Worcester, UK.

**Graham Twelftree** is Professor of New Testament at Regent University, Virginia Beach, USA.

**Peter Versteeg** is Project Coordinator at the Free University of Amsterdam, Holland, for the Institute for the Study of Religion, Culture and Society.

**Phillip H. Wiebe** is Professor of Philosophy at Trinity Western University, British Columbia, Canada.

**Nigel G. Wright** is Principal of Surgeon's College in London.

# Introduction

# Exorcism: Multi-Disciplinary Perspectives

## Robin A. Parry

Exorcism does not appear on the radar of many forms of Western Christianity. Typically believers will not encounter it in their churches, they will not see books about it, nor will they hear it spoken of in sermons or in prayers. It seems that the devil and his demonic hordes have been largely 'cast out' of many Western Christian worldviews – exorcised through the rite of deliberate amnesia.

The reasons for this loss of exorcism are many and varied but they certainly include the cultural marginalization of the Christian churches and traditions, horror stories in the media of abusive exorcisms past and present, the widespread rejection within the sciences of spirit-matter metaphysical dualism which was historically the framework within which talk of 'evil spirits' made sense, and the rise of alternative, psychological accounts of possession.

Critical here is the role of worldviews. Worldviews function as 'the glasses behind our eyes' *through which* we make sense of the world of our experience. Anthropologist Charles Kraft defines them as 'the culturally structured assumptions, values, and commitments underlying a people's perception of REALITY.'[1] Worldviews are normally accepted without question by those being brought up in a society. They equip people to explain things, to evaluate things, to assign priorities to things, and validate them in socially approved ways. Worldviews enable people to categorize reality, to know how to relate to different kinds of people, to

---

[1] C. Kraft, *Christianity With Power: Experiencing the Supernatural* (London: Marshall Pickering, 1990), 20. As is implicit in this quotation, Kraft is a critical realist in his epistemology.

understand the nature of causal relationships between events, and to conceptualize 'time', 'space' and 'material objects'. Normally we do not think *about* worldviews, we think *with* them; we do not look *at* them, we look *through* them. What strikes us as 'obviously true' or 'utterly unbelievable' is largely shaped by the worldviews into which we are inducted and through which we 'make sense' of things.

As far as demons go Western worldviews tend to classify them in the same category as 'goblins' and 'faeries'. For many modern westerners it does not seem remotely plausible to speak of angels and demons as *real* entities acting in the real world. So when it comes to explaining the cause of an event in the world westerners will instinctively explain it in terms of natural causes or human causes but will only turn to 'supernatural' causes as a last resort, if at all. And whilst westerners might make room for God as an explanation for an event they are less likely to appeal to a spirit (whether an angel, a demon, an animal spirit, or the spirit of a dead person). So when one comes to look at a case of apparent demonic possession and ask the question, 'What is causing this?' the natural inclination of the westerner will be to look for a *non-supernatural* explanation. And even if one cannot be found, many would still be inclined to believe that such an explanation is there awaiting discovery. It's a worldview thing.

In large part, the demonic now only remains in mainstream Western thinking as a metaphor (e.g., 'John wrestled with his inner demons') or within fictional genres such as horror, fantasy, or sf. The essay in this volume by Lucy Huskinson traces the presentation and perception of possession and exorcism in Western popular culture – movies, TV, literature, and music – from the early 1970s through to the 21st C. She shows very clearly how over a comparatively short space of time attitudes moved from a social context in which possession was viewed with genuine fear (with the possessing demon serving as a symbolic monster onto which society projected its anxiety and fear about disturbing social changes amongst the young – changes that people could not control) to one in which it was considered funny.[2] Huskinson's chapter illustrates very well how popular attitudes to possession and

---

[2] We ought to stress that Huskinson's psychological explanation for the function of representations of demons in popular culture does not rule out the existence of real demons and real possession. It is an attempt to account for the social function of popular representations of the demonic and the monstrous rather than an attempt to 'explain away' the phenomenon of possession per se. The account can be accepted wherever one stands on the reality of demons and possession.

exorcism must be socially located to be understood. Those who persist in maintaining the existence of actual demons outside of the world of fiction are treated as odd or perhaps even slightly dangerous – the kind of people liable to psychologically terrorize vulnerable people. There is very little social reinforcement for the 'superstitious' belief in possession outside of enclaves such as churches. Consequently, the default presumption of many, although often expressed with some degree of hesitancy, is that demonic oppression and exorcism can be explained psychologically. In such a context many Christians are understandably inclined to feel somewhat embarrassed about possession and to sideline the role of exorcism.

Given the minor role that deliverance ministry plays in many forms of contemporary Western Christianity (see chapters 4 and 12 for some exceptions to this) it comes as something of a shock for westerners to discover just how prominent it was in the ministry of Jesus, in the history of the Church, and indeed for perhaps most Christians in the Majority World today. In this volume, Wonsuk Ma shows that whilst we find little about exorcism in the Old Testament, the roots of later belief and practise can be clearly seen there. Moving into the New Testament Graham Twelftree's chapter demonstrates that exorcism was *the cornerstone* of Jesus' ministry. Even the most sceptical NT scholars acknowledged that the historical Jesus was known as an exorcist for whom casting out demons was integral to his message about the kingdom of God. Twelftree argues that this ministry of exorcism was taken up by Jesus' followers, although for various reasons it was more central in some early Christian circles than in others. Andrew Daunton-Fear explores the place of deliverance from demons in the early Church showing how important it was in the first five centuries and tracing the fascinating ways in which the ministry of deliverance developed in those formative years. Moving into the modern world Allan Anderson focuses on Majority World Pentecostalism and reveals just how significant freedom from the demonic is for many Christians in South America, Africa, and Asia. Anderson also shows that deliverance ministry as practised amongst different groups is culturally contextualized. James Collins examines the place of exorcism in certain streams of the Charismatic movement in the 20th century western world which resisted the flight from belief in spirit possession. And one could easily have supplemented the historical chapters in this book with many others on the period from 6th C to 19th C to reinforce the idea that deliverance from demons used to be far more prominent in Christian life than western Christians might imagine. Also, whilst this book focuses primarily on the Pentecostal and Charismatic movements (especially chapters 4 and 5), there is plenty that could also be said about contemporary trends in the more liturgical exorcistic traditions such as are found in the Roman Catholic Church.[3] Indeed, the iconic image of the exorcist in the West is still very much that of the Catholic priest. So we can safely say that the vast majority of Christians, past and present, have taken the command to 'cast out demons' very seriously indeed.[4] For this reason alone the topic ought to create interest and give contemporary western Christians pause for thought.

## Marks of possession

It is worth taking the time to outline some of the features that mark possession. In chapter 6 Peter Versteeg explains that amongst cultural anthropologists the notion of 'spirit possession' is a somewhat wider concept than it is in Christian theology. When Christians speak of 'possession' they are almost always referring to the idea that an evil spirit from Satan is afflicting someone in a harmful way. If someone is possessed then the spirit needs to be 'cast out'. Cultural anthropologists, however, view such possessions as a subset of a wider cross-cultural category of spirit possession.[5] For many peoples the spirits that possess *need not* be hostile spirits. Indeed possession by some spirits is viewed as a positive thing that is actively sought after. This idea is not wholly alien to Christianity for, as Versteeg points out, being 'possessed' by the Holy Spirit is viewed in some Christian circles as highly desirable. Montan, the founder of Montanism, purportedly speaking in the voice of the Holy Spirit, said, 'Behold, man is like a lyre, and I come flying into him like a plectrum – the man sleeps, and I am waking.'[6] Here the Spirit is playing the role of *possessing* spirit. One thinks also of the Old Testament stories in which the Spirit of God came upon various

---

[3] Exorcism and deliverance are an ongoing concern in such traditions. For instance, the Roman Catholic Church revised its official Latin rite of exorcism – 'De Exorcismus et Supplicationibus Quibusdam' ('Of All Kinds of Exorcisms and Supplications') – as recently as 1999.

[4] Bourguignon's 1973 study of 488 sample societies found some kind of possession belief in 77% of them (Bourguignon, 'Possession and Trance' in Carl Ember and Melvin Ember, *Encyclopaedia of Medical Anthropology: Health and Illness in the World's Cultures* (Springer, 2003), 137).

[5] Erika Bourguignon, 'Possession and Trance', 137-45.

[6] St Epiphanius, Haer., 48, 4, ii, quoted in Traugott K. Oesterreich, *Possession and Exorcism* (New York: Causeway Books, 1974), 75.

ecstatic prophets who seemed to lose control of themselves and began prophesying (1 Sam 10:1–13; 19:18–24). That said, it ought to be pointed out that most experiences of the Holy Spirit for most Christians – Charismatic and Pentecostal Christians included – are not of this 'possession trance' variety.

Traugott Oesterreich's work on *Possession and Exorcism*, first published in 1921, is still very helpful in getting a clearer grasp of the phenomena of possession.[7] Oesterreich examined hundreds of reports of possession and exorcism past and present and sought to distil from them common features.

The 'first and most striking characteristic is that the patient's organism appears to be invaded by a new personality; it is governed by a strange soul.'[8] This can be manifested in three ways: First, through a new physiognomy – the patient's features are changed. Second, through a changed voice with intonation that corresponds to the new personality – in particular, deeper voices are common. Third, the normal 'self' of the patient is displaced and a new 'ego' speaks in its place. This new 'person' is often foul mouthed and opposes socially accepted ethical and religious ideas.

> These important psychological phenomena are usually [N.B. not always] accompanied by others, foremost among which are strongly marked motor ones. The affective disorder of the possessed is translated by their movements, which equal in intensity those of veritable raving madmen . . . The movements are partially deprived of sense; they consist in a disordered agitation of the limbs, with contortions and dislocation in the most impossible directions – the body is bent backwards like a bow, etc. The proof that they are not due to simulation or voluntary action is that such contortions cannot, as a rule, be executed voluntarily.[9]

The *strength* of the possessed person is also beyond that of people in a non-possessed state and often, when religious rituals are brought to bear in exorcism, the violent movements of the patient increase.

The possessing spirit can speak as a demon or, less typically in Christian contexts, as the spirit of a dead person or an animal. The invading personalities speak through the patient in the first person. As far as the patient is concerned they may or may not be aware of what

---

[7] Oesterreich, *Possession*.

[8] Oesterreich, *Possession*, 17.

[9] Oesterreich, *Possession*, 22-23.

is happening. In some cases a person is fully conscious of switching back and forth between their normal personality and the spirit personality. Oesterreich refers to this as the 'Lucid form of possession'.[10] Here the patient is a passive spectator of what takes place within. She feels the switch from one personality to the other but these states have the character of compulsion and she cannot control it. One moment she is her normal self, the next she is the demon. Her soul feels divided.[11]

More typically, when the spirit is manifesting, the person loses consciousness and is not aware what is happening.[12] Oesterreich refers to this form of possession as 'the somnambulistic form of possession'.[13] On awakening they will have no memory of the activity of the spirit. In both cases the switch from one personality to the other is not gradual but instantaneous.

Oesterreich has been describing what anthropologists refer to as 'possession trance'. Peter Versteeg notes that anthropologists also speak of 'possession belief'. For physical changes to be interpreted as possession, a possession belief – a concept of spirit possession and what it looks like – must be available. Obviously nobody can observe a spirit directly and all that can be seen is the behaviour of the patient as described above. People – both the patient and observers – may interpret certain behaviour by a patient as spirit possession. And, as Versteeg points out, possession beliefs may be used to interpret non-trance behaviour, such as sickness or sterility, as being due to the interference of spirits. Such is referred to by some anthropologists as

---

[10] Oesterreich, *Possession*, 40-90.

[11] Oesterreich does not himself believe in spirit possession. He sees the lucid form of possession as the clue to what is going on. In lucid possession the states of consciousness of both the personalities belong to the patient. How else, he reasons, would the patient experience them both as it where 'from the inside'? He believes that all possession is best conceived of as a *division within the psyche of an individual* rather than an invasion from an alien consciousness.

[12] Oesterreich, *Possession*, 32. Although amnesia is frequently associated with possession trance it is not linked with trance where possession is absent (Bourguignon, 'Possession and Trance', 138). For instance, Peter's vision in Acts 10. Geographic and gender distribution is interesting here. 'While the most prominent form of sacred altered state of consciousness in North America is Visionary Trance, in Africa it is Possession Trance. Visionary Trance is more likely to be found among men. Possession Trance among women' (Bourguignon, 'Possession and Trance', 138).

[13] Oesterreich, *Possession*, 39.

'non-trance possession'. Certainly many Christians have also wanted to speak of demonic afflictions which are distinguished from possession proper. Pentecostals, for instance, would typically distinguish 'demonic possession' (in which a spirit takes control of a person from within) from 'demonic oppression' (in which a spirit afflicts a person from without).[14] Indeed, as Mark Cartledge discusses in chapter 12, some Charismatics have wanted to avoid the language of possession altogether and to speak instead of various degrees of demonization. Similarly the Church of England's Exeter Report, published in 1965, spoke in terms such as 'demonic interference' rather than 'possession'. Other Christians may retain the use of the concept of 'possession' but only for extreme forms of demonization. The point is that the influence of spirits upon people is often thought to be broader than the type of full scale possessions described by Oesterreich. This is evident in Andrew Daunton-Fear's chapter on the Early Church where we can see that the early Christians often believed that demons were to be found influencing most or all pagans whether or not they exhibited the 'classic' signs of possession (and one presumes that most did not). In this volume we will bear in mind 'non-trance possession' (i.e., demonic influence that falls short of full scale 'possession') whilst giving due attention to full scale 'trance possession'.

## Possession and exorcism as 'embodied' and 'enmeshed'

Why present *multi-disciplinary* studies on deliverance and exorcism? Is it not a topic that belongs to the realm of theology? Behind this question lies a suspicion that if we let 'secular' disciplines start messing around with 'religious' subjects they will undermine Christian theological accounts. There is some legitimacy to this concern because, as every good postmodern will tell you, academic disciplines are not worldview-free-zones and anti-theological bias can creep into the foundational assumptions of some studies.

Nevertheless, Christian theology itself legitimizes the attempt to draw on insights from non-theological disciplines. This is because a biblically-informed Christian theology sees human life as fundamentally *embodied* and *enmeshed*. In the Bible humans are not disembodied

---

[14] Different Pentecostals and Charismatics work with different typologies (e.g., M. Scanlan – temptation, opposition, bondage; H.A.M. Whyte – oppression, obsession, possession).

spiritual creatures who happen to sit inside bodies like drivers in cars. Humans are embodied, psycho-physical creatures. We are certainly more than mere physical beings (at least if 'physical' is understood in a reductionist way) but we are certainly *not less* than physical creatures.[15] So it is that Christian eschatological hope has always been for the resurrection of the *body* and not, contrary to popular belief, for the soul to leave the body and go to heaven.

Humans, biblically understood, are also completely *enmeshed* in social and cultural contexts. We are beings-in-relation. Contemplating humans in a Cartesian fashion apart from their historical, social, cultural, and geographical context is fruitless. Our very identities are, to a significant extent, narrative identities shaped by the social locations we inhabit. This biblical recognition of the embodied and enmeshed nature of human life has implications for openness on the part of theologians to insights from other disciplines for such disciplines can focus specifically on the bodily and social nature of being human. Whilst, from a Christian perspective, they can only offer incomplete accounts of phenomena they nevertheless offer real enlightenment. They offer insights that both Christian theology and Christian practice needs to take on board.

Coming back to demonic oppression and exorcism we need to appreciate the way in which those phenomena are embodied and enmeshed. Possession is something that happens to *embodied* people. If demons did nothing but sit on benches looking at the view they would be of no concern to us. Indeed, one wonders whether it even *makes sense* to think of demons sitting on benches.[16] As Tom Noble points out: 'we need to start here from the obvious, and consequently often unnoticed, fact that in

---

[15] This is the case whether one is a 'soft dualist' or a 'non-reductive physicalist'. On soft dualism see John Cooper, *Body, Soul and Everlasting Life: Biblical Anthropology and the Monism-Dualism Debate* (Grand Rapids: Eerdmans, 1989). On non-reductive physicalism see Warren S. Brown, Nancey Murphey and H. Newton Malony (eds.), *Whatever Happened to the Soul? Scientific and Theological Portraits of Human Nature* (Minneapolis: Fortress Press, 1998); Joel B. Green, *Body, Soul and Human Life: The Nature of Humanity in the Bible* (Milton Keynes: Paternoster, 2008).

[16] It may possibly be meaningful if we are talking metaphorically about the potential for demonization if one sits on the bench. To take a more serious example, it might be that a Christian could believe that demons dwell at a certain pagan altar. This might be taken to mean not that the demon is actually present when nobody else is there but that if someone participates in an altar-activity (which is understood by the Christian as an act of idolatry)

the Synoptics and Acts demons are never encountered in mid-air or anywhere other than in the human psyche. They are always found, without exception, inhabiting human beings and making them behave in ways which remind us of mental illness.'[17] Amos Yong similarly comments: 'A demonic spirit is nothing . . . if not personally incarnate in demoniacs and is irrelevant if not manifest concretely in time and space.'[18] People (and in one biblical case, pigs) get 'demonized' and therefore this condition – however we try to account for it – is utterly embodied. We must also bear in mind that 'possession' afflicts people and people are socially and culturally located. The *meaning* of what is happening to them – how they, and those around them, 'make sense' of it and deal with it – is construed within such contexts.

As such, possession and exorcism can be considered from a variety of disciplinary perspectives. For instance, it seems obvious to us that during 'possession' electro-chemical events are happening in the afflicted person's brain. That is simply part of what it is to be the kind of physical creatures that we are. So neurologists would have *something* of relevance to contribute to our understanding of possession and exorcism.[19] They would be able to offer perspectives of interest. It might be that certain parts of the brain are linked with the experience

---

(cont.) then one is opening oneself up to the demonic. In that sense it might be meaningful to speak of a demon being in a certain place at time x when that demon is not effecting any embodied people at time x. Alternatively, it might make sense to imagine a demon, which is not spatially located any where, focusing its attention on a certain spatial location and bringing about particular physical effects there. For instance, it might cause a door to slam in John's room. On such a view, assuming it is coherent, we might say that the demon is 'in John's room' even though it is not spatially located there.

[17] Tom Noble, 'The Spirit World: A Theological Approach' in A.N.S. Lane (ed.), *The Unseen World: Christian Reflections on Angels, Demons and the Heavenly Realm* (Carlisle: Paternoster/Grand Rapids: Baker, 1996), 209.

[18] Amos Yong, *Beyond the Impasse: Toward a Pneumatological Theology of Religions* (Grand Rapids: Baker/Carlisle: Paternoster, 2003), 138.

[19] There is very little work in this area but do see 'Electroencephalographic Measurement of Possession Trance in the Field,' by Tsutomu Oohashi, Norie Kawai, Manabu Honda, Satoshi Nakamura, Masako Morimoto, Emi Nishina and Tadao Maekawa in *Clinical Neurophysiology* 113 (2002), 345-445. In their study 'a portable . . . EEG telemetry system was developed to record the EEGs of three healthy male Balinese while they were performing a ritual dedicatory drama in the field . . . During the drama, one of the subjects became possessed while the others did not. The EEG of the

of 'demonization'. This in and of itself does not 'explain away posses-sion' because one *might* argue that demons act directly on the human brain, or perhaps indirectly through *naturally* caused brain malfunc-tions. And it is not just neurology. Very obviously, given the way in which possession is something that impacts a person's mental life and behaviour, the discipline of Psychology will have perspectives and insights worthy of serious reflection. There are some studies from cog-nitive psychologists, for instance, which strongly suggest that humans have a natural inclination towards body-soul dualism and towards belief in spirit beings – we have to be educated *out* of such beliefs more than *in* to them.[20] Now, of course, one cannot deduce the truth or fal-sity of those beliefs from such a fact, if fact it be. Nevertheless, such research does hold promise for a deeper understanding regarding beliefs about demons. Similarly possession and exorcism take place in historical and socio-cultural contexts. We would thus expect disci-plines such as History, Sociology, Cultural Studies, Religious Studies, and Anthropology to make insightful contributions to our under-standing.

Now none of this requires us to naively presume that these various disciplines are methodologically neutral. The psychology of Freud, for instance, was anti-theistic in its very roots and this foundational bias has implications for how reliable Christians and other theists will judge its proposals.[21] But even granted an awareness of the religious non-neutrality of such academic work this does not, in and of itself, mean that it can be dismissed out of hand. Christians still need to care-fully consider it because genuine insights onto aspects of God's cre-ation can still come that way. To take Freud as an example, whist his theories about belief in God and demon possession (on which see

---

(cont.) possessed subject did not show any pathological findings including epileptic discharges, but indicated enhanced power in the theta and alpha frequency bands during the trance. This finding was not observed in the other two subjects, who did not go into trances, with no pathological EEG findings' (Abstract).

[20] See the overview in Patrick Richmond, 'Scientific Explanations of Religious Experience and Their Implications for Belief', *Science and Christian Belief*, forthcoming.

[21] Indeed when Freud gets onto the topic of religion his theories seem to attract attention more for their shock and 'fun' value than because there is much by way of evidence to think that he is right (see Alvin Plantinga's cri-tique in *Warranted Christian Belief* (New York: Oxford University Press, 2000).

chapter 7) are not very plausible, some of his thinking on the unconscious is genuinely revolutionary and may be of some relevance to understanding possession and deliverance ministry.

One issue right at the heart of the theological appropriation of insights from non-theological disciplines concerns so-called 'methodological naturalism'. God will not form part of the explanations for phenomena offered by such disciplines. You won't catch, say, physicists, biologists, sociologists, historians, geologists, meteorologists, anthropologists, or neurologists saying, *when speaking in the capacity of their respective disciplines*, 'This happened because God did it'. God does not form part of the explanatory framework of such areas of scholarship. However, we must not imagine that this is because such disciplines actually presuppose the truth of *metaphysical atheism*. 'Methodological naturalism' historically developed amongst natural philosophers (what we now call scientists) who were metaphysical theists.[22] Christian theology has long embraced the idea that events that happen in the world have both secondary causes (i.e., causes *within the world*) and a primary cause (God). The natural sciences simply provided explanations of secondary causes and hence were no threat to theological explanations. So it made perfect sense for a scientist who was a Christian to explain a rain storm in meteorological terms without any reference to God, whilst at the same time acknowledging that God was indeed the primary cause of the rain storm.

However, things are not quite so simple when it comes to actions claimed to be caused by 'spiritual' beings that are part of the created order. For instance, Descartes famously saw a human being as essentially a non-physical (and hence, non-spatially-located) mind that intersected with the physical world through a body. Explanations for various actions on the part of human bodies would be found, according to Descartes, in the choices of the rational, non-physical minds controlling them. But, Descartes' dualistic interactionism *did* require gaps in the causal chain of events. For instance, consider the question, Why did John's hand wave? If there was a successful causal explanation (that made no appeal to a non-physical mind) for the hand on John's body to wave then John's 'mind', at least as understood by Descartes, was done out of a job. We have what could be called the 'mind of the gaps' where 'mind' is used to explain human behaviour for which we have no alternative scientific explanation. But, as science – especially

---

[22] See Denis Alexander, *Rebuilding the Matrix: Science and Faith in the 21ˢᵗ Century* (Oxford: Lion, 2001).

neurology – fills in the gaps and explains more and more in terms of brains there is less and less for the Cartesian mind to explain. The worry is that one day it may have nothing left to explain and will vanish into the ether. It is precisely such concerns, amongst others, that have led to a widespread rejection of Cartesian dualism and a plethora of alternative attempts to account for the mysterious reality of the human mind. No one can doubt the reality of mind. The tricky question concerns the nature of its reality? What is mind?

An analogous concern is raised with angels and demons if they are understood as something like 'non-physical, rational centres of consciousness'. Angels and demons are not, unlike God, the first cause of the universe. In Christian theology, they are very much a part of the created order – just as much as trees or goats or quarks. But how, as non-physical, non-spatially located beings, do they interact with the physical world? How do non-physical beings possess or afflict people? And, if we have an adequate scientific set of explanations for the behaviour of a 'demonised' person, is the demon done out of a job? To take the example from earlier – if we discover a physical cause for the brain events that underlie the possession experience, is an appeal to demons working through such physical causes rendered obsolete by Occam's razor? Is appeal to the demon no longer serving any explanatory role? If so, do we have a 'demon of the gaps' that is exorcized by science as those gaps are reduced and finally closed? Is there a need to rethink the nature of the demonic in the same way that many modern philosophers, scientists, and theologians are rethinking the nature of mind?

Here we are thrown into the heart of the issue regarding the ontology of the demonic. Possession is very obviously a real experience – we have countless well attested examples from all ages and cultures – but what kind of reality does the possessing spirit have? We might think of the options here in terms of three broad approaches:

1. traditional accounts of possession
2. reductionist accounts of possession
3. alternative accounts of possession

### Traditional accounts of possession

By 'traditional accounts of possession' I mean theological accounts according to which demons are non-physical persons that afflict human persons. Spirits – both good and evil – are here conceived as metaphysical substances that possess the capacity 'for thought, feeling, consciousness and volitional power'.[23] Their conscious states include sensations (obviously not caused by physical processes in the way that our perceptions of the world are, but more akin to dreams that correspond accurately to physical reality), thoughts, beliefs, desires, and acts of will.[24] Demons would not occupy physical space so if you cut open a person who was possessed you would not discover the demon inside. But they could be thought to be 'spiritually present' in a particular place by virtue of their focusing their attention on that place and exercising their will towards it in order to cause things to happen in that place. So it is the *activity* of a demon in a specific place that makes it 'present' there. This is not obviously an unintelligible idea.

These accounts will depend on some kind of ontological spirit-matter dualism with demons and human minds on the spirit side of the divide and bodies on the material side. Humans and perhaps some animals, occupying both spiritual and material dimensions of reality, will provide a doorway through which demons can manifest in the material world. Perhaps the demon will attach itself to the non-physical mind of the person and through that mind's interaction with its body it can engage the material world.[25] Alternatively, the demon might be thought capable of causing events *directly* in the physical world. They might, for instance, be thought to operate directly on the causal circuitry of the human brain in order to control people.[26]

There are some highly competent Christian philosophers and scientists who would defend the intelligibility and indeed probability of such an ontological dualism.[27] The case against dualism is not as overpowering as its critics often suppose and it is too soon to read the eulogy.

---

[23] J.P. Morland and Scott B. Rae, *Body and Soul: Human Nature and the Crisis in Ethics* (Downers Grove: IVP, 2000), 155.

[24] For an exploration of this see Peter S. Williams, *The Case for Angels* (Carlisle: Paternoster, 2002), 78-88.

[25] This is a Christian account. One could easily modify it to present an account from some alternative religion.

[26] This is the view of Christian philosopher Kevin Corcoran who has a materialist view of humans but sees demons as non-physical persons. Thus possession requires demons to directly cause physical events in the brain (email to me dated 15th February 2009).

[27] For instance, recent philosophical defenders of body-mind dualism include Richard Swinburne, Alvin Plantinga, and J.P. Moreland. Christians that are scientists tend to be more sceptical but science does not exclude the possibility of dualism. For instance, the esteemed Christian neuroscientist Sir John Eccles was a body-mind dualist.

Nevertheless, it remains very much a minority report amongst contemporary scientists and philosophers and the ever-present 'worry' as far as possession goes is that of the aforementioned 'demon of the gaps'. This is because the dualistic ontology means that 'any supernatural act in causal contact with the natural realm is a temporary exception to the natural causal order of things; that is, to what would have happened if the supernatural agent had not acted . . . "[Demonic actions] leave *scientifically detectable* gaps in the natural world".'[28] But, of course, this way of conceiving things means that a demonic explanation and a scientific explanation are placed in competition. If science is one day able to explain the apparent demonic activity then we must concede that it was not really demonic activity. Does dualism give a hostage to fortune?

A further problem with the idea of non-physical causes for physical events is that physical agents cause physical events by transmitting energy. The amount of energy in the universe is, according to physicists, constant and the energy being transmitted is already tied into a causal network. Where are the gaps in this physical web that allow a non-physical agent to either redirect energy or, more problematically, input new energy into the system? If non-physical agents are regularly inputting energy into the universe then the total amount of energy is increasing all the time (which runs counter to physics) and events will be regularly occurring for which there is no scientific explanation. This is a concern. However, many Christians have no problems whatsoever with the denial of causal closure and perhaps the dualist model is simply the sober truth about the world.[29]

---

[28]  Peter S. Williams, *The Case for Angels*, 84-85. Within this extract Williams quotes from J.P. Moreland. Body-mind dualists maintain that it is not only *possible* for physical events to be caused by immaterial things; it is, in fact, *very common.* Every time a human chooses to do something – such as pick up a pen – an immaterial thing (their mind) is causing a physical effect (in their brain which in turn causes their arm and hand to move). So if one accepts body-mind dualism as an intelligible and plausible position then one can accept the possibility of demonic action in the physical world as intelligible and perhaps plausible.

[29]  And there may be strategies to deal with the problem. It *might* be suggested, for instance, that there are open points of indeterminacy at a quantum level that are intrinsic to the nature of the world. *Perhaps* demons could determine certain quantum possibilities, which are fundamentally indeterminate, without adding new energy into the system. And whist the effects would be absolutely tiny, perhaps chaos theory (which is deterministic) could explain how such tiny events could end up having effects on a far bigger canvas.

## Reductionist accounts of possession

By 'reductionist accounts of possession' I intend that wide range of explanations of possession that reject the spirit-matter dualism presupposed by the traditional accounts and attempt to offer a plausible account in terms of natural causes. Such accounts will maintain that whilst possession *appears to be* the invasion of a person by an alien, non-physical entity, in fact *something else* is going on. The nature of that 'something else' will vary from one explanation to another, although it will almost certainly include some psychological element in it. Such accounts are offered as explanations of possession that do not appeal to demons ('possession is really *nothing but* x'). For instance, very few psychiatrists would seriously consider actual demons as part of an explanation for 'possession'. Indeed, the majority of phenomena associated with full blown possession – distinct personas within a single subject, convulsions, hearing voices, suicidal urges, deafness and dumbness, paranoia, hallucinations – can be readily explained in terms of psychiatric disorders. In chapter 7 William Kay overviews some of the attempts to offer such accounts from both psychology and psychiatry.

However, there remain features of some possession accounts which are very hard to account for in this way. Phillip Wiebe, in chapter 8, takes the case of the Gerasene/Gadarene demoniac as a paradigm example. What psychological explanation of possession can account for the 'suicide' of a herd of pigs at the very moment that Jesus exorcised the man from a legion of demons? David Instone-Brewer draws attention to possession stories in the gospels in which the demons knew things about Jesus which one would not expect the possessed people to know. Now in these cases it is always possible to argue that these features of the stories are literary and not historical. They are important in terms of communicating a theological point but they do not describe what actually happened. Perhaps. However, contemporary accounts of some possessions exhibit the same, hard to account for, features. Wiebe tells some stories of possessions which, if accurate, cannot be fully explained in terms of psychology. David Instone-Brewer similarly relates a story of how he abandoned his belief that *all* possessions are *purely* psychiatric disorders. He tells of the time that he was training as a medic with a special interest in psychiatry. He went to interview a patient who was lying on a bed, facing away from him. Instone-Brewer decided to pray silently for the man. The man, who could not have been aware of this, immediately sat bolt upright and said in a voice, not his own, 'Leave him alone – he belongs to us.'

Instone-Brewer was well aware that some hysterical conditions can mimic possession and that in such cases to treat a patient as if he really is possessed would simply compound the condition. So the trainee medic prayed silently. This prayer provoked a more violent outburst. To observers this would have appeared as a one-way conversation but after some non-audible prayer the man collapsed back on the bed with a scream. After that, he awoke with no memory of the event and 'in his right mind'. Instone-Brewer describes how on several subsequent occasions he has had similar encounters in which he would not speak audibly but would silently place questions to the spirits and they would answer them through the mouth of the possessed person.[30] It is very hard to adequately account for such things on the standard psychological explanations. As Wiebe argues, belief that something more – indeed something genuinely demonic – is going on in these cases is entirely rational.

This is not to suggest that defenders of traditional accounts would dismiss reductionist accounts out of hand. Indeed, they might be very happy to concede that many experiences of *apparent* possession are, in actual fact, nothing of the sort. Indeed, many who engage in exorcism would recognize that not everyone who *appears* to be demonized *really is*. For instance, Mark Cartledge shows in his examination of John Wimber's diagnostic for discerning the activity of demons that Wimber was clear that not all manifestations that *look* demonic *are* demonic (chapter 12). Kabiro Wa Gatumu's chapter also stresses the importance of discerning between true possession and other maladies which are very similar in appearance to possession. The dilemma for the practitioner then is the diagnostic problem. As Kay explains, 'It is very difficult to disentangle mental problems that present themselves with all the symptoms of demon possession from demon possession that induces mental problems.' And to cast a demon out of someone who does not have one could simply make their problem worse.

Indeed defenders of traditional accounts *might* think that reductionist accounts do not merely explain 'non-authentic possessions' but also shed *some* light on genuine cases of possession. Traditionalists might argue, for instance, that demons can create psychiatric problems in people and that the nature of those problems can be illuminated by insights from the human sciences (Wa Gatuma seems to take this view). To take

---

[30] David Instone-Brewer, 'Jesus and the Psychiatrists' in A.N.S. Lane (ed.), *The Unseen World: Christian Reflections on Angels, Demons and the Heavenly Realm* (Carlisle: Paternoster/Grand Rapids: Baker, 1996), 133-48.

an analogy, understanding something of the physical properties of water will illuminate the splash that a stone makes when thrown into a pond. In the same way, understanding something about the human mind may illuminate the way that it reacts to interference from a demon. Exploring exactly how insights from various disciplines might be integrated into traditionalist demonization accounts is a task which few seem to have undertaken. Perhaps that will change over the next few years.

### Alternative accounts of possession

By 'alternative accounts of possession' I mean accounts which seek to find ways to mediate between traditional accounts and reductionist accounts. There may be some very different ways in which this is attempted and this introduction aims simply to point towards a basic strategy rather than to offer an exhaustive typology. However, I would hazard to suggest that at the heart of alternative accounts is the idea of the demonic as something that would not exist without human minds and social structures but which cannot be simply reduced to them. So, on these accounts, demons were not 'sitting around' before the appearance of humanity waiting for something to do. Before humanity *there were no demons*. However, demons are real. They supervene upon human social structures and psyches and cannot be reduced to that upon which they supervene. They gain a reality that transcends it and they exercise real power over cultures and individuals. In the words of Tom Noble, 'It is rather as if a man's shadow, cast on the wall of a cave, has taken a life of its own as a terrifying genie which enslaves him.'[31]

Perhaps the most influential defender of this approach in Christian circles has been Walter Wink (on Wink see chapters 10 and 11). Wink describes how he moved away from the view that 'principalities and powers' could be '"demythologized", that is, rendered without remainder into the categories of modern sociology, depth psychology, and general systems theory.'[32] When all these reductionist explanations are finished there is always *more* to be said. There is something else about the demonic, something invisible, immaterial but, and Wink is at pains to stress this, *very real*.

To explore this 'surplus' Wink draws on the work of Carl Jung (on Jung, see chapter 7). Jung, following Freud, accepted the reality of

---

[31] Tom Noble, 'The Spirit World', 215.

[32] Walter Wink, *Naming the Powers* (Philadelphia: Fortress Press, 1984), 5.

'the unconscious', but Jung went further and spoke not only of the individual unconscious but of 'the *collective* unconsciousness'. We share this unconscious psychic reservoir with all humans across the globe. The collective unconscious is 'populated' with archetypes which might be thought of as potential patterns of thought, imagination, and behaviour. From the archetypes come the images which fill dreams, myths, and symbols. One of the archetypes Jung called 'the shadow' which is all that we refuse to accept about ourselves, repress, and project out onto others. For Wink, Satan and his demons are akin to archetypal realities. As they are rooted in the collective unconsciousness their reality transcends any individual. In other words, demons do not exist simply in the mind of an individual, even if they would not exist apart from human minds. And the demonic transcends the individual in another sense: 'Satan . . . is more than inner, because the social sedimentation of human choices for evil has formed a veritable layer of sludge that spans the world. Satan is both an inner and an outer reality.'[33] Here be 'demons as objective realities which are nevertheless in some way the function of the twisted perversion of fallen corporate humanity.'[34] In this volume Nigel Wright represents this tradition.[35]

Wink sees 'principalities and powers' as the spirituality and inwardness of institutions and social systems. When institutions such as governments act against divine intentions they behave in demonic ways and may be 'possessed'. Gordon Graham develops this idea through

---

[33] Walter Wink quoted in Cook, 'Devils and Manticores: Plundering Jung for a Plausible Demonology' in A.N.S. Lane (ed.), *The Unseen World*, 175. In this regard it is interesting to consider some of Michael Fishbane's comments on the serpent in Genesis 3: 'The serpent represents that part of the world and man resistant to a fixed order. It appears to be outside of man, stimulating his desires. But it is also a primordial, serpentine chaos coiled in the well of being. The serpent is with us in the world, without us in the world, and within us in the world.' *Biblical Texts and Texture: A Literary Reading of Selected Texts* (Oxford: One World, 1998, original edition, 1978), 23.

[34] Noble, 'The Spirit World', 213.

[35] Kabiro Wa Gatumu's proposal in chapter 11 that language about possession should be understood as irreducibly metaphorical – genuinely *referring* to demonic activity but not to be taken strictly *literally* – represents an interesting development of the traditional view (rather than an alternative account). It journeys a long way with Walter Wink's alternative account but refuses to embrace Wink's commitment to the ontological dependence of demons on human social structures.

reflection on the idea of 'the spirit of enterprise'.[36] If we wish to explain the economic development of the USA, part of such an explanation would be an appeal to 'the spirit of enterprise'. Graham argues that 'the spirit of enterprise' is no mere figure of speech since attempts to translate it into a non-figurative explanation fail.[37] Thus for Graham 'spirit of enterprise' has a real explanatory role, cannot be reduced to human agents (individually or collectively), and its operation can be described using the sort of language that we use of human agency. It is an irreducible *explanans*. Satan, as the 'spirit of evil', plays an analogous role in explaining how certain people, who are not obviously evil characters, can commit very evil acts (think of the Holocaust, Stalinism, the Rwandan genocide, the Columbine school shootings). Whilst explanations in terms of individual psychologies or sociological conditions give insight they fail miserably as complete explanations, and to point to Satan's work in seducing such people to sin has real explanatory power. This is one alternative account of the role of evil spirits in temptation and in the inspiration of evil acts that is not committed to a metaphysic in which demons would exist if humans did not.

When discussing *individual* possession alternative accounts might propose that the demonic spirits ruling over nations or smaller institutions can impact individuals in numerous ways, including in cases of classical possession. On this approach more leeway is given for the integration of psychological and theological accounts. Wink himself draws on the work of theorist René Girard.[38] He sees victims of 'outer personal demons' as people scapegoated by the pathological society in which they live. To take the case of the Gerasene demoniac: the local townspeople rage against Roman occupation but take out their fury against the man who serves as a scapegoat. The man internalizes their collective madness freeing them from their own symptoms. However, he now sees himself as occupied by the oppressive Roman Legions (note: 'my name is Legion') – understood as demonic hordes – and

---

[36] Gordon Graham, *Evil and Christian Ethics* (Cambridge: Cambridge University Press, 2001), ch. 5.

[37] He considers the following possibilities: 'spirit of enterprise' is really just (a) shorthand for the existence of large numbers of enterprising people, (b) a way of saying that lots of individuals subscribe to enterprising values and work together to realize their goals, (c) a way of referring to a cultural milieu. All these suggestions are problematic (*Evil*, 187-89).

[38] On Girard and Wink's use of him see Michael Willett Newheart, *"My Name is Legion": The Story and Soul of the Gerasene Demoniac* (Collegeville: Liturgical Press, 2004), ch. 5.

gashes himself with stones (seeking to cast out the demons?). The demons are the spirituality of the people. Outward possession is, in this case, the personal pole of a *social* malady. Freedom can only come when Jesus casts the Legion of demons out – unclean spirits fittingly sent into unclean pigs. Now these demons are clearly 'in the man's head' but they are not *merely* 'in his head'. Their reality transcends his individual psyche. But is there *even more* to demonic possession than this? Wink is agnostic but does admit that there does seem to be more to demonic evil than 'the collective shadow projected onto the scape-goat.'[39]

On alternative accounts the psyche of the possessed person as well as their social and cultural contexts will flavour their experience of possession. By analogy one might think of the way in which blue paint (the 'demonic spirit') can be mixed with yellow paint (aspects of a person's socially-located psyche) to create green paint (the demonic personality). If such a view could be developed intelligibly then one who held it would expect aspects of the possessed person's psyche and socio-cultural context to be taken up into the demonic personality. They would also expect genuine insight on the phenomena to be shed by psychology, sociology and so on.

One of the goals of this collection of multi-disciplinary studies is to further inform the ongoing reflection of the churches on the lessons that can be learned for the understanding of possession and the practise of deliverance ministry. We are not recommending specific conclusions so much as informing the debate and inviting further thought.

## The practise of deliverance

The stance one takes on the nature of possession will influence one's practise of exorcism. It should come as no surprise that the vast majority of those who see value in deliverance ministry will hold to a traditional account of possession. It is also not surprising that many of those who do not believe in demons think that exorcism is, at best, ineffective and, at worst, positively harmful. That said, some psychiatrists, who are themselves atheists, believe that the rite of exorcism can help some patients who believe themselves to be possessed. Not because these psychiatrists believe that God is at work

---

[39] Wink, *Unmasking the Powers*, 187.

overpowering the devil but because a patient who believes that exorcism will help them may indeed find that it can play a role in their healing.[40]

Do those who hold to alternative accounts make space for exorcism and deliverance? There is certainly some caution but also an openness. In chapter 10 Nigel Wright defends what he calls a non-ontological and yet realist view of demonic. However, whilst denying that there are personal creatures called 'demons' Wright believes that there is still a place for exorcism, albeit in a chastened form, in the ministry of the churches. In the planning stages of this book I talked to Dominic Walker, Bishop of Monmouth (and co-chair of the Church of England's Christian Deliverance Study Group). He has been involved in many cases of deliverance ministry over the years and tells some genuinely hair-raising stories of some of his experiences. Interestingly, he was clear that he was not inclined to believe that the demons he encountered were non-physical persons, but tended towards quasi-psychological explanations. Nevertheless he was firm in his conviction that God chooses to use the deliverance ministry to liberate some people from oppression.

> My position is that I believe that possession by some external evil is possible but in the thousand of cases that have come my way I cannot say that I have definitely seen it, (although I have had cases that defy explanation and where a person has responded to the rite of exorcism). I see deliverance ministry as embracing a number of therapeutic, sacramental, and healing practices rather than as some kind of Christian magic. I [think] that to reject [the view that] demons . . . are some kind of alien invaders is not to reject the demonic or the value of deliverance ministry or God's power to rid people of the effects of evil.[41]

Now it might well be that some readers will believe that Bishop Walker has actually been encountering some real demons without recognising it. Be that as it may, what is perhaps more interesting is that here we have a practitioner active in delivering people from 'the demonic' in the name of Christ, who has seen some real success in this ministry *even though* he is inclined to understand 'the demonic' in non-traditional ways.

---

[40] 'Exorcism: Abuse or Cure?' *The Guardian* 2nd May 2001.
[41] Email to me dates 13th Feb 2009.

*Wise practise*

Two critical issues of pastoral concern in this area are (a) knowing when someone needs deliverance ministry, and (b) knowing how to minister to a person in a responsible, accountable way. There are no shortage of real life 'horror' stories of enthusiastic Christians seeking to exorcise people who did not need it or of performing exorcisms in truly inappropriate ways. Mark Cartledge and Kabiro Wa Gatumu begin to touch on this their chapters. Cartledge examines John Wimber's diagnostic and seeks to improve on it in light of the earlier chapters of this book. In particular he suggests that what psychologists refer to as Dissociative Identity Disorder makes some of Wimber's criteria for discerning demonic activity inadequate and in need of refinement.[42]

More traditional churches offer an interesting model here and Pentecostals and Charismatics would be wise to consider their guidelines. For instance, the Church of England seeks to walk the fine line between rejection of exorcism and irresponsible practise. Through the 20th century there was some embarrassment about the subject within the Church but during the 1960s there was an explosion of interest in the occult and possession and Church of England priests were inundated with requests for exorcisms. In 1963 the Bishop of Exeter convened a group of theologians and clergy to consider the question of exorcism and in 1972 *Exorcism: The Report of a Commission Convened by the Bishop of Exeter* (edited by Dom Robert Petitpierre) was made available to the public. It has proven to be a landmark document, the impact of which is still felt in the Church of England. Amongst its recommendations were the following:

---

[42] Of course, one perennial problem for any attempt at diagnosis is that there are no unequivocal criteria for determining whether the diagnosis of demon possession is accurate. Most of the typical symptoms of possession can also be symptoms of conditions other than possession. And even a failure to achieve permanent recovery is not a sure guide. If the diagnosis of demonization *is* accurate, then delivered people may return to wrongdoing and be reinhabited by demons (seven spirits return to the clean house, Matt. 12:45); if it is *inaccurate*, then the person receiving ministry is either going to feign deliverance to escape the situation or respond in some pathological way to the treatment to which he or she has been subjected. This diagnostic conundrum is one of the ongoing challenges for responsible deliverance ministry.

- Until one has reason to believe otherwise, one should assume that the patient's illness has a physical or psychological cause. Even in cases where medical treatment fails to alleviate the condition, one should not rush to a diagnosis of demonic interference.
- The individual should be referred to a 'competent physician in psychological medicine' (p. 23). Only after the patient has undergone a thorough psychological and physical examination, and has then been examined by a licensed exorcist, should an exorcism be performed, if it is then deemed necessary.
- The examining exorcist should be experienced in such matters, acting under the authority of the Bishop. The Report stressed the importance of getting permission from the diocese Bishop for each exorcism of persons.[43]
- the other members of the exorcism team should consist only of 'mature Christian people who are sympathetic to this ministry' (p. 35). There should be individuals present capable of restraining the subject if in the course of the exorcism it should become necessary. Furthermore, if the individual to be exorcised is a woman, there ought to be at least one other woman present in the event that restraint is required.
- animals and children should be removed from the house beforehand, after first giving them a blessing.
- Preferably, a deep armchair should be provided for the subject during the service in order to minimize the risk of injury.
- It is recommended that a physician and/or psychiatrist be present, if possible.
- In addition, the exorcist must be ready to dismiss at any time any individual whose presence proves inappropriate, including himself, should he discover that he is incapable of dealing with the demands of the exorcism. For this reason, it is advisable to have another priest present.
- 'The exorcist should be open to the possibility that after the exorcism other sacramental means of grace would be appropriate: e.g. Holy Communion, Holy Unction, and perhaps even Baptism' (p. 37).[44]

---

[43] In the Roman Catholic Church the guidelines are much the same. Canon 1172 states 'No one may lawfully exorcise the possessed without the special permission of the local Ordinary [Bishop]. This permission is to be granted by the local Ordinary only to a priest who is endowed with piety, knowledge, prudence and integrity of life.'

[44] I was helped in this section by Linda Malia, 'A fresh look at a remarkable document: *Exorcism: The report of a commission convened by the Bishop of Exeter'*. *Anglican Theological Review* (Winter 2001).

The Report recommended the appointment of a diocesan exorcist for each diocese; and, the establishment of centers of training for each diocese. Since the 1980s, the majority of Church of England dioceses possess a deliverance ministry team. There is also an annual training conference arranged by the Christian Deliverance Study Group (formerly Christian Exorcism Study Group) to which Bishops send suitable priests and lay people for training. The training conference is staffed by priests experienced in deliverance ministry and also by psychiatrists so as to provide a holistic training.

After the infamous Barnsley case,[45] the House of Bishops in 1975 produced five guidelines for the exorcism of people. They are that this ministry must be done:

1. in collaboration with the resources of medicine
2. in the context of prayer and sacrament
3. with the minimum of publicity
4. by experienced people authorized by the Bishop
5. with continuing pastoral care after the exorcism[46]

These guidelines were again commended in the report *A Time to Heal* published in 2000 and approved by the General Synod so they are the current guidelines for the Church of England and constitute 'good practice'.[47] They would be the benchmark for any legal action that might be taken following an exorcism.

The Church of England's approach will strike many Pentecostals and Charismatics as over-cautious, over-controlling, and in danger of missing some demonic attacks through fear of misdiagnosis. Perhaps it is. On the other hand, many, though by no means all, Pentecostal and Charismatic groups suffer with the opposite problem and are in danger of harming as many people as they help. The task of discerning and dealing with demons – however they are conceived – is often left to

---

[45] In 1974, 31 year old Michael Taylor of Barnsley returned home after a night in which an exorcism had been performed on him at a church in the town. The exorcism had not been authorized by the Bishop. On returning home he killed his wife by mutilating her, and then in court claimed that he was sane until he was exorcised.

[46] *Report of Proceedings*, General Synod, 6 no 2 July 1975.

[47] Chapter 9 of *A Time to Heal* (Church House Publishing, 2000) provides the latest authoritative position of the Church of England on Deliverance Ministry. My thanks to Bishop Dominic Walker for help with this section on the Church of England's Guidelines.

people who are ill prepared and poorly accountable. The ministry of deliverance has always been an important part of the ministry of the churches but precisely because of its potential for abuse it is critical that it is exercised with responsibility. Pentecostal and Charismatic churches need to give more attention to safeguarding good pastoral practice in this important area. If these multi-disciplinary studies can initiate some further reflection on, amongst other things, good and bad practice then that can only be for the good.

Christians from the period of the New Testament church and on through the first centuries did not follow a single, fixed approach to exorcism (see chapters 2 and 3). Different churches placed different emphases on the practice, understood it in slightly different ways, and engaged in it in a variety of manners. Thus it was and thus it remains. And diversity is no bad thing because exorcism, like Christian theology and praxis in general, must always seek to be contextualized. Allen Anderson's chapter shows us how the understanding of possession and the practice of exorcism is culturally contextualized in modern day Majority World Pentecostalism. That is precisely why such Spirit-Christianity has been so successful in allowing the gospel to impact the felt needs of diverse peoples across the globe. One task for the church in all times and places is to ask afresh how demonic evil should be understood and opposed in the name of Christ. Our prayer is that this book will in some small way contribute to such ongoing reflections for contemporary churches.

# Chapter 1

# The Presence of Evil and Exorcism in the Old Testament

*Wonsuk Ma*

**Abstract**

This study examines selected passages to determine how ancient Israelites understood the root of evil particularly with reference to supernatural forces such as demons, spirits, and Satan. Such forces are presented within an overwhelming theological framework of God's sovereignty and superiority, and so they operate under God's strict control. Therefore, Israel's religious tradition did not develop a systematic response to them, although a few suggestions may be drawn from the passages. Only in the post-exilic era is a spiritual force opposing God's authority introduced.

This present study examines Old Testament reflections on evil – often conceptualized in terms of demons, evil spirits, and Satan – and how the people of God understood it and countered its presence. Their understanding certainly reflects their worldview, shaped by their religious traditions, with influence from neighboring cultures and religions. It also reflects their own identity as they related to their God Yahweh.

Several groups of relevant passages will be studied in their literary and, if it is discernable, their social context. The latter concern is important, although often challenging because of the developmental nature of any Old Testament concept due to its long period of evolution through various social and religious settings. Also several parallels will be drawn from the religions/worldviews and general folkloric traditions of the people groups that surrounded Israel. For several obvious reasons, the New Testament will not be included in this discussion. Chapter 2 will fill that gap, but more importantly the Old Testament evidence should be interpreted in its own right without any heavy influence of New Testament usage.

## Evil in the Old Testament

The Old Testament presents at least two distinct levels of thought. The first is the official theology constructed by the hands of the religious and social establishments, represented by prophets and priests, and scribes. All the major theological ideologies are such official products. The existence of good and evil according to this established theology is under God's absolute control, as evidenced by the lack of any primordial struggle motif in the act of creation in Genesis 1 – light and darkness are *both* God's creation. This is, no doubt, part of Israel's constant effort to claim the absolute supremacy of its God, Yahweh. The Yahwist's monotheistic presentations of God leave no room for any spiritual beings other than God and his messengers. In this level, even if the existence of personified evil is admitted, its work comes under God's strict control, and little room is left for any dualistic notion of good and evil, or God and his foe, in conflict.

However, the other important source of Israel's thoughts is folkloric traditions, often freely shared with its surrounding cultures. Evidence of its constant influence on Hebrew theological construction is often found in phraseologies and imageries. Although often 'refined' or appropriated by established theological hands, nonetheless traces of folkloric influence are evident. In many allusions to creation, for example, not only is there such a foe as a deep sea, dragons, and other forces, but also God is presented as having to subdue such before creation properly takes place. It is in this 'popular' level of Israel's thought where a lively interaction with the forces of evil is expected and negotiated. Many Psalms such as Ps 74 include such popular level beliefs.

> It was you who split open the sea by your power; you broke the heads of the monster in the waters. It was you who crushed the heads of Leviathan and gave him as food to the creatures of the desert (Ps. 74:13–14).

The most common representation of the evil force is by water, especially deep sea water which sea monsters are believed to inhabit.[1] Deep water is also associated with the idea of darkness and chaos. Often scholars point out a parallel with Mesopotamian creation myths such as Enuma Elish where Marduk, the creation deity, has to slay Tiamat, the deep sea goddess.[2] However, it was Hermann Gunkel who explored the powerful influence of folklore as perhaps being the oldest form of narrative, to the Old Testament.[3] Folklore by nature is universal or international. This universal commonality springs from two sources, according to Gunkel: first, striking cross-cultural similarities in story-making and thought process, and secondly similarities in human experiences, such as life's struggles with its surroundings, illness, misfortune, disaster and war.[4] Folklore is an expression of such common experiences of life, and so is the problem of evil, as well as human efforts to counter its effect on human life.

## Demons and demonic presence

The idea of demon(s) is not commonly known to the Old Testament world nor does the word *'āzā'zēl* provide an undisputed meaning.[5] However, the presence of 'demonic' power is widespread, especially in folkloric expressions. They are often associated with darkness, the desert, or death. Their appearance is sometimes presented in the form of animals, especially imaginary ones.[6] Egyptians described such a

---

[1] J. Petersen, *Israel: Its Life and Culture* (London: Humphrey Milford, 1926), I–II, 471 argues that the negative view of water is not of Israelite origin.

[2] 'The Creation Epic' found in 'Akkadian Myths and Epics', trans. E.A. Speiser, in *Ancient Near Eastern Texts Relating to the Old Testament*, 3rd ed., ed. James B. Pritchard (Princeton, NJ: Princeton University Press, 1969) 60–72. The book is henceforth referred to as *ANETOT*.

[3] Hermann Gunkel, *The Folktale in the Old Testament*, trans. Michael D. Rutter with an introduction by John W. Rogerson (Sheffield: Almond, 1987), 27.

[4] Gunkel, *The Folktale*, 31–32.

[5] All four appearances are found in Lev 16:8, 10, and 26 in the context of atonement. The word, therefore, refers to a scapegoat. However, C.F. Keil and F. Delitsch, *The Pentateuch*, Biblical Commentary on the Old Testament 2, trans. J. Martin (Grand Rapids: Eerdmans, 1956), 398 identify this as a desert demon, as the goat is to be sent to *'āzā'zēl*. The book of Enoch uses this for a chief demon (1 En. 8:1; 9:6; 10:4–8).

[6] For a useful discussion of various demonic figures and their non-Israelite traces, see Walter Eichrodt, *Theology of the Old Testament*, trans. J.A. Barker, vol. 2 (Philadelphia: Westminster, 1967), 223–24.

ghost 'with nose behind him, with his face reversed (or turned back-
wards).'[7] Often when including folkloric elements, such ideas tend to
be old. 'Demons' are perceived to bring minor disruptions such as con-
tamination of water.[8] We shall examine Genesis 32:23–32 as an example
of this folkloric influence on Hebraic thinking. We shall also briefly
consider the Israelite idea of death as another concept commonly
shared with the ancient world. These will provide a snap-shot of the
popular picture of demonic presence, which ancient people felt surrounded by.

### Jacob's struggle (Gen. 32:23–32)

In this saga, where folkloric elements are cast in a mysterious historical figure, Jacob wrestles with an unidentified man through the night.
When the unknown figure becomes aware that he cannot overpower
Jacob and the daybreak is drawing near, he takes desperate action to
rid himself of the persistent Jacob. At the end of the struggle, he pro-
nounces blessing so that he can be released before light appears. This
assailant is believed by Gunkel to be a night 'demon' or the 'demon' of
the river apparently in a human form (*'îš*), nonetheless a divine being.
It was only later connected with Yahweh (e.g., Hos 12:5 and also Gen
32:30).[9]

But why think this character to be a 'demon'? Several features illustrate the general perception of the demonic among ancient Israelites. It
appears only at night and must disappear before daybreak.[10] It cannot
withstand light. This nocturnal orientation of such figures is also found
elsewhere (e.g., Gen. 19:15–16). Also knowing a name implies control
or power over the person and the 'man' refuses to reveal his name.
Further, he has something supernatural at his disposal, such as granting a blessing by changing Jacob's name. At the same time, a human

---

[7] This 'Magical Protection for a Child' is found in 'Egyptian Rituals and
Incantations', in *ANETOT*, 328, col. 1.

[8] 2 Kgs. 2:19–20. Salt is universally believed as potent against demons and
their damages. Theodor H. Gaster, *Myth, Legend and Custom in the Old
Testament*, vol. 2 (New York: Harper & Row, 1969), 516.

[9] Gunkel, *The Folktale*, 86. A good number of commentators agree on the 'distinct animistic traits' in this 'local story', e.g., Claus Westermann, *Genesis
12–36: A Commentary*, trans. John J. Scullion (Minneapolis: Augsburg, 1985),
515.

[10] The nocturnal nature of mysterious 'men' is found in many places in the
Old Testament, e.g., Gen. 19:15–16; Ex. 12:22.

can wrestle and gain control over the 'demon', clearly indicating his inferior state as a divine being. Interestingly, the 'demonic' figure, although hostile to Jacob since his territory is violated, can nonetheless be both benevolent and malevolent.

References to such unknown and mysterious persons abound in the Old Testament. Their actions range from harm to favor. Often referred to as a 'messenger' (of God), they bring destruction to a city (e.g., Gen. 19), and at the same time rescue God's people (Gen. 19). Often connected with locations such as deserts, rivers, mountains, and the like, they appear to be more malevolent than benevolent.

### Death in popular belief

As in any culture, death is an unknown and thus often-feared realm of reality. Ancient Egyptians thought that at the death of a child a spirit in the form of a ghost comes to 'kiss', 'silence', 'injure', or 'take away' the child.[11] Eichrodt believes that the concept of a demon is closely associated with the dead, as the spirit of a deceased does not belong either to heaven or earth.[12] The word *'iṭṭim* (Isa. 19:3), appearing only once, brings a strong connect with death: It is commonly translated as 'ghosts' or 'spirits of the dead' (NIV, NRSV), although the KJV renders it as 'charmer'. Such spirits are consulted in times of crisis. Also a good burial for unjustly murdered countrymen was considered an act of honour which is generously rewarded by God (cf. Tobit). In ancient Israel, and many ancient civilizations such as Egypt, some kind of continuing existence after death was recognized. For Israelites the dead were believed to be confined in an underworld, often called 'Sheol'. Therefore, it is not difficult to assume that necromancy was a common practice in the ancient world.[13] However, Israel had been sternly warned against this practice and Saul himself strictly administers this rule (1 Sam. 28:9).

In the scripture, there is no evidence that the spirits of the dead are an 'evil' force, although they are not to be disturbed as seen in the story of the witch of Endor. Sheol, their abode, was believed to be a nether land and this is clearly separate from the land of the living.[14] They were

---

[11] 'Magical Protection for a Child', in *ANETOT*, 328, col. 2.

[12] Eichrodt, *Theology of the Old Testament*, vol. 2, 223.

[13] Helmer Ringgren, *Israelite Religion*, trans. David E. Green (Philadelphia: Fortress, 1966), 242.

[14] More on Sheol, see Luis I.J. Stadelmann, *The Hebrew Conception of the World* (Rome: Biblical Institute Press, 1970), 165–76.

believed to know what the living may not, and can give out such knowledge to the living. This process required the assistance of a medium who called the dead from Sheol and communicated with him. Thus, the medium of Endor calls Samuel, but Samuel's appearance is concealed from her clients. She had to *describe* the appearance of Samuel (that only she could see) to ascertain his identity (1 Sam. 28:14). Nowhere throughout the passage is there any evidence that the reality of Samuel's presence or the truth of his words were questioned. Although strictly prohibited among Israelites, this leaves a strong impression that such a practice was widespread in the ancient world, including ancient Israel.

There is little to learn about the origin of evil or human measures to counter misfortunes in such stories. However, this brief survey reveals an aspect of the ancient thought-world – the way in which people felt surrounded by mysterious forces.

## Evil and malevolent spirits

There are several mentions of the spirits of a malevolent nature associated with God. If we isolate those with a clear reference to an entity, they are the 'evil spirit' placed between Abimelech and people of Shechem (Judg. 9:23), also the one that came upon Saul (1 Sam. 16:15, 16, 16:23; 18:10; 19:9); and the 'lying spirit' upon Ahab's prophets (1 Kgs. 22:22, 23; 2 Chr. 18:21, 22). Other references such as a 'spirit of judgment' and a 'spirit of fire' (Isa. 4:4), a 'spirit of dizziness' (Isa. 19:14), and a 'spirit of prostitution' (Hos. 4:12; 5:4) lack a reference to a distinct entity. Two passages deserve a closer look as they have sufficient details for discussion.

### The evil spirit upon Saul (1 Sam 16; 18–19)

The coming of the evil spirit upon Saul coincided with the departure of God's Spirit from him (1 Sam 16:14), as well as the coming of the Spirit upon David (1 Sam 16:13). This strongly suggests that the nature and function of the divine Spirit here is not life-giving, but leadership-empowering with a particular link to royal status. Therefore, the coming of the evil spirit was not a natural consequence of the departure of God's Spirit from Saul. The fact that the evil spirit was *from* Yahweh requires our attention. The Hebrew word *mē'ēt* ('from within' in a literal sense) strongly suggests the evil spirit's close link with Yahweh.

It came from God's presence. In 1 Sam. 18:10, the link between God and the evil spirit is even closer by calling it *rûaḥ ʾĕlōhîm rāʿa*, 'evil spirit of God'. One useful parallel may be found in the discussion of the 'lying spirit' (see below), although other interpretations may be possible.

The work of the evil spirit is quite clear from the verb used. The piel form of *bʿt* means 'to terrify', while its niphal form means 'to be overtaken by sudden terror' as seen in Dan. 8:17. The forcefulness of its movement and effect is evident. The effect of the presence of the evil spirit was both internal as well as external. Internally it tormented Saul (1 Sam. 16:15) requiring an urgent relief (16:16, 23). The belief that mental disturbance was caused by an evil spirit or demon was a widespread notion throughout the ancient Near East.[15] For example, headaches were often attributed to the activity of an evil spirit.[16] The external manifestation of its presence is also interesting. The first was to cause Saul 'to prophesy' (18:10) – the hithpael form of *nbʾ* has a strong reference to an external and behavioral aspect of spirit-possession, thus, meaning 'to have prophetic ecstasy'.[17] A similar behavior is reported in 1 Sam. 19:23–24, although it is caused by the Spirit of God: 'But the Spirit of God came upon him [Saul], and he walked along prophesying [hithpael form] until he came to Naioth. He stripped off his robe and also prophesied [again, hithpael form] in Samuel's presence.' The evil spirit also urged Saul to kill David (19:9). In his emotionally heightened, disturbed and uncontrollable state, he was prompted to take a spear to pin David to the wall.

Although the exact nature of the evil spirit remains to be further explored, a few things are quite clear. First, its role was to bring mental disturbance and to urge the actions of harm and evil. This evil was at least its intention and effect, but it is difficult to conclude that the spirit itself was evil. It is interesting that Saul's courtiers recognize the presence of the evil spirit immediately (16:15). Secondly, the

---

[15] E.g., 'The Legend of the Possessed Princess' in *ANETOT*, 30, col. 1 records that the wise man found the princess 'in the condition of one possessed of spirits' . . . and he 'indeed found an enemy with whom to contend.'

[16] In a Hittite inscription, we see the following incantation, 'Loosen the evil tension of [his] head, his hands (and) his [feet]. Give it to (their) wicked adversaries!' 'Purification Ritual Engaging the Help of Protective Demons' found in 'Hittite Rituals, Incantations, and Description of Festivals', trans. Albrecht Goetze, in *ANETOT*, 348, col. 1.

[17] Robert R. Wilson, 'Prophecy and Ecstasy: A Reexamination,' *Journal of Biblical Literature* 98 (1979), 321–37.

presence and activity of the evil spirit was immediately recognized by people around Saul. Mental disturbances are easily attributed to the work of a spirit in the ancient world. Third, there is evidence that not only could the effect of the evil spirit's presence be reduced or soothed, but also that the very presence of the evil spirit could be eliminated by human effort. As soon as Saul was found to be affected by the evil spirit, his courtiers recommend that Saul search for a skillful harp player who could calm and sooth his disturbed mental state (16:16). David was able to sooth the disturbed mental state of Saul, and, on one occasion, the evil spirit actually left (16:23). Fourth, related to the preceding discussion, the role of music as a cultic element was a common feature throughout the ancient world. The association of various musical instruments with the coming of God's Spirit is particularly relevant (1 Sam. 10:5), as music played an important role in the activity of the spirit, be it God's Spirit or an evil spirit. There are several musical instruments that appear more often than others, such as lyres, tambourines, flutes, and harps (10:5), although others such as the trumpet are also mentioned.

### The lying spirit upon Ahab's prophets (1 Kgs. 22:22–23//2 Chr. 18:21–22)

This may be the most useful passage in answering several important questions, if this can be considered as a typical representation of an Israelite worldview. In this detailed conflict between Micaiah, a lone prophet of God, and the four-hundred court prophets of Ahab, the whole narrative is extremely entertaining as each party claimed to be a true prophet(ic group). A true prophet was marked by a true prophecy, and true prophecy was tested by the presence and activity of God's Spirit (22:24). The prophetic possession by a god or a spirit and the disclosure of a secret through a prophetic utterance were widespread phenomena throughout the ancient Near Eastern world, as attested by the Wen-Amon's journey report.[18]

Micaiah's claim for genuine prophethood stemmed from his own witness to the heavenly council scene, an extremely common literary image in the ancient Near East.[19] Although not part of the council itself,

---

[18] 'The Journey of Wen-Amon to Phoenicia' found in 'Egyptian Myths, Tales, and Mortuary Texts', trans. John. A. Wilson, in *ANETOT*, 25–29.

[19] There are many studies available, e.g. R.N. Whybray, *The Heavenly Councilor in Isaiah xl 13–14: A Study of the Source of the Theology of Deutero-Isaiah* (Cambridge: Cambridge University Press, 1971).

the prophet was allowed to observe the proceeding.[20] This experience set Micaiah apart, as the messenger of God's true word, from the multitude and from the elaborate cultic prophets of Ahab.

In the heavenly council scene in this passage, the courtiers are called 'spirits'. The agenda was to determine a strategy to entice Ahab to begin a war to recapture a 'no man's land' in the northeastern region of Ramoth Gilead. The plan was to lead to Ahab's final defeat and death. In this council meeting, among other suggestions, a member (or a 'spirit') proposes to become an 'evil spirit' in the mouths of Ahab's prophets so that Ahab can be enticed to go for a war (22:22–23). Two things become immediately clear. First, 'enticing' in 22:20 (or 'fooling', 'deceiving', or 'seducing') – the meaning of the piel form of *pth* – is not viewed as morally negative, thus, justifying this decision of God. The later parallel in the Chronicler's account does not significantly differ (2 Chr 18:21–22). Second, in the same vein, one of God's 'spirits' now becoming a 'lying spirit' does not pose any moral dilemma in the ancient Hebrew mind. The net result is that the lying spirit is not lying by its own nature but by simple 'assumption' or 'assignment'. This neutral view of demons and spirits was widely shared in the ancient world. For example, Volz argues that such a neutral view of demons is the origin of Israel's concept of God's Spirit.[21] This is in accordance with the preceding discussion where everything, both good and evil, belongs to God.

### Summary

Whether this case of the lying spirit can be stretched to explain other experiences such as the 'evil spirit of/from God' upon Saul or the 'evil spirit' that God placed between Abimelech and the Shechemites, at least a tentative conclusion can be made: The 'evil spirit' was not evil by nature but by assignment. The spirit was indeed 'of/from God' as it proceeded from Yahweh's council.

Now when it comes to exorcism, there is little evidence of any effort to deal with this lying spirit. If exorcism is a human measure or attempt to counter the evil activities of presumably malevolent

---

[20] Sometimes the observer forgets his invited status and participates in the proceeding, e.g., Isa. 6.

[21] Paul Volt, *Der Geist Gottes und die verwandten Erscheinungen im Alten Testament und im anschliessenden Judentum* (Tübingen: J.C.B. Mohr, 1910), 2–4.

spiritual forces/beings, there are two problems in applying the concept to this case. First, it is *God's* plan or a 'divine conspiracy' one was dealing with. Therefore, even if one was afflicted by a 'lying spirit' it is still *God* that one needed to deal with, not a demon or Satan. Second, in the case of Ahab's prophets, their priority task appears to have been to ascertain that the Spirit of God was upon them, not on Micaiah, as the source of prophecy, which may require discernment or detection. Often 'blinding' or 'deafening' was a part of God's deliberate plan for an individual's or a group's demise.

However, in the case of the evil spirit upon Saul, there was an active response to counter the effect or even the presence of the evil spirit. David's skillful playing of the harp not only soothed Saul's mental state, but also causes the evil spirit to leave him (1 Sam. 16:23). Although the inherent quality of good music is recognized in calming minds, its spiritual value as a cultic element cannot be ignored. The passage, for the first time, suggests the role of music or cult in countering the presence of the evil force; perhaps a step towards the 'spiritual warfare' spoken of by the Third Wave advocates of today.

## Gods of the nations

There is a group of passages in the Old Testament which refers to spiritual beings connected to non-Israelite entities. Various national deities such as Baal can be included here; however, the present discussion is limited to two representative passages: one on the non-Israelite practice of cursing and the other on a spiritual being connected to a territory or domain.

### Balaam (Num. 22–24)

As the Israelites approached the Jordan, Balak, King of Moab, hired Balaam for a great fee to curse the advancing Israelites (22:6). Balaam, a non-Israelite seer, was known for his effectiveness as a Mesopotamian diviner to bless or curse a group of people. Cursing was a regular part of the ancient world, be it against an individual or a nation. For example, many magical inscriptions have been found among ancient Egyptian materials that impose a curse upon their enemies, such as 'The ruler of Jerusalem . . . and all the retainers who are with him'.[22]

---

[22] 'The Execration of Asiatic Prince' in *ANETOT*, 329, col. 1.

Often such names were inscribed in a piece of pottery which was then smashed in the belief that the power of their enemy would be broken.[23] In this case, Balaam was to invoke the name of his or Balak's god to curse Israel. However, he was so quickly overcome by Yahweh, Israel's God, that he called him 'Yahweh my God' (22:18). He further declared, 'I must speak only what God puts in my mouth' (22:38). Balaam never succeeded in cursing Israel; instead, he blessed them.

This provides a window onto the ancient practice of cursing, and although numerous rituals were offered, Baalam was not to place a curse against Israel, but was to receive an oracle from God or to obtain his permission.[24] Ancient records reveal an endless array of ritual prescriptions and prayers used to place a curse or to counter one, and to invoke the help of protective spirits. In spite of various objects used to represent the target of a curse, the power of incantation and prayer stands out. The collection of eight prayers of blessing and curses from the Sakkarah pyramid of the pharaoh Unis (25th century BCE) is a fine example.[25] The power of such an oracle is also exemplified in a curse against such curse oracles including 'every evil word, every evil speech, every evil slander, every evil thought, every evil plot . . . all evil dreams, and all evil slumber.'[26]

In the current passage, there is no evidence of any action taken by the Israelites, if they ever even knew of this plot, to counter Balaam's curse. The inclusion of the Balaam episode is intended to demonstrate Yahweh's sovereignty over all the nations and their gods.

### Prince of Persia (Dan 10)

This chapter has raised serious questions as Third Wave thinkers such as Peter Wagner have defended the idea of territorial spirits using it. Even a casual reading of the chapter would reveal that the word 'prince' (*śar*) appears five times (10:13, 20, 21). In a visionary encounter with the divine world, Daniel was told by an angelic being that his prayer was heard by God at the moment of utterance and the messenger was immediately dispatched (10:12). However, the messenger was

---

[23] John A. Wilson's comment on 'The Execration of Asiatic Princes' in *ANE-TOT*, 328, col. 2.

[24] Philip J. Budd, *Numbers*, Word Biblical Commentary (Waco, TX: Word, 1984), 264.

[25] 'Curses and Threats' found in 'Egyptian Rituals and Incantation', in *ANE-TOT*, 326–28.

[26] 'The Execration of Asiatic Princes', in *ANETOT*, 329, cols. 1–2.

detained for twenty-one days as the prince of Persia resisted him. It was only through the intervention of Michael that the messenger was now in Daniel's presence (10:13). It is evident that the word 'prince' is not used here in an earthly sense. The same word is used for both the (spiritual) authority of Persia and God's angelic beings.

Here, we have an explicit reference to a direct and active opposition from a spiritual force against God and his angels. Ancient minds perceived an earthly event as a reflection of a parallel heavenly occurrence. A war between Israel and its enemy was easily understood as a battle between Yahweh and the god of the enemy. Therefore, Israel's unlikely victories were credited to the work of Yahweh (e.g., Num. 10:35–36; Judg. 5:19–20). What is unique in this passage, however, is the presence of supernatural beings that are not under God's total control. In fact, there is a force *actively opposing Yahweh and his people*. The twenty-one day struggle of Daniel is described in 10:2–3, and is now explained in a heavenly term, 'Since the first day that you set your mind to gain understanding and to humble yourself before your God, your words were heard, and I have come in response to them. But the prince of the Persian kingdom resisted me twenty-one days. Then Michael, one of the chief princes, came to help me, because I was detained there with the king of Persia' (10:12–13). The exact nature of this conflict is not clear. Goldingay presents three possible interpretations: 1) a verbal/legal conflict with the Persian representative, 2) a warrior halting a messenger,[27] or 3) a literal struggle between supernatural armies.[28]

Related to the discussion is the identity of the 'prince of Persia'. Israel claims the absolute supremacy of Yahweh, and other national deities are reduced to serving Yahweh. As the same word, *śar*, is used for both the Persian 'prince' and God's angels (v. 13 where Michael is described as 'one of the chief princes'), it is natural to understand the 'Persian prince' as a spiritual force too. It is Yahweh who assigned them their territory of dominion (Deut. 4:19; 32:8–9; Ps. 89:6), and this leads to the conclusion that the 'prince' is the national deity of Persia. This supreme rule of God over the nations, however, does not rule out the possibility of their rebellion and conflict. Regardless of the exact nature of the conflict, it is a conflict between two heavenly powers. The

---

[27] A presence of God's angel to oppose Balaam's way (Num. 22:21–35) may be compared to this passage.

[28] John E. Goldingay, *Daniel*, Word Biblical Commentary (Dallas: Word, 1987), 292.

opposition of the prince of Persia was successful for twenty-one days. The supremacy of Yahweh is never questioned, but it is his 'prince' who counters this opposition. Their evil rule or opposition to God's authority will be punished (cf. Nebuchadnezzar's destruction in Dan. 4:14).

In this scene of a heavenly conflict, was there any role for a human (in this case, Daniel) to play? The passage reveals that the first day when Daniel prayed, God's messenger was deployed (10:12), and only delayed by the hindrance of the prince of Persia. If this is the case, then Daniel's three week experience should be viewed as a consequence of delay. His own struggle, perhaps without knowing the heavenly scene, suggests this: 'I, Daniel, mourned for three weeks. I ate no choice food; no meat or wine touched my lips; and I used no lotions at all until the three weeks were over' (10:2–3). Although the exact point of Michael's appearance is not clear, the impression is that Michael overcame the resistance of the Persian prince and released God's messenger from detention. Whether Daniel's continuing prayer played a role in God's deployment of Michael cannot be concluded with any certainty, although the ancient Near East was full of rituals and incantations to influence heavenly conflicts.

### Satan

The earlier Yahwistic religion constructed a theology according to which Yahweh is the only true God. In this absolute monotheism, he is responsible for everything that exists, and this includes evil. However, in the later period, Yahweh was understood to be exclusively good without any involvement in evil. This required the origin of evil to be sought elsewhere, and this is where the figure of Satan appeared as God's antagonist, although God's sovereignty continued to be affirmed.[29]

There are three passages with references to *śāṭān*: it is used fourteen times in the prologue of Job, three times in Zechariah, and once in the Chronicler's account of David's census. Except for the Chronicler's use, all the occurrences are with the definite article. It should also be observed that all the occurrences are from later periods; that is, from the post-exilic era.

---

[29] Ringgren, *Israelite Religion*, 313.

*Job's prologue (1:6–11; 2:1–7)*

As the word *śāṭān* appears with the definite article, it is to be taken as
a common noun (the adversary), not a proper noun (Satan). When
used for human (e.g. 1 Kgs. 5:18) and superhuman figures it is an
'adversary' or 'accuser'. In Job we assume it is used to indicate the
*function* of a spirit in God's court.[30] In the prologue of Job, the accuser
stands with the 'sons of God' before the Lord. However, the sequence
of the sons of God followed by the appearance of the accuser leaves
unanswered the question of whether the accuser is a regular member
of the council or an unexpected visitor.[31] The language does not necessarily present the accuser as evil in nature. If 1 Kings 22 can be used as
a guide in a heavenly court scene, various spirits are assembled around
God 'probably thought of as his own particular duties'.[32] His accusation of Job also comes only at the urging of God. Nonetheless, he
accuses Job without evidence, leading to a 'possible conflict between
the domains of heaven and earth' which is 'typical of biblical leg-
ends'.[33] Job 1:12 makes it clear that he can bring harshness and misfortune only by God's permission and to the extent set by God.

Now the agents of evil that bring disaster to Job's children and his
possessions are both human and natural, and supernatural forces. The
accuser can cause the Sebeans (1:15) and the Chaldeans (1:17) to attack
Job's children and servants, and raid his livestock. He also brings the
'fire of God' (1:16) from the sky as well as a mighty wind (1:19) and
causes physical disease (2:7). As a supernatural being, and part of
God's heavenly council, he was believed to have natural and supernatural forces at his disposal to harm humans. However, it should also
be noted that not every evil is caused by him: the verbal assault from
Job's wife and the long and painful accusatory confrontations of the
three friends are not attributed to the instigation of the accuser.

His role is twofold. One is bringing charges before the Lord against
an individual, and consequently provoking God's permission for an
action against against Job (2:3). The same verb is used to describe
Jezebel's instigation upon Ahab to act out evil (1 Kgs. 21:25). The other
is executing the permitted evil against the individual, and the

---

[30] H.H. Rowley, *Job*, New Century Bible (London: Marshall, Morgan & Scott,
1978), 31.

[31] Norman C. Habel, *The Book of Job: A Commentary*, Old Testament Library
(Philadelphia: Westminster, 1985), 89.

[32] Rowley, *Job*, 30.

[33] Habel, *The Book of Job*, 27.

adversary has human, natural and supernatural elements at his disposal. It is also noted that his role is found only in the beginning of the story and the rest is left to its own (human) course, with little evidence of supernatural intervention until the thick curtain is raised and God shows his face to Job and the three friends.

Nowhere do we find Job taking any action to counter the evil. Job consistently maintains a long-standing faith that both good and evil come from God. His only 'exocistic' action is to have a firm faith in God, his sovereignty, his justice to vindicate the righteous at the end, and that God's deep mystery is hidden to humans. In fact, in the dramatic conclusion of the story, the adversary is nowhere to be found. Job's vindication is not against the accuser but in God's faith in Job's righteousness. This passage maintains a mid-way between the absolute belief that everything, including evil, comes from the Lord and the dualistic notion of God vs. Satan which is found in extra-biblical writings and the New Testament. It also continues the familiar heavenly council scene as the backdrop for this revelation.

### David's census (1 Chr. 21:1)

This is the Chronicler's version of David's fateful national census. This is the only incident that the noun *śāṭān* appears without the definite article, thus being a proper noun. It may be argued that by the time the Chronicles were completed, Satan as the chief adversary of God had been established. Nonetheless, a comparison between this and the older pre-exilic records yields a useful insight. This pair provides a rare window into the developmental process of the concept of Satan and the motivation behind it.

> Again the anger of the LORD burned against Israel, and he incited David against them, saying, 'Go and take a census of Israel and Judah' (2 Sam. 24:1).

> Satan rose up against Israel and incited David to take a census of Israel (1 Chr. 21:1).

The earlier text identifies God himself as being responsible for David's decision for a census. In fact, it was God's anger that led him to provoke (the same verb as used in Job and Jezebel, see above) David to carry out this disastrous plan. As seen in the 'evil spirit' and the 'lying spirit' stories above, pre-exilic minds are willing to live with this dilemma in order to project Yahweh as the supreme deity. However, in the post-exilic era, having affirmed the supremacy of Yahweh over the nations, the figure of God's adversary emerges. Ringgren and others strongly argue that the Persian influence encouraged the increasing dualistic trend in the Jewish mind. However, he argues that it was the common human inquiry into the origin of evil, rather than Persian thought, that was responsible for the concept of Satan.[34]

In this extremely scanty evidence, the provocative role of Satan is in line with our observation above. The presence or absence of the definite article hardly makes any difference; but of interest is the fact that Satan's work in Chronicles, unlike in Job, was mediated exclusively through natural causes – no direct supernatural actions are involved.

Now with regard to exorcism, the passage does not give any clue about ways to counter the act of Satan. The only evidence is a common-sense objection of Joab, which is quickly overruled by the king (21:4):

> But Joab replied, 'May the LORD multiply his troops a hundred times over. My lord the king, are they not all my lord's subjects? Why does my lord want to do this? Why should he bring guilt on Israel?' (21:3)

### Night vision of Zechariah (3:1–5)

The vision of Zechariah presents another heavenly council scene where Joshua the high priest stands before the angel of the Lord, while the adversary (with the definite article, thus, not a proper noun), standing on God's right, brings his charge against Joshua. The filthy clothes of the high priest indicate his unworthiness in the presence of God's angel, and the adversary accuses him of this filthiness. However, it becomes quickly evident that the high priest represents the nation of Israel. The Lord's reaction is rather surprising, if we consider the two passages we studied above. In spite of clear evidence to support his accusations, the accuser is rebuked by the Lord himself. Nonetheless, he is a member of Yahweh's heavenly council.

As in Job, God is the advocate of his servants. In this passage, God's advocacy comes in spite of the high priest's sinfulness. In God's sight, his filthiness is compared to destruction by fire. It is God's act of salvation and restoration that causes him to snatch Joshua (or Israel) from complete annihilation.

---

[34] Ringgren, *Israelite Religion*, 315.

In this heavenly council vision, the prophet interrupts the council proceedings by joining the conversation. This prophetic interruption is not uncommon (e.g., Isa. 6). Although this intervention is not against the accusation or the accuser, the prophetic voice of Zechariah becomes part of Joshua's restoration. There is no evidence of human measure to counter the accuser's activity. After all, he is part of God's heavenly council.

## Summary: Human response to evil

The preceding discussion makes it quite clear that 'exorcism' is not a relevant term for the Old Testament, if it is defined as 'the practice of expelling evil spirits from persons or places by means of incantations and the performance of certain occult acts.'[35] A clear dualism in the balance of universal power only has a trace of its development in the Old Testament. The sudden surge of references to exorcism after the Old Testament period is a stark contrast. For example, Qumran documents attest to a significant development of the theology of evil spirits and Satan during the inter-testamental period. Therefore, it is more appropriate when discussing the Old Testament to speak about the problem of evil and human response to it.

Ancient Israelites were aware of the presence of adverse forces in operation, and they are often supernatural in nature. Terms ('demon', 'spirit', 'prince' and 'Satan') are not clearly defined and clarified at all. Often 'foreign' ideas have become part of Israelite psyche as seen in the idea of some demonic elements and Balaam's (planned) curse.

What is consistently clear is the absolute supremacy of Yahweh, leaving little room for other spirits to function as full blown deities; they were often seen as members of the heavenly council of Yahweh. They become evil only as they assume an evil assignment, as in Saul's case. In the religious world where God's goodness is firmly upheld, this is a handy way to explain the presence of evil without hurting God's sovereignty and supremacy.

Although any proactive or even preemptive measure to counter the presence of evil is rare in the OT, there is evidence that God's people were not just passive spectators of what was taking place in the divine

---

[35] I. Mendelsohn, 'Exorcism', *Interpreter's Dictionary of the Bible*, vol. 2 (New York: Abingdon, 1962), 199–200.

world (as discussed above in the case of Saul, as well as Daniel).[36] Firm faith in God, often expressed in devout prayer, is the foundational measure. However, cultic activity (or worship) is unmistakably suggested in countering evil forces. All having been said, however, it is ultimately the all loving and all powerful God who holds the key to all the problems of evil, and the Old Testament is consistent in establishing this truth.

---

[36] Although Jacob's wrestling with the unidentified figure may suggest a human measure, it may also be treated as part of an unswerving commitment and piety.

# Chapter 2

# Deliverance and Exorcism in the New Testament

## *Graham H. Twelftree*

'But if by the Spirit of God I cast out demons, the kingdom of God has come upon you'                                              *Jesus of Nazareth*

### Abstract

Exorcism was understood as a way of removing unwanted supranatural beings from people. Perhaps as the first charismatic healer and taking up the methods of magicians, Jesus made exorcism the cornerstone to his ministry, claiming that in them the kingdom of God was being realized. For Paul, with salvation focussed in the cross, exorcism was of peripheral interest, perhaps only using it exceptionally. In contrast to the synoptic gospels, the Fourth Gospel removes all reference to exorcism. Then, after little interest in exorcism across the church, the longer ending of Mark signals the return of the practice.

## Introduction

The purpose of this chapter is to describe the practice and purpose of exorcism in the writings of the New Testament in the context of the immediate period.[1] We will see that, on the one hand, exorcism was

---

[1] I am grateful to Richard H. Bell and Alicia M. Eichmann for their comments on an earlier version of this paper. For a more detailed treatment of exorcism among early Christians see Graham H. Twelftree, *In the Name of Jesus: Exorcism Among Early Christians* (Grand Rapids: Baker Academic, 2007), parts 1 and 2.

central to the ministry of Jesus yet, on the other hand, it was of varying interest to early Christians and, for reasons that will be explained,
of no interest to Johannine Christians.

By the time of Jesus exorcism was widely practised as one of the
ways to deal with human suffering, though some writers readily
expressed scepticism about demons and their control.[2] Generally, however, Jews and Greeks alike had come to share the popular view,[3] established among the philosophers by Xenocrates in the fourth century BC,
that some of the demons (*daimōn*) were evil,[4] or at least that there were
intermediaries between humans and the gods (e.g., *Corpus Hermetica*
XVI.18) whose actions could be good or bad.[5] Those who were evil or
acted badly were firmly associated with human suffering[6] and, for the
Jews, could cause evil tendencies and sinfulness.[7]

Nevertheless, not all human suffering or sickness was attributed to
spirits or demons and possession was sometimes seen to be beneficial
– Plato mentions prophecy and creativity in particular.[8] Hippocrates
of Cos (born c. 460 BC) is an example of a writer in antiquity who

---

[2]  See, e.g. esp., Lucian of Samosata, *Lover of Lies* 8, 15–16; cf. F. Gerald Down-
ing, 'Access to Other Cultures, Past and Present (on The Myth of the Cultural Gap)', *ModChurchman* 21 (1977–78), 28–42; and the literature cited by
Craig S. Keener, *The Gospel of John* (2 vols.; Peabody: Hendrickson, 2003),
1.261–63. See also the discussion by Richard H. Bell, *Deliver Us from Evil:
Interpreting the Redemption from the Power of Satan in New Testament Theology*
(WUNT 216; Tübingen: Mohr Siebeck, 2007), 342–44.

[3]  Cf. Sophron (5th century BC), Fragments 3 and 4A–D. See J.H. Hordern,
*Sophron's Mimes: Text, Translation, and Commentary* (New York: Oxford
University Press, 2004), 124–42 and the discussion by H.J. Rose, *Religion in
Greece and Rome* (New York: Harper & Row, 1959), 42–43.

[4]  On the evolution of the notion of demons see Walter Burkett, *Greek Religion*
(Cambridge, Mass.: Harvard University Press, 1985), 187–81, 329–32 citing
Xenocrates, Fragment 23 and 24; more generally see Amin Lange, H.
Lichtenberger and K.F.D. Römheld, (eds.), *Die Dämonen Demons* (Tübingen:
Mohr Siebeck, 2003).

[5]  See, e.g. Joesphus, *Ant.* 13.415; 16.76, 210; *JW* 1.556, 628.

[6]  Graham H. Twelftree, 'Demon', *NIDB* 2: 92–93.

[7]  E.g., Zech 13:2; *Jub.* 10.8; 4Q444; 11Q5; *T. Ben.* 5.2–3 on which see Amin
Lange, 'Considerations Concerning the "Spirit of Impurity" in Zech 13:2',
in Lange, Lichtenberger and Römheld (ed.), *Demons*, 254–68.

[8]  Plato, *Phraedrus* 244A–245B. See also, e.g., Herodotus, *History* 9.33–42;
Plato, *Timaeus* 71D–72B; Acts 16:16–18. See Eric Sorensen, *Possession and
Exorcism in the New Testament and Early Christianity* (WUNT 2/157;
Tübingen: Mohr Siebeck, 2002), 91–103.

considered illness to have causes other than spirits and demons.[9] Plato includes guilt associated with one's forebears as a cause of disease (Plato, *Phraedrus* 244D). Also, although Paul equates his thorn in the flesh with a messenger from Satan (2 Cor. 12:7), he gives no suggestion that his other troubles were of demonic origin (cf. 4:8–9; 6:4–5).

When troubles were deemed to be of demonic origin a number of responses were possible. Early Greeks could undertake for themselves purification rituals in their temples to pacify the god seeking retribution for some sacrilegious act.[10] Throughout their history, Greeks also shared the practice of driving out an unwanted spiritual presence from their community through a ceremony that involved brutally killing individuals or expelling them from the city.[11]

Importantly for this chapter, if a spirit entered and possessed a person, and the person's health was impaired, exorcism could be used. Alternatively, as the use of amulets, for example, attests, a person thought to be externally afflicted by a spirit could take apotropaic action.[12] In the Pauline corpus, at least some of the discussions of

---

[9] Cf., Hippocrates, *On the Sacred Diseases* 1.1–29; also, e.g. Herodotus, *History* 2.173; 6.84. On the gospel writers distinguishing between sicknesses see Christopher J. Thomas, *The Devil, Disease and Deliverance: Origins of Illness in New Testament Thought* (JPT Supp 13; Sheffield: Sheffield Academic, 1998), 199–201, and the brief discussion by Graham Dow, 'The Case for the Existence of Demons', *Churchman* 94 (1980), 199–208. See 200, 202.

[10] E.g. Aeschylus, *Choephori* 71–74; Herodotus, *History* 1.43; Plato, *Phraedrus* 244E; cf. Timaeus Locrus, 224 line 8 (see Walter Marg, *Timaeus Locrus: De Natura Mundi et Animai: Überlieferung, Testmonia, Text und Übersetzung* [Leiden: Brill, 1972], 148–50 and Thomas H. Tobin, *On the Nature of the World and the Soul* [Chico, Calif.: Scholars Press, 1985]) and the Selinous *lex sacra* (c. 460–450 BC), on which see Michael H. Jameson, David R. Jordan and Roy Kotansky, *A* Lex Sacra *from Selinous* (Durham N.C.: Duke University Press, 1993), esp. ix, cf. 103, and the brief discussion by Sorensen, *Possession*, 110.

[11] E.g., Aristophanes, *Equites* 1405; *Ranae* 733; Plutarch, *Moralia* 693 E–F; Philostratus, *Life of Apollonius* 4.10. See Dennis D. Hughes, *Human Sacrifice in Ancient Greece* (London: Routledge, 1991), 139–65; Jan Bremmer, 'Scapegoat Rituals in Ancient Greece', *HSCP*, 87 (1983), 299–320; Sorensen, *Possession*, 113–114, esp. n. 209. Cf. James G. Frazer, *The Golden Bough*, 3rd edition, 1913; *Part VI: The Scapegoat* (New York: St Martin's, 1966).

[12] See the evidence assembled in Graham H. Twelftree, 'Jesus the Exorcist and Ancient Magic', in *A Kind of Magic: Understanding Magic in the New Testament and its Religious Environment* (European Studies on Christian Origins; LNTS, 306; Michael Labahn and Bert Jan Lietaert Peerbolte [eds.], London and New York: Sheffield Academic, 2007), 57–86 (see, 61–62).

'principalities and powers'[13] relate to believers needing to take protective measures against such powers (note Eph. 6:10–17).

Yet, as we will also see, the distinction between exorcism and other forms of healing in the New Testament cannot be explained simply as different responses to demonic possession on the one hand, and demonic affliction on the other.[14] For, in the Fourth Gospel we will see that demonic possession – expressed in sinfulness or human error – was countered without an exorcist. Then, when discussing Luke's perspective, we will see that there could be a blurring of a distinction between possession and other sicknesses and the response could be either healing or exorcism.

We turn now to sketch out how exorcism was understood in the New Testament period before outlining exorcism in the ministry of Jesus, Paul, and other New Testament writers. By the end of this chapter we will be able to see that New Testament writers understood deliverance not to be combating some forms of demonic attack (perhaps oppression),[15] but as the salvation that exorcism sometimes expressed.

### Exorcists and their exorcisms

The term 'exorcist' (*exorkistōs*), found only once in the New Testament (Acts 19:13), its earliest known occurrence,[16] comes from the verb *exorkizō*, to command or adjure (only in the New Testament at Matt 26:63). If, as is reasonable, exorcism is understood as forcing an unwanted

---

[13]  See Peter T. O'Brien, 'Principalities and Powers: Opponents of the Church', in D.A. Carson (ed.), *Biblical Interpretation and the Church* (Exeter: Paternoster, 1984), 110–50; Clinton E. Arnold, *Ephesians: Power and Magic: The Concept of Power in Ephesians* (SNTS Monograph Series 63; Cambridge: Cambridge University Press, 1989).

[14]  Nevertheless, Bell, *Deliver Us*, 320 n. 2 is right to correct me that New Testament writers see a distinction between those possessed and those considered to be otherwise suffering from Satan or demonic attack. Cf. Graham H. Twelftree, *Christ Triumphant* (London: Hodder and Stoughton, 1985), 177.

[15]  As described by, e.g., Francis MacNutt, *Healing* (Notre Dame, Ind.: Ave Maria, 1999), 167.

[16]  Roy Kotansky, 'Greek Exorcistic Amulets', in Marvin Meyer and Paul Mirecki (ed.), *Ancient Magic and Ritual Power* (Boston and Leiden: Brill, 1995), 249 n. 14.

spiritual entity to leave its host,[17] its success was seen to depend on varying understandings of the relative importance of three factors: the innate power of the exorcist, the potency of the power-authority used by the exorcist, and the words or activity (or both) used to bring into operation suitable adequate preternatural force.[18] The varying importance attributed to these factors gave rise to a range of kinds of exorcists and approaches to exorcism, a range that only reached its full extent after the New Testament period. Being aware of the kinds of exorcisms involved in this range helps us understand both the exorcisms of Jesus, as well as those of his immediate followers, and later Christians represented in the New Testament.

At one end of this range, and the most commonly known form of exorcism in New Testament times, were those in which it was thought that an offending demon could be evicted simply by what someone said or did.[19] Although this form of exorcism had been long and widely established,[20] the most notable source of information for these exorcisms comes from what are known as the magical papyri;[21] hence the exorcisms are reasonably called magical.[22] It needs to be stressed, however, that in designating them 'magical' they are not being denigrated or measured against other supposedly better or more successful methods. These magical exorcisms were well known across the New Testament world, including in Palestine.[23]

---

[17] More fully see Graham H. Twelftree, *Jesus the Exorcist* (WUNT 2/54 Tübingen: Mohr Siebeck, 1993), 13. On defining exorcism see Sorensen, *Possession*, 1–2.

[18] Cf. the classification of Jewish exorcisms by Gideon Bohak, *Ancient Jewish Magic* (Cambridge: Cambridge University Press, 2008), esp. 88.

[19] In more detail on this form of exorcism and a discussion of the primary data see Twelftree, 'Ancient Magic', esp. 63–78.

[20] See Sorensen, *Possession*, chapters 2–4.

[21] Cf. *Sepher Ha-Razim* 2.95–103, 124–27; 5.38–42, on which see Michael A. Morgan, *Sepher Ha-Razim* (Chico: Scholars Press, 1983), esp. 51–52, 54, 76 and Philip S. Alexander, 'Incantations and Books of Magic', in Emil Schürer, *The History of the Jewish People in the Age of Jesus Christ* (175 BC–135 AD) revised by Geza Vermes, Fergus Millar and Martin Goodman, vol. 3 Part I (Edinburgh: T.&T. Clark, 1986), 347–50.

[22] On the problem of defining 'magic' see, e.g. A.F. Segal, 'Hellenistic Magic: Some Questions of Definition', in R. van den Broek and M.J. Vermaseren (eds.), *Studies in Gnosticism and Hellenistic Religions* (Leiden: Brill, 1981), 349–75 (349); C.A. Hoffman, 'Fiat Magia', in Paul Mirecki and Marvin Meyer (ed.), *Magic and Ritual in the Ancient World* (Leiden: Brill, 1995), 179–94.

[23] See the discussion by Esther Eshel, 'Genres of Magical Texts in the Dead Sea Scrolls', in Lange, Lichtenberger and Römheld (eds.), *Demons*, 395–415.

Material in the Dead Sea Scrolls, the New Testament, Josephus, Justin Martyr, as well as the magical papyri show that in these exorcisms an unwanted spirit could be evicted[24] by engaging a god or power-authority, or a person could use a second spiritual being as a power-source.[25] In some cases, under the assumption that the mere presence of supranatural power was sufficient (cf. Minucius Felix, *Oct.* 27.7), spiritual power could be transferred or linked to an object (such as an amulet) for use in driving out a demon.[26] There are also examples where no words were uttered; actions or activities (such as using fumigation or a ring) were considered sufficient to contain and convey spiritual power.[27]

As well as using this power to evict a demon, some magical material assumes a person could be externally troubled or harassed by a spiritual entity rather than be its host. Therefore, there is the attempt to control the spirit, cause it to flee, or to provide protection for the person.[28]

---

(cont.) On the relative stability of the ideas and practices found in the magical papyri see Alexander, 'Incantations', 344; Susan R. Garrett, 'Light on a Dark Subject and Vice Versa: Magic and Magicians in the New Testament', in Jacob Neusner, Ernest S. Frerichs and Paul Virgil McCracken Flesher (ed.), *Religion, Science and Magic in Concert and Conflict* (New York and Oxford: Oxford University Press, 1989), 142–65, esp. 162.

[24] There is some evidence (esp. Tob 3.17; cf. 6.15 [G¹]) that an exorcism may have been seen as issuing a bill of divorce to a demon. See Paul E. Dion, 'Raphael L'exorciste', *Bib* 57 (1976), 399–413, esp. 407–08 and Dan Levene, '"A Happy Thought of the Magicians", The Magical *Get.*', in Robert Deutsch (ed.), *Shlomo: Studies in Epigraphy, Iconography, History and Archaeology in Honor of Shlomo Moussaieff* (Tel Aviv-Jaffa: Archaeological Center Publications, 2003), 174–84.

[25] E.g., Tob 6.7–8; 8.2–3; 4Q196 I 12; 4Q197 4 I 13–14; 4Q510; 4Q511; 4Q511 frag. 63, col. 4.1–3; 6Q18; 8Q5 1; 11Q5 (11QPsª) XXVII, 9–10; 11Q11; Mark 9:38/Luke 9:49; Acts 19:13–19; Josephus, *Ant.* 8.45–49; cf. *JW* 7.180–85; Justin Martyr, *Dialogue* 85.3; and, e.g. *PGM* IV. 1227–64, 3007–86; V. 96–172.

[26] E.g. *PGM* IV. 1240, 3019; XII. 281–82; cf. XXXVI. 275–83; also Kotansky, 'Greek Exorcistic Amulets', 242–77.

[27] E.g., Josephus, *Ant.* 8.47; *Pesiqta de Rab Kahana* 4.5 on which see See Jacob Neusner, *Development of a Legend* (Leiden: Brill, 1970), 167, 182.

[28] E.g., Tob 6.1–8.3; 4Q510 and 4Q511; also 11Q11; *LAB* 60; *PGM* I. 96–132, 195–222; III. 1–164; IV. 86–87; IV. 2145–240; VII. 579–90; CXIV. 1–14; Roy Kotansky, *Greek Magical Amulets: The Inscribed Gold, Silver, Copper, and Bronze 'Lamellae': Text and Commentary. Part I: Published Texts of Known Provenance* (Abhandlungen der Nordrhein-Westfälischen Akademie der Wissenschaften. Sonderreihe Papyrologica Coloniensia vol. 22.1; Opladen: Westdeutscher Verlag, 1994), I.38, 52, 67.

Although these magical exorcisms could be performed by any-one, there were also highly regarded professional, often peripatetic, practitioners.[29] Along with performing exorcisms they were also sought to help find a lover, restrain anger, get rid of a friend, produce a trance, gain control of a god, acquire business and cus-tomers, and cause sickness, for example. These professionals, liter-ate and sometimes bilingual, and religiously well informed, gave attention to their personal diet as well as to ritual purity. Working with their assistants, who were sometimes family members, they collected, copied, amalgamated and preserved a great range of texts, sometimes in multiple copies, perhaps for giving to col-leagues. Aside from tools for writing prescriptions, they also had on hand a wide range of materials: vegetable matter, insects and ani-mal body parts, sheets of papyrus and metal, as well as containers and utensils that facilitated the preparation of their prescriptions. Sometimes they would perform exorcisms using incantations alone or include activities or, perhaps, dispense some article or phylactery (or both) that was already charged with spiritual power in order to drive away, or provides the patient ongoing protection from, a spir-itual being.

Next, along this range of kinds of exorcists, are what we could call charismatic magicians whose success was thought to depend on their personal force as well as on what they said or done. For example, Josephus (b. 37/38 AD) tells a story of David in a way that describes him as a charismatic magician.[30] Saul is said to be beset by 'strange disorders and evil spirits' that required a search to be made for someone 'with power to charm away spirits and to play upon the harp'. David is found and, Josephus says, whenever the evil spirit tormented Saul, David stood over the king and played his harp and chanted his songs so that Saul's 'illness was charmed away' (*Ant*. 6.168–69). It was not only David's presence but also his playing that was considered important in removing an evil spirit.[31]

At the other end of the range of exorcisms from those we have called magical are those carried out by charismatics. Instead of the

---

[29] On what follows, in more detail, see Twelftree, 'Ancient Magic', 76–78.

[30] Josephus, *Ant*. 16.166–69; cf. 1 Sam 16. Also see 1QapGen XX. 28–29.

[31] For a nuanced discussion of the understanding of the removal of the demon in relation to this passage see Roland Deines, 'Josephus, Salomo und die von Gott verliehene τεχνή gegen die Dämonen', in Lange, Lichtenberger and Römheld (eds.), *Demons*, 368–69 n. 10.

locus of power-authority being in what was said or done, it is the personal or charismatic force alone of the exorcist that is thought to bring about the eviction of the unwanted spirit. A number of examples are found in the literature.[32] In the rabbinic literature there is a story concerning Simeon ben Yose, a fourth generation tannaitic rabbi. A demon, Ben Temalion, is said to be cast out of the Emperor's daughter by Simeon simply calling out to the demon, 'Ben Temalion, get out! Ben Temalion, get out!' (*b. Me'ilah* 17b). This exorcism is described as depending entirely on the personal or charismatic force of Simeon. Also, Flavius Philostratus (c. 170–c. 245 AD) tells of Apollonius of Tyana[33] casting out a demon from a lad by reprimanding the demon and ordering it to quit the youth (Philostratus, *Life of Apollonius* IV. 20). Further, Lucian of Samosata (born c. 120 AD) says a Syrian from Palestine performed exorcisms for a large fee. He is said to stand beside the person and ask the spirit about his entry into the sufferer. The spirit would answer, sometimes in a foreign language. To drive out the spirit, Lucian says the Syrian would adjure and, if necessary, threaten it (Lucian, *Love of Lies* 16).

In none of the material that we have noted is there any explicit suggestion that the exorcisms had any significance beyond the healing of the individual involved or, in the case of the charismatic healings, enhancing the reputation of the healer. However, in the Qumran literature there are already hints of what will become the defining characteristics of the exorcisms of Jesus: the evil spirits, who have a leader,[34] are enemies of God's people being driven out on his authority.[35] Turning to the New Testament, the subject of exorcism is dominated by reports of Jesus' exorcistic activity.

---

[32] In more detail see Twelftree, *Name*, 44–45.

[33] Apollonius probably lived from 40 AD to about 120 AD. See Maria Dzielska, *Apollonius of Tyana in Legend and History* (Rome: L'erma, 1986), 32–38, 186.

[34] 1QS 3.24; also, e.g., 1Q13 2.12–13; 4Q387 3.ii.4, most commonly Belial (e.g., 1QS 1.16–2.8; CD 4.12–15; 1QM 1.4–5, 13–16), but also Mastema (e.g., CD 16.5; 1QM 13.11), Melchereša (4Q280 1.2), Satan (11QPs[a] 19.15), Abaddon (11Q11 4.10; 4QBer[a]) and, depending on how 4Q560 is restored, Beelzebul on which see D.L. Penny and Michael O. Wise, 'By the Power of Beelzebub: An Aramaic Incantation Formula from Qumran (4Q560)', *JBL* 113 (1994), 627–50; J. Naveh, 'Fragments of an Aramaic Magic Book from Qumran', *IEJ* 48 (1998), 252–61.

[35] See the discussion of 4Q560; 11Q5; 11Q11; 4Q510 and 4Q511 in Twelftree, 'Ancient Magic', 63–64.

## Jesus and exorcism

In considering the exorcisms of Jesus against this background a number of aspects of his approach stand out. To begin with, at first sight, it seems that Jesus is most like the charismatic exorcists in relying on his own personal or charismatic force to evict demons.[36] For, in telling a demon, for example, to 'Be silent, and come out of him!' (Mark 1:25), he appeared to be relying on his own resources. However, when asked about his method, Jesus said that he cast out demons 'by the Spirit (or finger) of God.'[37] And, in the question, 'If I cast out demons by Beelzebul, by whom do your sons cast them out?' (Matt. 12:27//Luke 11:19) Jesus assumes he is, like his contemporary exorcists, relying an external power-authority. That is, even though he appeared to act on the basis of his own personal force, like the magicians, Jesus was confidently assuming the right to use, at will, his chosen power-authority. The cultural proximity of Jesus to the approach of the magicians is also apparent in that every incantation Jesus is reported to have used in exorcism is paralleled in the magical literature.[38]

However, secondly, there are some marked differences between the exorcisms of Jesus and those of the magicians.[39] Jesus does not 'charge,' 'adjure' or 'bind' the demons by another power-authority. Instead, so confident is Jesus in his ability to use or, even, be identified with the Spirit or finger of God – his power source – that he uses only the emphatic 'I'. Also, from the evidence available to us, Jesus did not collect, maintain or (save from the episode of the pigs in Mark 5:1–20) use artefacts or a library of incantations. Apart from exorcism, he expressed no interest in either the control of, or protection from, unwanted demons that are frequently found in ancient magic. Jesus does not rebuke sickness,[40] reserving exorcistic language and technique for the removal of demons, nor does he show any interest in exorcising buildings or places, and at no point is Jesus reported as using prayer in his exorcistic technique. Taking into account the proximity of Jesus'

---

[36] So, e.g., Geza Vermes, *Jesus the Jew* (London: SCM, 2001), 60, cf. 195.

[37] Matt. 12.28//Luke 11.20. On the historical reliability of this saying see Graham H. Twelftree, *Jesus the Miracle Worker* (Downers Grove, Ill, IVP, 1999), 268.

[38] See Twelftree, 'Ancient Magic', 83 n. 124.

[39] Further, see Graham H. Twelftree, '*ΕΙ ΔΕ . . . ΕΓΩ ΕΚΒΑΛΛΩ ΤΑ ΔΑΙΜΟ-ΝΙΑ . . .*', in David Wenham and Craig Blomberg (eds.), *The Miracles of Jesus* (Sheffield: JSOT, 1986), 383–86.

[40] On Luke 4:39 see below.

approach to the magicians, as well as his differences from them, and his self-confidence in – even identification with – his power-authority, places Jesus somewhere between the charismatic magicians and the later charismatics. Indeed, he is probably to be considered the first of the charismatic healers.[41]

Thirdly, we know of no other healer in antiquity for whom miracles appear to dominate as they do Jesus' activity[42] and for whom exorcism is reported to have been one of the most obvious and important aspects of his public life.[43] Nevertheless, fourthly, given the general prevalence at the time of exorcisms similar to his, as well as Jews not considering such miracles as eschatologically significant, it is astonishing that Jesus made the unprecedented claim that his exorcisms were both the spearhead of his defeat of Satan and, in themselves, an important part of the realization of the kingdom of God.[44] In other words, for Jesus, exorcism delivered a person from Satan and became an expression of the kingdom of God (Matt. 11:5; Luke 7:22).

Although the evidence is not as clear as we would wish, it is most probable that before Easter Jesus sent his immediate followers on a mission to announce the coming of the kingdom of God.[45] However, it does not seem that he gave them a specific charge to perform exorcisms. Only one of the gospel sources, Mark, says that Jesus 'gave them authority over the unclean spirits.'[46] However, from the vocabulary and style of the statement, as well as Mark's considerable interest in exorcism, it is probably a later addition to the tradition.[47] Nevertheless, even though Jesus' command has little support, it remains highly

---

[41] See Peter Brown, 'The Rise and Function of the Holy Man in Late Antiquity', *JRS* 61 (1971), 100.

[42] John P. Meier, *A Marginal Jew*, vol. 2 (New York: Doubleday, 1991), Part 3, esp. 970.

[43] See Graham H. Twelftree, 'The Miracles of Jesus: Marginal or Mainstream?' *JSHJ* 1 (2003), 104–24.

[44] Matt. 12:28//Luke 11:20; cf. Matt. 10:6–8//Luke 9:1–2; Mark 3:21–30. See Twelftree, 'Marginal or Mainstream?' 120.

[45] See the discussion by F.C. Hahn, *Mission in the New Testament* (London: SCM, 1965), 41–46; Joachim Jeremias, *New Testament Theology* (London: SCM, 1971), 231; John P. Meier, *A Marginal Jew: Rethinking the Historical Jesus*, vol. 3 (New York: Doubleday, 2001), 148–62.

[46] Mark 6:7, followed by Matt. 10:8 and Luke 9:1.

[47] In more detail see Twelftree, *Name*, 50–51; cf. those cited by E.J. Pryke, *Redactional Style in the Marcan Gospel* (SNTSMS 33. Cambridge: Cambridge University Press, 1978), 14.

likely Jesus' followers conducted exorcisms on their pre-Easter mission, and the story of the unknown exorcist assumes, inadvertently, they were already exorcists.[48] Further, that they were expected to announce the kingdom of God (Luke 10:9) – and they would have been aware of the connection Jesus made between exorcism and the arrival of the kingdom – strongly suggests both that they engaged in exorcism and that it would have been considered as delivering people from Satan.

However, Jesus' followers did not take up his method of confidently using, to the point of identifying with, the Spirit or finger of God and commanding the demon to depart. Rather, the story of the unknown exorcist carries the hint that the disciples were using the more magical methods of other exorcists. That is, their technique involved making it obvious that they were casting out demons 'in the name of' a power-authority, in their case, Jesus (Mark 9:38). Yet, the apparent brevity reported of these exorcisms, though not exceptional, stands in contrast to what is generally known about exorcism in the period. Like Jesus' exorcisms, they were probably understood as delivering people from Satan and as expressions of the arrival of the kingdom of God.

## Paul[49]

With the high profile the synoptic gospels give to exorcism in the ministry of Jesus it is, at first, surprising when we turn to Paul – the Christian writer closest in time to Jesus – that he appears to say nothing whatsoever about either Jesus being an exorcist or about his own possible involvement in the practice. Of course, the absence of any clear reference to exorcism could be due to the nature of Paul's writings. They are occasional letters dealing with specific issues that do not naturally lend themselves to mentioning exorcisms he may have performed.

Paul's letters are equally silent about exorcism in his churches. At first sight it might be expected that the list of gifts of the Spirit would include exorcism. However, Paul describes the *charismata* as being for

---

[48] See Mark 9:38–39//Luke 9:49–50; cf. Luke 10:17.

[49] For recent literature see Craig A. Evans, 'Paul the Exorcist and Healer', in Stanley E. Porter (ed.), *Paul and his Theology* (Leiden and Boston: Brill, 2006), 363–79 and those cited 363 n. 1.

'the common good' (1 Cor. 12:7) or for the benefit of 'one another' – believers (Rom. 12:5). Therefore, the *charismata* being for use within the church, and Paul viewing people as related either to Satan or Christ[50] – and Christians having passed from Satan to Christ[51] – it would be inconceivable for him to mention exorcism, or even evangelism, among the gifts.[52]

Nevertheless, in Galatians 3:5 Paul assumes that his readers are being supplied with the Spirit resulting in miracles being worked 'in' (*en*) or among them. As he uses the same language at 1 Corinthians 12:6, where the *charasmata* are activated 'in' (*en*) the believers, this suggests that the Galatians are able to carry out or perform miracles. Whether or not this included exorcism we cannot say, though it seems likely.

Positive indications that Paul was involved in exorcism come from noting that he probably knew and modelled Jesus' ministry,[53] including performing miracles (Rom. 15:18–19). More particularly, in using the term 'power' (*dunamis*) to characterize his ministry (1 Cor. 4:20) Paul is probably conveying the idea that miracles, including exorcisms, were involved. For, in the period, the plural, 'powers' (*dunameis*), was used for miracles[54] and healing,[55] as well as exorcism.[56] Also, Paul's use of the phrase 'signs and wonders'[57] as a description of his ministry is a further strong suggestion that miracles were part of his ministry. Although none of this is irrefutable evidence that Paul was involved in exorcism, it makes it probable that exorcism was part of his ministry.

Indeed, Paul portrays the pre-Christian state as one in which a person is 'enslaved to the elemental spirits' (Gal. 4:3; cf. Eph. 2:1–2).

---

[50] 1 Cor. 5:5; 2 Cor. 6:15; Gal. 5:16–26.

[51] 2 Cor. 6:14–15; cf. Rom. 13:12; 2 Cor. 4:6. See also Col. 1:13.

[52] Cf. J. Christopher Thomas, 'Spiritual Conflict in Illness and Affliction', in A. Scott Moreau et al. (ed.), *Deliver us from Evil* (Monrovia: MARC, 2002), 47.

[53] See 1 Cor. 4:16–17; 11:1; cf. 1 Thess. 1:6; 2:14; Willis Peter De Boer, *The Imitation of Paul* (Kampen: Kok, 1962), esp. chapter 5; Elizabeth Anne Castelli, *Imitating Paul* (Louisville: WJK, 1991), chapter 4.

[54] E.g. Matt. 7:22; 11:20–21//Luke 10:13; Matt. 11:23; Mark 6:2//Matt. 13:54; Matt. 13:58; Luke 19:37; Mark 6:5, 14//Matt. 14:2; Mark 9:30; Gal. 3:5; Justin, *1 Apology* 26.2.

[55] Mark 5:30//Luke 8:46; Luke 5:17; 6:19; P. Oxy. XI. 1381.90–91 (2nd century).

[56] Luke 4:36; 6:18–19; 9:1; 10:19–20.

[57] Rom. 15.18–19; 1 Cor. 4:20; 2 Cor. 12:12; 1 Thess. 1:5. See Molly Whitaker, 'Signs and Wonders: The Pagan Background', *SE* 5 (1968), 155–58; Graham H. Twelftree, 'Signs, Wonders, Miracles', in *DPL*, 875–77.

Although he only once mentions demons (1 Cor. 10:20), and on another occasion a 'messenger' (*angelos*) of Satan (2 Cor. 12:7), Paul uses the language of 'principalities and powers' to refer not only to the Jewish idea that supernatural powers motivated the pagan world order,[58] but also to sinister rebellious beings in league with Satan.[59]

However, Paul gives no suggestion that freedom from these 'spirits' came through exorcism. Instead, he says, it is in knowing God or in being known by God (Gal. 4:9) – in other words in salvation – that deliverance from the sinister powers has taken place for the Galatians (cf. Eph. 2:8). In particular, salvation was not located in his ministry or any aspect of it as it was for Jesus. Rather, salvation, notably from the powers of darkness, was located in the cross-event (Col. 1:13–14; 2:15). Moreover, the approach Paul takes in responding to the experience of the ongoing activity of these sinister beings is not exorcism but more an apotropaic approach: an appeal to the Lord's grace (2 Cor. 12:9), to knowledge of the love of God in Jesus Christ (Rom. 8:38–39), and to living in the Spirit (Gal. 5:16). Again, in that believers have passed from Satan to Christ (see above), this is not surprising.

Thus, so far, on the one hand, all we have are hints that Paul and his readers probably conducted exorcisms. On the other hand, however, we have seen that, for Paul, freedom from the demonic comes not from exorcism but in salvation. Before we attempt to solve this conundrum, Acts can be taken into account. However, being a secondary source by an author with an unclear relationship with Paul, Acts is to be used with care in recovering the historical Paul.[60]

There are just two stories in Acts that are of particular interest to us. In one story the seven sons of a Jewish high priest named Sceva attempt to cast out a demon 'by Jesus whom Paul proclaims' (Acts 19:13). That Paul's name is said to be invoked as part of the incantation for an exorcism is corroborative evidence that Paul was an exorcist.

Another story, Acts 16:16–18, is of more direct use in telling us about Paul and exorcism. For many days, Paul is said to be followed by a slave girl crying out, 'These men are slaves of the Most high God, who

---

[58] Deut. 32:8; Isa. 24:21–22; Dan. 10:13, 20; 1 Cor. 2:6–8.

[59] Cf. 1 Cor. 15:24–25. See also Gal. 4:3, 9, on which see Clinton E. Arnold, 'Returning to the Domain of the Powers: *Stoicheia* as Evil Spirits in Galatians 4:3,9', *NovT* 38 (1996), 55–76.

[60] See S.M. Praeder, 'Miracle Worker and Missionary: Paul in the Acts of the Apostles', *SBLSP* 22 (1983), 107–29; William O. Walker, 'Acts and the Pauline corpus reconsidered', *JSNT* 24 (1985), 3–23; Stanley E. Porter, *Paul in Acts* (Peabody: Hendrickson, 2001), esp. 60–62.

proclaim to you a way of salvation' (Acts 16:17). Annoyed, Paul turned and exorcised a spirit of divination (*pneuma puthōna*, 16:16) from her. That this story comes in one of the so-called 'we-passages' in Acts[61] probably adds to its value for it is reasonable to take these as implying Luke's first hand knowledge of the reported events.[62] In any case, it is unlikely that Luke would create a story in which one of his heroes was motivated by annoyance (*diaponeomai*, Acts 16:18; cf. 4:2).[63]

The method of exorcism Paul is said to use is, 'I order (*parangellō*) you in the name of Jesus Christ to come out of her' (Acts 16:17). This declared reliance on an outside power-authority is the same as what we have seen is likely to have been used by the followers of Jesus before Easter. Moreover, the use of *parangellō*, with its overtones imply-ing the handing on of a command,[64] confirms that Paul was not, as a charismatic might, relying on his own resources to carry out the evic-tion of the annoying spirit. Rather, as was common at the time, a figure who was thought to have preternatural or exorcistic powers – often Solomon,[65] but in this case Jesus[66] – was invoked.

The evidence is not as fulsome or as clear as we would wish, but it does point to a simple solution to the puzzle of Paul's involvement in exorcism. That is, while Paul understood freedom from slavery to the elemental spirits to take place in salvation, that salvation was focussed in the cross-event not, as for Jesus, in his ministry or an aspect of it. At best, therefore, exorcism could only be of peripheral interest to him. However, as suggested by Acts, as well as by his own writing, having

---

[61] Acts (11:28 in the Western text, see D [itp] [cop^G67]); 16:10–17; 20:5–15; 21:1–18; 27:1–28:16.

[62] Over against the scepticism of, e.g., Vernon K. Robin, 'By Land and by Sea: The We-Passages and Ancient Sea Voyages', in C.H. Talbert (ed.), *Perspectives on Luke–Acts* (Danville: Association of Baptist Professors of Religion and Edinburgh: T.&T. Clark, 1978), 215–42, see Colin J. Hemer, 'First Person Narrative in Acts 27–28', *TynBul* 36 (1985), 79–109 and Colin J. Hemer, *The Book of Acts in the Setting of Hellenistic History* (Tübingen: J.C.B. Mohr; 1989), 308–34.

[63] For a more detailed defence of the historical reliability of this story see Twelftree, *Name*, 72–73.

[64] E.g., Xenophon, *Anab.* 1.8.3; Plato, *Phaed.* 116C; Jos. (LXX) 6:7; Josephus, *Ant.* 2.311; 3.29; 6.140; 7.329; Philo, *Legat.* 1.98; 3.151; *Sacr.* 1.64.

[65] E.g., 11Q11 II.2; Josephus, *Ant.* 8.45–49. See D.C. Duling, 'Solomon, Exorcism and the Son of David', *HTR* 68 (1975), 235–52.

[66] See also, most notably, *PGM* IV. 1231–39 and IV. 3020. Further, and on other figures, see Twelftree, 'Ancient Magic', 79–81.

Jesus as a model, he performed exorcisms, perhaps in exceptional cases or when so directed by the Spirit. We turn now to discuss how exorcism was understood by the gospel writers.

## Mark

The earliest gospel, perhaps written in Rome around 70 AD,[67] contains a great deal of material related to exorcism.[68] Contrary to the view of some modern interpreters,[69] Mark portrays the demonic battle as being against Satan not Rome.[70] In turn, for Mark, exorcism is significant because it both personalizes, as well as provides a cosmic arena to, the battle of ministry.

There are a number of signals in the narrative that the interpretive key for Mark's readers to hear what he has to say, including about exorcism, is his discipleship motif. In concluding Jesus' teaching, and applying it to his readers, Mark has Jesus say, 'And what I say to you' – the historical disciples (Mark 13:3) – 'I say to all', the readers (13:37). That is, Jesus' teaching is intended to be taken as applying to the readers. Also, some stories conclude with instruction to the disciples that readers would, therefore, have taken to be for them. Of particular interest are the instructions on how to conduct an exorcism that conclude the story of the lad with epileptic-like symptoms (9:28–29). In using the theme of discipleship to challenge his readers to take up and enter the same discipleship,[71] a number of aspects of Mark's views on exorcism become clear.

First, Mark sees exorcism as the highest priority in the ministry of his readers. Even though the report of the work of the Twelve includes curing the sick (Mark 6:12), in the stories of their call (3:14–15) and their sending (6:7), along with proclaiming the message, exorcism is their

---

[67] Cf. John S. Kloppenborg, '*Evocatio Deorum* and the Date of Mark', *JBL* 124 (2005), 419–50.

[68] Note esp. Mark 1:21–28, 32–34; 3:7–30; 5:1–20; 6:7–13; 7:24–30; 9:14–29, 38–39.

[69] E.g., Paul W. Hollenbach, 'Jesus, Demoniacs, and Public Authorities: A Socio-Historical Study', in *JAAR* 49 (1981), 567–88; Ched Myers, *Binding the Strong Man* (Maryknoll: Orbis, 1994), 31; Santiaogo Guijarro, 'The Politics of Exorcism', in *The Social Setting of Jesus and the Gospels*, Wolfgang Stegemann, Bruce J. Malina and Gerd Theissen (eds.), (Minneapolis: Fortress, 2002), 165–67, 171–72.

[70] See the discussion of the politics of possession in Twelftree, *Name*, 105–11.

[71] Cf. Ernest Best, *Following Jesus* (Sheffield: JSOT, 1981), 246.

only assigned task. Also, the authority which arises out of being called (3:14–15; cf. 6:7) is frequently associated with exorcism (1:22, 27; 3:15; 6:7). Even the parable of the doorman and the slaves (13:34), where the slaves are also given authority (*exousia*),[72] may be intended to convey the idea that exorcism was to be the dominant work of ministry for followers of Jesus. In turn, exorcism is important because, according to the story of the Beelzebul controversy (3:21–30), it is God's promised eschatological deliverance of people, no less significant or miraculous than raising the dead. In other words, in their exorcisms, their compassionate God is eschatologically active delivering people from a mighty enemy.

Mark, along with the other synoptic gospel writers, reinforces this by describing a demon as being 'cast out' (*ekballō*). For, in the Septuagint *ekballō* is most often used when an enemy, frustrating or standing in the way of God fulfilling his purpose for his chosen people, is cast out so that God's purposes can be fulfilled.[73]

Secondly, the story of the Beelzebul controversy also functions to establish that the power-authority for exorcism is the Holy Spirit not Satan, as antagonistic observers probably asserted (Mark 3:23). It is likely, then, that the ministry of exorcism was associated with fear or caused turbulence in the church. This impression is also gained from the story of the stilling of the storm which is likely to have been read as an assurance that, when facing (demonic?) storms – about to be illustrated in the story of the Gerasene demoniac (5:1–20), the church (the boat?) would be kept safe by Jesus being with them, and by their faith in him (4:35–41).

Thirdly, Mark seems to advocate a number of different methods of exorcism for his readers. In modelling Jesus, his followers would be expected to rebuke, muzzle, use the name of the demon to gain preternatural control, transfer demons from a person to an external habitat, and order demons to leave their host. Also, in the cases of mute sufferers, Mark advocates prayer (Mark 9:29) that is, a faith-filled statement – dependent on the Holy Spirit – directed to the demon. Further, Mark also endorses the method of exorcism 'in the name of Jesus' (9:38). This was to perform an exorcism as if it had been carried out by Jesus himself.[74] All three of these approaches to exorcism

---

[72] Cf. Best, *Following*, 152–53.

[73] Cf. Exod. 23:30; Deut. 33:27–28. See the discussion in Twelftree, *Christ*, 104–5.

[74] See the discussion in Twelftree, *Name*, 127.

amount to directing faith-filled statements to demons as if Jesus were the exorcist.

## Luke

Luke also holds the view that exorcism is to be part of the mission of the church. Not only does portraying the followers of Jesus as parallel-ing and therefore modelling and maintaining his ministry (Acts 1:1) show this (Luke 22:20, 27),[75] but so also does the story of the mission of the Seventy (10:1–12, 17–20) in prefiguring the universal mission of the church.[76] However, the relatively low profile of exorcism in Acts[77] shows that, for Luke, exorcism was not the only, nor the most impor-tant, aspect of the ministry of the church.

Concomitantly, Luke broadens the scope of the demonic. Notably, Luke recasts the story of Jesus' healing Simon's mother-in-law (cf. Mark 1:29–31) so that a 'high' (*megalō*) fever is said to 'trouble' (*sunechō*) her. Then, rather than Jesus taking the woman by the hand, exorcistic meas-ures are described in that Jesus stands over the woman and rebukes the fever (Luke 4:38–39).[78] Yet, on the one hand, in another story, a crippled woman who is said to 'have' (*echō*, 13:11) a spirit is not described as being exorcised. Instead, Jesus declares she is free from her ailment and puts his hands on her (13:12–13). On the other hand, at the beginning of the Sermon on the Plain Luke does not say Jesus rebuked or cast out the unclean spirits but that those who were troubled with unclean spirits were 'healed' or 'cured' (*etherapeuonto*, 6:18).

It is not that Luke is being governed by a distinction between oppres-sion and possession; he uses oppression to refer to the whole range of demonic activity rather than an aspect of it (Acts 10:38). Instead, Luke

---

[75] Robert F. O'Toole, 'Parallels between Jesus and his Disciples in Luke–Acts: A Further Study', *BZ* 27 (1983), 195–212; William S. Kurz, 'Narrative Models for Imitation in Luke-Acts', in David L. Balch, Everett Ferguson and Wayne A. Meeks (ed.), *Greeks, Romans, and Christians: Essays in Honor of Abraham J. Malherbe* (Minneapolis: Fortress, 1990), 171–89.

[76] Helmut Flender, *St Luke: Theologian of Redemptive History* (London: SPCK, 1967), 23; I. Howard Marshall, *The Gospel of Luke* (Exeter: Paternoster, 1978), 415.

[77] See Acts 5:12–16 (summary of apostles' ministry); 8:4–8 (Philip in Samaria); 10:36–43 (summary of Jesus' ministry); 16:16–18 (possessed slave girl); 19:11–20 (the Sons of Sceva).

[78] Further, see Twelftree, *Name*, 132.

is blurring the distinction between demon possession and other kinds of sickness, suggesting that all sickness has a demonic dimension or is evil, even though not thought to be caused by a demon.[79] In turn, performing exorcism takes its place in a balanced approach to ministry involving word and deed (cf. Luke 9:1–6; Acts 8:38).

Even though Jesus was seen as the pattern for the life and ministry of the church, Christians were not expected to emulate precisely the methods of Jesus. What appears critical to Luke is not the person conducting the exorcism or the method used, but the powerful presence of God (often through his Spirit) driving away the demonic. For example, in the stories of Paul's clothing and the sons of Sceva (Acts 19:11–20), Luke says that 'handkerchiefs or aprons were carried away from his body to the sick, and diseases left them and the evil spirits came out of them' (19:12). While this may seem bizarre to twenty-first-century readers, in the ancient world it was thought that objects could be imbibed with, as well as transmit, spiritual power.[80] This included a person's clothing which was thought to carry the wearer's authority and power.[81] On the other hand, while accepting a variety of kinds of Christian exorcism (cf. Luke 9:49–50), he condemns text-based healings or exorcisms because they are not empowered by God or the Spirit (Acts 19:11–20).

In any case, for Luke, techniques were not the key to successful exorcism, but a person filled and empowered by the Spirit bringing about the preliminary, though ongoing, defeat of Satan and his kingdom. Likewise, Luke also does not condone payment for this ministry for that would, presumably, detract from seeing exorcisms as vehicles or expressions of God's salvation (Acts 8:18–24).

## Matthew

Reading between the lines it seems that, perhaps late in first-century Antioch,[82] Matthew considered that peripatetic ecstatic Christians, whose ministry involved exorcism, were 'savaging' (*harpax*) his

---

[79] Further, see Leo O'Reilly, *Word and Sign in the Acts of the Apostles* (Rome: Editrice Pontifical Università Gregoriana, 1987), 217 and the discussion in Twelftree, *Miracle Worker*, 178–81 and Twelftree, *Name*, 133–34.

[80] Cf. Josephus, *Ant.* 8.45–49, 353–54; *PGM* V. 159–71 XII. 301–6.

[81] E.g. Gen. 35:2; Num. 20:25–26; 1 Sam. 18:4; 1 Kgs. 19:19–20; 2 Kgs. 2:8; Ezek. 44:19 and Hag. 2:12–14. See also Luke 8:43–48.

[82] David C. Sim, *The Gospel of Matthew and Christian Judaism* (Edinburgh: T.&T. Clark, 1998), 33–40.

community (Matt 7:15). What Matthew objected to was their libertine lifestyle (7:15–27) and, probably, their taking money for their services.[83]

Though not suspicious of exorcism,[84] Matthew has probably, therefore, given miracles, including exorcism, their low priority behind the spoken word which takes pride of place in ministry. Exorcism is not mentioned until 4:23–25 in a summary and there is no healing story until after the Sermon on the Mount (cf. Matt 9:2–8). Yet, the command at the end of the gospel to teach all nations 'to obey everything that I have commanded you' (28:20) assumes a role for exorcism. In that 'to obey' (*tērein*) is to preserve or guard something[85] rather than keep a law, and a 'command' (*entellō*) is a general instruction as much as a law (cf. 4:6; 17:9), Jesus' final words commission his followers to take up all that is included in the gospel,[86] including exorcism (cf. 10:1).

Matthew implies that exorcism had neither been very successful for his community (Matt 17:14–21) nor, as was the experience for Jesus, had they been well received (12:22–29). His readers were, therefore, in need of encouragement (17:20). Indeed, Matthew invested Christian exorcisms with the same significance as those of Jesus: they were modelled on Jesus,[87] they were the deliverance of people from Satan's hold and, hence, the first stage of the destruction of Satan (12:28). Complementarily, they expressed the eschatological coming of the powerful presence of God (10:7; 12:28). The simple method of exorcising 'in the name of' Jesus[88] involved using faith-filled statements empowered by the Spirit directed against the demons (17:20). The removal of the unclean spirit was to be followed by the healed person adopting the lifestyle of a disciple otherwise the person was susceptible to further demonic attack, resulting in a worse state than before (12:43–44).

---

[83] See Matt. 10:8–9; cf. Acts 20:29, 33; 1 Thess. 2:5; *Didache* 11:6.

[84] Contra John M. Hull, *Hellenistic Magic and the Synoptic Tradition* (London: SCM, 1974), 116–41.

[85] Cf. Matt. 19:17; 23:3; 27:36, 54; 28:4, 20.

[86] W.D. Davies and Dale C. Allison, *The Gospel According to Saint Matthew* (3 vols.; Edinburgh: T.&T. Clark, 1988, 1991, 1997), 3:686; cf. Dorothy Jean Weaver, *Matthew's Missionary Discourse* (Sheffield: JSOT, 1990), 151.

[87] Matt. 10:7–8; cf. 4:17, 23–25.

[88] Matt. 7:22. Cf. 10:41–42; 18:5; 21:9.

## Johannine literature

From the synoptic gospels it seems that exorcism was of central importance in the ministry of Jesus and of varying importance in the churches they represent. Coming to the Johannine literature, therefore, it is
a surprise that there is no mention of the subject. With all the gospels
likely to have been written for wide circulation,[89] it cannot be that the
Fourth Gospel and its readers were unaware of exorcism being associated with Jesus and his followers. In fact, not only is it likely that the
Fourth Evangelist was aware of the synoptic traditions[90] but also, in
particular, there are hints of a knowledge of the exorcism material.[91]

The reason for the Fourth Gospel not mentioning exorcism is probably to be found primarily in noting that exorcisms would have been
viewed much differently from the miracles described by the Fourth
Evangelist. On the one hand, although exorcisms were taken to show
that Jesus was empowered by the Spirit, and understood to be part of
the actualization of the kingdom of God, they were seen as common
(e.g. Luke 11:19) and of ambiguous origin (e.g. Mark 3:22). Also, for the
synoptics, we have seen that the exorcisms were the focal point of the
battle with, and defeat of, Satan. On the other hand, for the Fourth
Evangelist, the cross is the scene of Jesus' battle with Satan.[92] Further,
though, there are far fewer miracles or signs in the Fourth Gospel, and
they are consistently spectacular and considered unambiguously divine both in origin and revelatory capacity.[93] Moreover, even though
Jesus is self-sufficient, his miracles reveal God to be at work.
Nevertheless, the miracles are not so much significant in themselves
but as signs, pointing to the true identity or glory of Jesus, and so to his

---

[89] On the intended wide readership for the gospels see Richard Bauckham
(ed.), *The Gospel for All Christians* (Grand Rapids and Cambridge: Eerdmans, 1998) and the discussion by Wendy E. Sproston North, 'John for
Readers of Mark? A Response to Richard Bauckham's Proposal', *JSNT* 25
(2003), 449–68.

[90] For a summary discussion see Andrew T. Lincoln, *The Gospel According to
Saint John* (Peabody: Hendrickson and London and New York: Continuum,
2005), 26–38.

[91] Edwin K. Broadhead, 'Echoes of an Exorcism in the Fourth Gospel?' *ZNW*
86 (1995), 111–19; also see Barnabas Lindars, 'Rebuking the Spirit: A New
Analysis of the Lazarus Story of John 11', *NTS* 38 (1992), 84–104.

[92] John 6:70; 12:31; 13:2; 14:30; 16:11. Cf. Heb. 2:10–18 on which see Bell,
*Deliver Us*, 292–318.

[93] See the discussion in Twelftree, *Miracle Worker*, chapters 7 and 8.

death and resurrection.[94] In other words, for the Fourth Evangelist, exorcisms would have been able neither to reflect clearly the divine origin, nature and destiny of Jesus nor the grand cosmic scale and otherworldly-setting of the battle involved in Jesus' ministry.

Yet, the Fourth Evangelist not only maintains the category of demon possession, but does so through having – at least at first sight – Jesus, and Jesus alone, repeatedly charged with having a demon.[95] But the great irony in the charge is particularly obvious in John 8:48–52. The readers are alerted to the irony of the accusation in the incredulous question that prefaces the charge: 'Are we not right in saying . . .?' (John 8:48). Readers know the 'Jews' could be anything but right in what they are about to say. For, in the narrative, the 'Jews' have been cast in a negative light as having the devil as their father, who does not stand in the truth because he is a liar.[96]

In answer to the two-part accusation that follows ('you are a Samaritan and have a demon') Jesus gives a simple catch-all response: 'I do not have a demon' (John 8:49). Irony continues in Jesus not denying being a Samaritan. Although the accusation of being a Samaritan was meant as a charge of being responsible for false prophecy (cf. 8:52),[97] over against the 'Jews', the Samaritans in the Fourth Gospel recognize Jesus and invite their new-found Saviour to live or dwell with them in intimacy (4:1–42). Ironically, this charge becomes a negative reflection of the 'Jews" own inability to identify and accept Jesus. In short, the charge brought against Jesus turns out to be both an ironic charge of the 'Jews" own inability to accept Jesus and a shorthand description of their own plight: the 'Jews', not Jesus, are to be taken as demon possessed.

In turn, in the Fourth Gospel, demon possession, or to be in error, is combated through knowing the truth. In the period, this was not an unfamiliar notion (cf. 1QS 2.13–26) and it was also important for churches sharing the same pool of ideas as the Fourth Gospel.[98] Of

---

[94] Twelftree, *Miracle Worker*, 227.

[95] John 7:20; 8:48, 49, 52; 10:20, 21.

[96] John 2:23–25; 3:1–12; 4:1–3; 7:20; 8:42–44.

[97] John Bowman, 'Samaritan Studies', *BJRL* 40 (1957–58), 306–8.

[98] See *Shepherd of Hermas* 14.2; Justin Martyr, *1 Apology* 56; Athenagoras, *Embassy* 27.2; Irenaeus, *Against Heresies* 2.31.2–3; Clement of Alexandria, *Exhortations to the Greeks* 1.1; 11.117.3–4. Cf. *T. Ben.* 5.2–3 on which see Amin Lange, 'Spirit of Inpurity', in Lange, Lichtenberger and Römheld (ed.), *Demons*, 262–63.

course, for the Fourth Evangelist knowing the truth was knowing Jesus.[99] Also, notably, the discussion centring around the charge of demon possession in 8:48–52 – which frequently touches on the issue of truth and falsehood (8:40, 44, 45, 46) – has its origin in the statement of Jesus, 'you will know the truth, and the truth will make you free' (8:32).[100]

Therefore, the Fourth Evangelist proposes that Satan has a deep and all encompassing hold not on a few but on the many. In turn, demon possession is not fought with the hand of a healer but with accepting Jesus (1:12), his truth and honouring God as one's Father (cf. 8:49). Salvation – knowing and remaining in Jesus and the truth he brings – is the required antidote to error and the demonic, not a healing encounter reserved for a few.

Also in the Johannine letters, where there are concerns about evil or false spirits (cf. 1 John 3:24; 4:1–6), exorcism is not mentioned. Rather, in the face of deception (1:2–3), knowing God, loving him, and in having the word of God abiding in you (2:14), the evil one is overcome (2:14–16). Consistent with these conclusions, in Revelation Satan's hold is not over a few individuals but over all the deceived who have not accepted the truth in Jesus (cf. Rev 9:20; 12:9).

## Other New Testament writings

In seeking to understand the place of exorcism in the New Testament there are some references of interest to us in Hebrews and James, as well as in the longer ending of Mark (Mark 16:9–20).[101] Hebrews 2:3–4 says 'God added his testimony by signs and wonders and various miracles [*dunamesin*], and by gifts [*merismois*] of the Holy Spirit, distributed according to his will.' The all encompassing phrase ('signs and wonders and various miracles')[102] suggests that exorcism was an ongoing part of the life of Christian ministry for Hebrews in confirming the

---

[99] John 1:14, 17; cf. 14:6; 15:26.

[100] B.C. Lategan, 'The truth that sets man free. Jn. 8:31–36', *Neot* 2 (1968), 70–80.

[101] The cryptic reference in 1 Pet. 3:18 to the resurrected Christ making 'a proclamation to the sprits in prison' connects dealing with the demonic not with exorcism but with Easter. Further on these passages see Twelftree, *Name*, §8.

[102] Acts 2:22; Rom. 15:18–19; 2 Cor. 12:12 and see n. 57 above.

message of the preachers and as an expression of the presence of the Spirit in the believer.

In James 2:19 there is the statement, 'You believe that God is one; you do well. Even the demons believe – and shudder (*phrissein*).' In the light of a general interest in evil or the demonic that is consistent with an interest in exorcism (Jas. 1:13–14; 3:15; 4:7), it is just possible that this brief statement echoes exorcistic activity. For Justin echoes this verse in the context of mentioning exorcism (*Dial.* 30.3; cf. Minucius Felix, *Oct.* 27.7). Also, the idea of shuddering, in the sense of frightening demons away, is found in the magical papyri (*PGM* IV. 3014–19). Further, 'God is one' is also a statement found in the vocabulary of Jewish exorcists in identifying their source of power-authority.[103] At the risk of pressing this text in James too far, it may be possible to see in it a reflection of exorcisms that were carried out in the name of God (cf. Jas. 5:14).[104]

The longer ending of Mark – perhaps written in Rome in the second quarter of the second century[105] – is evidence of the fluctuating fortunes of exorcism in the early church.[106] For this is the first clear reference to interest in exorcism since Matthew, written in the last quarter of the first century.[107] Here we need to note that in using the term 'cast out' (*ekballō*, Mark 16:9, 17) exorcism continues to be an expression of salvation – the casting out of an enemy of God so that his purposes could be fulfilled.[108] Also, not only are the exorcisms salvific but they provide evidence of faith (*pistueō*, 16:17; cf. John 14:12) and of the veracity of the message (Mark 16:20). From the mention of speaking in tongues alongside of exorcism we can extrapolate that exorcism was considered a 'gift' (cf. 1 Cor. 12:9–10, 28–30). The longer ending also maintains the view (cf. Mark 9:37–41) that the exorcisms were performed as if by Jesus (16:17) – perhaps understood to be through his Spirit.

---

[103] Justin Martyr, *Dial.* 85.3; cf. *PGM* IV. 1231–39; Origen, *Contra Celsum* 1.24–25; 4.33–34.

[104] Cf. *PGM* IV. 3014–20 and Justin, *Dial.* 85.3.

[105] See G. W. Trompf, 'The Markusschluss in Recent Research', *ABR* 21 (1973), 15–26 and Steven Lynn Cox, *A History and Critique of Scholarship Concerning the Markan Endings* (Lewiston: Mellen, 1993).

[106] Cf. Mark 16:9, 17, cf. 20. What follows depends on the discussion in Twelftree, *Name*, 235–37.

[107] See Twelftree, *Name*, esp. 229.

[108] Twelftree, *Jesus the Exorcist*, 109–10.

## Summary

The theme of exorcism in the New Testament is dominated by the reports of this aspect of Jesus' ministry in which he appears extraordinarily prolific and successful. So confident is he in his relationship with God that he identifies with God's Spirit and, using incantations familiar at the time, simply orders the demons to leave individuals. Such an approach identifies Jesus as the earliest known charismatic figure of this type.

However, for Jesus, his exorcisms are more than individual healings. Because of the position he presumed to have in God's economy, and because of the assumed relationship of the unwanted spirit to a demonic leader, the exorcisms are an assault on and deliverance from the kingdom of Satan and, concomitantly, one of the major expressions of the arrival of the kingdom or powerful presence of God.

Before Easter, Jesus sent his followers on a mission that extended his own. However, they resorted to more magical means in exorcising 'in the name of Jesus'. Paul is also most likely to have been involved in similar forms of exorcisms, at least occasionally. However, for Paul, with the prime locus of salvation taken to be in the past (the cross event) and in another figure (Jesus), deliverance from enslavement to the elemental spirits was understood to come not directly through his ministry or any part of it, but in the relationship with God possible in Christ. Having passed from Satan to Christ, a believer withstood ongoing attack from sinister powers by appealing to God's grace, for example.

The Christian communities represented by the gospels were involved in exorcism to varying degrees. On the one hand, in Mark exorcism was of high importance in mirroring the ministry of Jesus. On the other hand, in Luke exorcism was part of a balanced ministry of word and deed where the deeds of healing against those oppressed by the devil were not always distinguished from exorcism. In the Johannine literature, so deep and all encompassing is Satan's hold not on a few but on the many that demon possession (manifest in error and sin) is not dealt with in individual exorcisms but with the truth or salvation – knowing and remaining in Jesus.

Perhaps because of the difficulty in distinguishing their approach from those of others, Christian exorcism suffered fluctuating fortunes. After no mention of it for around half a century, at the time of the circulation of the longer ending of Mark in the middle of the second century, exorcism was revived and continued to be one aspect or expression of deliverance or salvation.

# Chapter 3

# Deliverance and Exorcism in the Early Church

*Andrew Daunton-Fear*

Yet all this sovereignty and power that we have over the demons derives its force only from the naming of Christ, and this reminder of what they expect to come upon them from God at the judgement seat of Christ.

*Tertullian*

**Abstract**

This study looks at the believed origin and nature of 'demons ', their claimed activities, and the means by which early Christians sought deliverance from their influence. It then focuses specifically on exorcism, considering first the approach of pagan magicians and Jews before examining in greater detail that of Christians in the period of the Early Church. Christian exorcism was clearly valued both for the relief it brought to sufferers and for its apologetic power in demonstrating the supremacy of Christ over the gods of the Greco-Roman Empire; it is still relevant today.

## The Early Church

The period of the Early Church begins with the first Christian Pentecost and lasts until the Western Roman Empire was overrun by savage tribes from beyond its frontiers in the fifth and sixth centuries. This period is then subdivided by the Council of Nicea (325) into Pre-Nicene and Post-Nicene. The leaders and theologians of the Early Church are known as the 'Church Fathers'. 'Patristics ' (Lat. *patres*, 'fathers ') is the study of their lives and writings. As the previous chapter in this symposium is devoted to examining the evidence of the New Testament, this chapter will touch on it but lightly.

## The demons

Evil spirits are rarely mentioned in the Old Testament and, when they are, they are said to come 'from the Lord'.[1] In contrast they feature prominently in the New Testament gospels where they are called 'unclean ' spirits[2] or 'demons ' (Gk. *daimonia*).[3] It is common to trace this new emphasis to the influence of Persian Zoroastrianism during Judah 's exile after Babylon fell to the Persians c.539 BC.[4] Jewish inter-testamental literature shows a considerable interest in angels and evil spirits. In *1 Enoch* 6 (pre-170 BC) the 'sons of God ' referred to in Genesis 6:2 are interpreted as angels, sent by God to watch over mankind, who fell in love with beautiful women; from their illicit intercourse came the giants whose souls are the evil spirits which afflict and oppress mankind (*1 En.* 15).

In Greek literature 'demon' (Gk. *daimōn* and its later derivative *daimonion*) long bore a positive connotation. By the first centuries of the Christian era, however, the general trend was to associate demons with evil.[5] In the writings of the second-century Fathers we find this view entrenched. Clement of Alexandria (c.150–c.210) chides the Greeks: 'Your gods are inhuman and man-hating demons who not only exult over the insanity of men, but go so far as to enjoy human slaughter.'[6]

Tertullian (c.170–c.230) says they attach themselves to pagan children from birth;[7] they are devoted to the deception of humans and preventing them from faith;[8] they are the power behind idolatry, their

---

[1] Judg. 9:23; 1 Sam. 16:14–23; 19:9. See chapter 1.

[2] E.g. Mark 1:23; 5:2; Matt. 10:1; 12:43.

[3] E.g. Luke 9:1; 10:17.

[4] J.M. Hull, *Hellenistic Magic and the Synoptic Tradition* (London: SCM, 1974), 29; E. Sorensen, *Possession and Exorcism in the New Testament and Early Christianity* (Tübingen: Mohr, 2002), ch. 2.

[5] E. Ferguson, *Demonology of the Early Christian World* (Lewiston, NY: Mellen Press, 1984), 49–51.

[6] *Exhortation* 3.42.1, cf. 4.55.5 (Butterworth); cf. Justin Martyr, *1 Apology* 5, Tatian, *Oration* 8–9, 12.

[7] Via the idolatrous practices to which new-born babies are subjected – *Soul* 39.

[8] *Nations* 2.13, *Apology* 22.4, 6, *Soul* 57.

special enterprise,[9] feeding on the odours and blood of the sacrifices,[10] and revelling in the savagery of the amphitheatre.[11] According to Justin (c.100–c.165), it was when the demons came to know the prophecies concerning Christ, such as Isaiah 35:5–6, that they raised up pagan counterparts such as Asclepius;[12] they also inspired heretical sects to confuse people,[13] and brought about the persecution of Christians.[14] These points were re-echoed by later Fathers.

## Deliverance

Christians aware of the demonic realm today tend to distinguish between states of oppression, where evil spirits are afflicting people from outside, and states of possession, where spirits have invaded their victims' minds, often suppressing their consciousness, rendering them helpless. 'Deliverance' is often used of release from the former, 'exorcism' of liberation from the latter. We shall see that this distinction has its counterpart in the Early Church.

St. Paul says of the salvation brought by Christ to those committed to him, 'He has delivered us from the dominion of darkness and transferred us to the kingdom of his beloved Son' (Col. 1:13). This took place, the Early Church declared, when a person came to faith in Christ and was baptised. Clement quotes with approval the statement of the so-called *Epistle of Barnabas*: 'Before we believed in God, the dwelling-place of our heart was unstable, truly a temple built with hands. For it was full of idolatry, and was a house of demons, through doing what was opposed to God.'[15] But he goes on at once to qualify this by saying it is not that demons actually dwell in the heart of an unbeliever but that the unbeliever sins *like* the demons.

---

[9] *Shows* 4, *Idolatry* 1, *Military Crown* 7. Association with idolatry makes the circus (*Shows* 4) and theatre (*Shows* 10) prohibited for the Christian.

[10] *Scapula* 2.

[11] 'It is the temple of all demons. There are as many unclean spirits gathered there as it can seat men.' (*Shows* 12.7)

[12] *1 Apol.* 54, *Dialogue* 69; cf. Tertullian, *Apol.* 22.4, 6, 11, *Soul* 46.

[13] *1 Apol.* 26 (Simon Magus), 56 (Menander), 58 (Marcion); cf. Tertullian, *Prescription against the Heretics*, 40.

[14] *1 Apol.* 57, *2 Apol.* 1; Tertullian, *Apol.* 27.3–5, 28.1.

[15] *Barn.* 16, qu. Clement, *Miscellanies* 2.116.4 (2.20 ANCL). The 'Epistle of Barnabas' appears to have been written in the period 70–150 AD, but is thought unlikely to be the work of the Barnabas of the New Testament.

The demonic realm was consciously rejected by the believer at baptism as Tertullian relates: 'When we enter the water and profess the Christian faith in terms prescribed by its law, we profess with our mouths that we have renounced the devil, his pomp and his angels.'[16]

Origen (c.185–c.254) declares a person's conversion chastises the demons;[17] baptism brings freedom from them.[18] That the human soul is attended by demons from birth he regards as a justification for infant baptism.[19] It seems likely that it led to the development of ritual exorcism as part of the baptismal procedure.[20] After baptism, Origen believed, Christian children were protected by the angels from further demonic assault until they reached puberty when, like adults, they had to join in battle against the demons.[21] He saw in Israel's wilderness wanderings a picture of the lifelong spiritual warfare all Christians engage in. To prove victorious Christians must defend themselves by prayer, fasting, reading the Scriptures, participation in the Eucharist, and virtuous living.[22] Throughout these battles, he believed, angels are at work on the side of good.[23] The person who gives in to temptation falls into the demons' power, but deliverance is possible through repentance.[24] Other Fathers speak of the protective power for a Christian of making the sign of the cross on one's forehead.[25]

In the Post-Nicene Church battles against demons appear to have been a constant preoccupation of the fourth and fifth-century Desert Fathers.[26]

---

[16] *Shows* 4.1 (Loeb), cf. *Crown* 3.

[17] *Homily on Numbers* 27.8.

[18] *Commentary on John* 20.340–41.

[19] *Hom. Lev.* 8.3.5.

[20] *Apostolic Tradition* 20–21. Whilst the original document is thought to be the work of Hippolytus of Rome c.215, much if not all of its prescribed exorcistic ritual may date from the fourth century, see P.F. Bradshaw, M.E. Johnson and L.E. Phillips, *The Apostolic Tradition: A Commentary* (Minneapolis: Fortress Press, 2002), 109–11.

[21] *Hom. Ezek.* 6.8, cf. *Hom. Jud.* 6.2

[22] *Hom. Ex.* 2, *Hom. Lev.* 6.6.5, *Hom. Josh.* 1.7, 8.7, 20, *Hom. Jud.* 6.2, *Comm. Song of Songs* 3.12, *Prayer* 13.3.

[23] *Hom. Num.* 5.3 *et passim.*

[24] *Hom. Ex.* 8, *Hom. Jud.* 7.1.

[25] Tertullian, *Crown* 2.42; *Apostolic Tradition* 42 (Cuming).

[26] C. Stewart, *The World of the Desert Fathers: Stories and Sayings* (Oxford: SLG Press, 1986), ch. 7.

## Exorcism

The word 'exorcism' is from the Greek *exorkizō*, 'I bind by oath'. It reflects the forceful commands used to evict the spirit-invader. In the New Testament story of the mute boy (Mark 9:14–27) the violence of the possessing spirit appears to be episodic (9:18, 22). Contemporary experience today would suggest that many victims of possession experience periods of unconsciousness interspersed with periods of relative lucidity, though not happiness.

### Pagan magical exorcism

In chapter 2 of his important monograph *Possession and Exorcism in the New Testament and Early Christianity,* Eric Sorensen considers the history of magical craft for dealing with demonic affliction in ancient Mesopotamia. It is first mentioned on tablets dating from 1500–1200 BC. In the fifth-century BC Herodotus (*History* 1.101) declares the word 'magic' (Gk. *mageia*) was first used of the craft of the magi (Gk. *magoi*), one of the six tribes of the Medes, a priestly tribe. Egypt, however, became reputed as the home of magic. Whilst the magic of other nations sought to invoke benevolent spiritual powers to counteract the powers of darkness, it seems Egyptians alone commanded their gods to work for them.[27] Much of our information comes from the Greek Magical Papyri (*PGM*) dating from the second century BC to the seventh century AD. The most comprehensive collection has been made by H.D. Betz.[28] In brief, the exorcistic procedure consisted of three parts: (1) the invocation of one or more powerful deities, (2) the command to the demon to depart from its victim, often using a succession of sonorous nonsense words and accompanying ritual, (3) the giving of an amulet to wear containing further terrifying words to seal the cure.[29]

---

[27] E.A.W. Budge, *Egyptian Magic* (London: Kegan Paul, 1901), ix.

[28] H.D. Betz, *The Greek Magical Papyri in Translation including the Demotic Spells* (Chicago: Chicago University Press, 1986, 1992). Whilst Betz omits predominantly 'Christian' magical texts a collection of these has been published by M. Meyer and R. Smith (eds.) as *Ancient Christian Magic: Coptic Texts of Ritual Power* (San Francisco: Harper, 1994).

[29] The three parts are clearly seen in *PGM* IV.1227–64, no. 19 in Meyer and Smith, *Ancient Christian Magic*. See also H.C. Kee, *Medicine, Miracle and Magic in New Testament Times* (Cambridge: Cambridge University Press, 1986), ch. 4.

## Jewish exorcism

Jewish elements are found throughout the magical papyri. Jews were in Egypt from at least the sixth century BC when the remnant of Judah, who had not been exiled to Babylon, fled there (Jer. 43:4–7). They appear to have prospered and, influenced no doubt by the surrounding cultural milieu, themselves developed a reputation for magical practices.[30] Josephus relates an exorcism in the second half of the first century AD which he had witnessed, performed by the Jew Eleazar in the presence of Vespasian. This was its method

> He put to the nose of the possessed man a ring which had under its seal one of the roots, prescribed by Solomon and then, as the man smelled it, drew out the demon through his nostrils, and when the man at once fell down, adjured the demon never to come back into him speaking Solomon's name and reciting the incantations which he had composed. Then wishing to convince the bystanders and prove to them that he had this power Eleazar placed a cup or foot basin full of water a little way off and commanded the demon, as it went out of the man, to overturn it and make known to the spectators that he had left the man. And when this was done the understanding and wisdom of Solomon were clearly revealed. (*Jewish Antiquities* 8.45–9, Loeb)

A considerable literature grew up attributing esoteric powers to Solomon, and indeed Moses,[31] enabling Jews to use at least quasi-magical techniques with a clear conscience. With some justice then did Justin in the second century berate Trypho the Jew for his countrymen's use of a craft which was just like that of the Gentiles with fumigations (incense) and incantations (spells).[32] It appears they were exorcising in the name of 'the God of Abraham, and the God of Isaac, and the God of Jacob'. By Origen's time they also used the epithets 'the God of Israel ', 'the God of the Hebrews', and 'the God who drowned the King of Egypt and the Egyptians in the Red Sea.'[33]

---

[30] Pliny, *Nat. Hist.* 30.2.

[31] See M.E. Mills, *Human Agents of Cosmic Power in Hellenistic Judaism and the Synoptic Tradition* (Sheffield: Sheffield University Press, 1990), chs. 3, 4.

[32] *Dial.* 85.3.

[33] *Contra Celsum* (Against *Celsus*) 1.22, 4.33–34.

### Christian exorcism

How different were Jesus' own exorcisms! He invoked no divine names and used no ritual but simply, on his own authority, ordered the demons to depart. The story of Legion shows him in conversation with a spirit and demanding its name (Mark 5:9).[34] In the story of the mute boy Jesus asks his case history (Mark 9:21). Responding to the Syrophoenician woman Jesus exorcises her daughter at a distance (Mark 7:29–30). All these stories present examples of how to exorcise in different circumstances. Did the evangelist have the instruction of his audience in mind when he included such a range?[35] In the only account of an exorcism in Acts Paul indeed, like Jesus, issues a direct command to the fortune-telling spirit to leave the slave girl, only he does it not on his own authority but in the name of Jesus Christ (16:18).[36] The eviction was instantaneous.

### After the apostles

#### Continuity

Did similar exorcisms continue in the Post-Apostolic Church? Very few Christian writings survive from the period 100–150 AD and those that do make no mention of exorcism, or indeed of miracles at all. B.B. Warfield inferred that miraculous powers were intended for the apostolic age alone.[37] Twelftree notes that, even in the New Testament interest in exorcism appears to decline[38] (though in fact this may relate more to the mindset of the evangelists than to what was actually happening

---

[34] Considered to be a means of gaining power over a spirit; cf. *PGM* I.162–3, IV.3081–84.

[35] Dibelius suggested this with regard to the healing stories, *From Tradition to Gospel*, tr. B.L. Woolf (Tübingen, 1934), 86–87; Twelftree is well aware of this motif in the exorcisms, *In the Name of Jesus: Exorcism among Early Christians* (Grand Rapids: Baker Academic, 2007), 117–18 *et passim*.

[36] Twelftree is surely wrong to refer to this exorcising 'by some greater source of power-authority' as 'magical', contrasting it with the 'charismatic' method of Jesus (see chapter 2 of this volume and *Name of Jesus*, 141 *et passim*). The method is essentially the same as Jesus' only susbstituting his name for his physical presence. We have seen how very different was the approach of magicians.

[37] B.B. Warfield, *Counterfeit Miracles* (Edinburgh: Banner of Truth, 1918, repr. 1983), 6.

[38] Luke, and especially Matthew, appear relatively less interested in exorcisms than Mark, and John has none at all, *Name of Jesus*, chs. 5–7, 9 and see chapter 2 in this volume.

'on the ground'), and he believes this trend continued afterwards until interest revived in Rome following the republication of Mark with its longer ending (16:9–20) in the period 120–150 AD.[39] But, as the post-apostolic Church clearly continued to spread the words of Christ, is it not likely they also continued to do his works? Tertullian gives this impression in his *Prescription against the Heretics* when he scoffs at Marcionites and Valentinians for claiming that people had to wait until the teaching of their founders (mid-second century) to hear the truth.

> During the interval [from the founding of the Church to the mid-second century] the gospel was wrongly preached; men wrongly believed; so many thousand thousands were wrongly baptized; so many works of faith were wrongly wrought; so many miraculous gifts (*virtutes*), so many spiritual endowments (*charismata*) were wrongly set in operation . . . (29.3, ANCL)

Moreover Justin, in the early 160s, declares that Jesus was made man to bring people to faith *and to destroy demons*, and he continues

> And now you can learn this from what is your own observation. For numberless demoniacs throughout the whole world, and in your own city [Rome], many of our Christian men exorcising them in the name of Jesus Christ, who was crucified under Pontius Pilate and have healed and do heal, rendering helpless and driving the possessing devils [demons] out of men, though they could not be cured by all the other exorcists and those who used incantations and drugs. (2 Apol. 6.5–6, ANCL)

This surely suggests both continuity and long experience in this task. This impression is reinforced by Irenaeus (c.140–c.200), bishop of Lyons, when in his great work *Refutation and Overthrow of Falsely-Called Knowledge*[40] (180s), after listing an array of supernatural gifts (in which he places exorcism first, implying perhaps it is the most common), he concludes

> It is not possible to name the number of the gifts (*charismata*) which the Church, throughout the whole world, has received from God, in the

---

[39] Ibid., 236–37, 286.
[40] Generally known by the briefer title *Against the Heresies* (the title of its Latin translation).

name of Jesus Christ, who was crucified under Pontius Pilate, and which she exerts day by day for the benefit of the Gentiles, neither practising deception upon any, nor taking any reward from them. For as she has received freely from God, freely does she minister. (2.32.4, ANCL)

By the end of the second century Tertullian can boldly taunt the magistrates of the Roman Empire

But who would rescue you from those secret enemies that everywhere lay waste your minds and your bodily health? I mean, from the assaults of demons, whom we drive out of you, without reward, without pay. Why, this alone would have sufficed to avenge us – to leave you open and exposed to unclean spirits with immediate possession![41] (*Apol.* 37.9, Loeb)

That exorcism had achieved such public prominence by then is surely best explained by assuming it had been practised with increasing confidence from Pentecost onwards.

### Further aspects

Earlier in the passage quoted above (*A.H.* 2.32.4) Irenaeus says that frequently those freed from evil spirits believed in Christ and joined the Church. How such people first came to the Church's attention is not stated, but perhaps for some it was through an experience similar to that related by Origen in the next century. He was preaching on 1 Samuel but when he quoted the words of Hannah, 'My soul exults in the Lord' (1 Sam. 2:1) demonic cries of protest burst from one listening. He proceeded to repeat the words time and again to chastise the spirit, urging those who had gathered round the person to do the same. We do not hear whether the spirit was driven out but Origen went on to say that such situations often led to a person's conversion.[42] P. and M-T. Nautin remark that Origen is here the first

---

[41] In 212 writing to Scapula, Proconsul of Africa, Tertullian lists some instances of the Church's exorcism: 'The clerk of one of [the local advocates] who was liable to be thrown upon the ground by an evil spirit, was set free from his affliction; as was also the relative of another and the little boy of a third.' (*Scap.* 4).

[42] *Hom. Sam.* 1.10.

to enable us to re-live the impact of the preaching of the patristic age.[43]

One would expect baptised, practising Christians to be safe from demon possession, but Tertullian reveals it was not always so.

> What is to save such people [Christians who attend shows] from demon-possession? For we have in fact the case (as the Lord is witness) of that woman, who went to the theatre and returned devil possessed. So, when the unclean spirit was being exorcised and was pressed with the accusation that it had dared to enter a woman who believed: 'and I was quite right, too', said he boldly; 'for I found her on my own ground'. (*Shows* 26.1–2, Loeb)

Apart from these incidents no accounts of exorcisms are recorded in the writings of the Pre-Nicene Fathers. This suggests a certain lack of interest in miraculous works. Certainly Clement[44] and Origen[45] disparage too much interest in physical healing, and Eusebius (c.260–339), in the early fourth century, admits he is more at home with reasoned argument than miraculous 'proofs' for defending the truth of Christianity.[46] A series of novelistic Apocryphal Acts, however, from the late second and third centuries,[47] revel in the supernatural, attributing many fanciful miracles to their apostle heroes. These commonly include exorcisms. Let me summarise one:

Virinus, the proconsul of Macedonia, sends soldiers to arrest the apostle Andrew for sorcery and opposing traditional religion. One of them, who is possessed, draws his sword in Andrew's presence and cries, 'What have I to do with you, Virinus, that you send me to one who can not only cast me out of this vessel, but burn me by his power?' The demon leaves him but he drops dead. The proconsul angrily confronts Andrew (who becomes invisible for a while), accuses him of sorcery and does not relent though the apostle raises the dead soldier in the name of

---

[43] P. and M-T. Nautin, *Origène: Homélies sur Samuel* (Sources Chrétiennes, Paris: Edit du Cerf. 328), 67.

[44] *Misc.* 7.46.4 (*ANCL* 7.7).

[45] *Prayer* 17.1; in *C.C.* 2.48 he interprets the 'greater works' of John 14:12 as referring to people's conversions.

[46] *Demonstration of the Gospel* (*D.E.*) 3.4.

[47] The *Acts* of Andrew, Peter and Paul date from the late second century, those of John and Thomas are thought to come from the first half of the third century. See J.K. Elliott (ed.) *The Apocryphal New Testament: A Collection of Apocryphal Literature in English Translation* (Oxford: Oxford University Press, 1993).

'my God Jesus Christ'. He then retires but next day has Andrew dragged to the stadium to contend with a series of wild animals. They ignore the apostle but one kills Virinus' son. Andrew raises him and Virinus is confounded (*Epitome of the Acts of Andrew* by Gregory of Tours, ch. 18).

The Apocryphal Acts were written as popular literature apparently to replace erotic pagan narratives.[48] However, since they paid scant attention to history and some at least came from a mildly heretical milieu, they were quickly marginalised by the mainstream Church.

## Methods

The Pre-Nicene Fathers do indicate some of the methods that were employed in Christian exorcism. The essential element was a command in the name of Jesus Christ to the possessing demon to leave its victim.[49] Sometimes this command had to be repeated perhaps several times. Cyprian indicates this when he speaks of demons 'howling and groaning at the voice of men and the power of God, feeling the stripes and blows . . .'[50] To this command various Fathers add other elements. Justin almost invariably says demons were exorcised in the name of Jesus 'who was crucified under Pontius Pilate', once adding a veritable creed (*Dial.* 85.1–2). Origen, in answer to Celsus' charge that Christians used incantations in their exorcisms, declared Christians used only the name of Jesus 'with the recital of the histories (Gk. *historia*) about him' (*C.C.* 1.6) – a reference perhaps to gospel narratives or creedal statements like those of Justin.[51] Origen goes on to say this method is particularly successful when used by those with 'real sincerity and genuine faith' though sometimes it is effective even when pronounced by bad men. In 7.4 he mentions the use of prayer. Tertullian tells of the effectiveness of a Christian's mere touch or breath[52] and says that fasting is a weapon for battling with tenacious demons.[53] By touch he may mean the laying on of hands, for Origen once specifies this.[54] Blowing was used in magical exorcisms[55] but for Christians,

---

[48] J. Quasten, *Patrology* I (Utrecht: Spectrum, 1950), 129.

[49] Acts 16:18; Justin, *2 Apol.* 6.5–6; Tertullian, *Apol.* 23.15–16; Origen, *C.C.* 1.6, 25; Lactantius, *Divine Institutes* 4.27.1–3; Eusebius, *D.E.* 3.6.34–36 *et passim*.

[50] *To Demetrianus* 15 (AD 252).

[51] H. Chadwick, *Origen: Contra Celsum* (Cambridge: Cambridge University Press, 1953, 1980), *loc. sit.*

[52] *Apol.* 23.16; cf. *Apostolic Tradition* 20.8.

[53] *Fasting* 8.3.

[54] *Hom. Josh.* 24.1.

[55] *PGM* IV.3081–84.

indwelt by God's Spirit (Rom. 8:9, 1 Cor. 6:19), it might have held special significance, delivering as it were a 'blast' of the *Holy* Spirit to evict an *impure* spirit. In the early fourth century Lactantius (c.250–c.325) speaks of the powerful effect of making the sign of the cross. These extra elements are never mentioned all together giving the impression that, apart from commanding in the name of Christ, there was no fixed procedure for Christian exorcism. It must have remained then essentially simple. Origen declares that since it is 'without any curious magical art or sorcerer's device' it can be performed by the simplest person (*C.C.* 7.4).[56] Sometimes, however, even the prolonged exertions of exorcists were unsuccessful. In such cases, according to Cyprian, only the possessed one's coming to faith and being baptised can evict the demon.[57] He also warns that, should a person's faith subsequently falter and he fall into sin, the demon might return.

### The Post-Nicene Church

From the Post-Nicene Church there are numerous, generally brief, accounts of exorcisms, particularly associated with various monks or the relics of martyrs. Let us look at some cases.

### Performed by monks

Pachomius (c.290–346), held to be the founder of communal monasticism, is said to have sent blessed oil to a father who anointed his possessed daughter, freeing her.[58] Macarius of Alexandria (d. 394) is said to have cured 'countless demon-ridden people'[59] and in one case laid hands on, anointed with oil, and poured water over a possessed boy to free him, but there would seem to be legendary accretions within the story for the boy is said to levitate and swell up in the course of his cure.[60] Palladius, author of the *Lausiac History* (c.419), says that Innocent, his first instructor in monasticism, once

---

[56] Twelftree, then, is not justified in saying from *C.C.* 1.6 and 6.40, 'It is reasonable to conclude that, in the latter part of the second century, exorcism among "orthodox" Christians in [Alexandria] was "indistinguishable from other exorcisms"', *Name of Jesus*, 288, cf. 269–73. For a more detailed response see my *Healing in the Early Church* (Milton Keynes: Paternoster, 2009), ch. 4, n. 145.

[57] *Ep.* 69.15–16; cf. Origen, *Hom. Josh.* 24.1.

[58] *Life of Pachomius* 43.

[59] *Lausiac History* 18.11.

[60] Ibid. 18.22.

healed a possessed, paralysed young man in Palestine by praying continuously for six hours.[61] In the West Sulpicius Severus tells how Martin of Tours (c.330–397) cured a possessed boy by the laying on of hands.[62]

### Through contact with relics of martyrs

From the beginning of the Church those who had died as martyrs were deeply admired. With the empire-wide persecutions of the Church in the mid-third and early fourth centuries, this intensified. The martyrs began to be viewed as endowed with special spiritual power. In the Post-Nicene Church touching their holy relics became seen as a means of drawing on their prayers, or more immediately their power.[63] Huge shrines were built around martyrs' graves in the cemeteries which became centres of pilgrimage. Sometimes martyrs' remains were transferred elsewhere.

Augustine of Hippo (354–430) speaks of a demon-possessed boy with a damaged eye who was cured through contact with the bones of Protasius and Gervasius in Milan, and of a convulsive brother and sister healed through contact with the relics of the first Christian martyr Stephen, which had been transferred to North Africa.[64] But the practice of touching martyrs' relics scarcely fostered faith in Christ's direct power to heal, rather it encouraged superstitious awe little removed from that associated with magic.

### 'Christian' magic

It does in fact appear that in the fourth and fifth centuries there were church members who participated in magical practices. Church Fathers of that time vehemently denounced the use of amulets in curing the sick.[65] In their *Ancient Christian Magic: Coptic Texts of Ritual Power*, Meyer and Smith publish a number of such amulets. These portray sickness, and especially chills and fevers, as the work of evil spirits and invoke God, Christ, the Holy Spirit, words of Scripture, and

---

[61] Ibid. 44.2–3.

[62] *Life of Martin* 17.

[63] See P. Brown, *The Cult of the Saints* (London: SCM, 1981); R.A. Greer, *The Fear of Freedom* (Pennsylvania: Pennsylvania University Press, 1989), ch. 5.

[64] *City of God* 22.8.

[65] E.g. Cyril of Jerusalem (c.315–87), *Catechesis* 19.8; Augustine, *Tractate on John* 7.6; cf. Woolley, *Exorcism and the Healing of the Sick* (London: SPCK, 1932), 60–61, 67.

the prayers of the saints to drive these spirits away.[66] Text 15, a fourth-century amulet, includes the term 'Abraxas' (= Abrasax) indicating heretical Gnostic provenance.[67] Text 19 is a full-blown magical exorcistic spell and amulet (*PGM* IV.1227–64) believed to date from the fourth century. It incorporates Christian and pagan divine names, sonorous nonsense words and ritual, but its Christian elements appear to sit somewhat awkwardly within an older pagan text dating perhaps from the second century.[68] Certainly any Christian involved in such an exorcism had strayed far from Christian orthodoxy.

## Who were the exorcists?

Who then performed (orthodox) exorcisms within the Early Church? In the New Testament it was the apostles (Acts 5:17, 16:18, 19:12, cf. 2:43?), some of 'the Seven' (Acts 8:7, cf. 6:8?), possibly the presbyter/ elders (cf. Jas 5:14–16), and perhaps some laity with the gifts of 'working miracles' and 'distinguishing between spirits' (1 Cor. 12:10, 28). We have noted that Irenaeus refers to the ability to drive out spirits as a 'gift' (*A.H.* 2.32.4) but his younger contemporary Tertullian declares *any* Christian may exorcise (*Apol.* 23.4), presumably because of his faith in Christ and having received the Holy Spirit. But in fact how many would dare? It is understandable then that those who regularly did exorcise should be regarded as having a special gift.[69] It is likely that bishops sometimes exorcised, perhaps especially when the person thought to be possessed had a high profile in the community. In the late second century in Phrygia in Asia Minor various bishops sought to refute the Montanist prophetess Maximilla,[70] and Sotas of Anchialus is said to have tried to exorcise her fellow prophetess Priscilla but been prevented by her supporters.[71] Yet people of humble status could also exorcise. Clement advises wealthy Alexandrian Christians to enlist for their own benefit 'an army of God-fearing old men, of God-beloved orphans, of widows armed with gentleness, of men adorned with love ... Through them ... the violence of demons is shattered, reduced to impotence by confident commands' (*Who is the Rich Man that is Saved?*

---

[66] E.g. no. 16, a 5th C amulet (Oxyrhynchus 1151).

[67] Irenaeus, *A.H.* 1.24.7.

[68] See Twelftree, *Name of Jesus*, 263.

[69] So also *Ep. to Virgins* (from 3rd C Syria) 1.12.

[70] Eusebius, *H.E.* 5.16.16–17.

[71] Eusebius, *H.E.* 5.19.3; for Sotas to be called '(blessed) Sotas of Anchialus' without qualification surely suggests he was bishop of that place.

34.2–3, Loeb). And Origen tells us that generally exorcisms were performed by uneducated people who were people of prayer (*C.C.* 7.4). Sometimes, he says, Christians drove out demons from places and even animals (*C.C.* 7.67).

Towards the middle of the third century we first hear of the office of exorcist.[72] It was one of the lower ranks of ministry in local churches. Cornelius, the new bishop of Rome, in a letter to Fabius of Antioch (c.251) lists those ministering in his church as 'one bishop . . . forty-six presbyters, seven deacons, seven sub-deacons, forty-two acolytes, fifty-two exorcists, readers and doorkeepers' (Eusebius, *H.E.* 6.43.11–12). The number 'fifty-two' comes after 'doorkeepers' in the Greek so exorcists, readers and doorkeepers are all included, but perhaps as many as twenty of them were exorcists for they are mentioned first.

In the Post-Nicene Church the order of exorcist continued but seems to have been gradually subsumed by the higher orders. The *Apostolic Constitutions* (probably Syrian, c.350–80) states that, while the exorcist is not ordained because his gift is one of God's grace that reveals itself, if there is an occasion, he should be ordained bishop, presbyter or deacon (8.26). Canon 3 of the *Canons of Hippolytus* (Egypt, fourth century) gives a prayer for the consecration of a bishop which contains the petition, 'Give him, Lord . . . power to loosen every bond of the oppression of demons, to cure the sick and crush Satan under his feet quickly . . . ' Canon 4 says the same prayer is to be used in the ordination of presbyters. In the Western Church bishops Martin of Tours[73] and Felix of Nola[74] were earlier exorcists. Woolley points out that in the old Roman rites there was no form of ordination as an exorcist was simply 'given a commission' by the bishop. Only in the fifth/sixth-century document from Gaul, *Ancient Statutes of the Church*, did he find a form of ordination in which a bishop handed to the candidate a book of written exorcisms saying: 'Receive and commit to memory (this), and have power to lay hands on him that is possessed, whether he is baptised or a catechumen.'[75] Clearly the spontaneity (and power?) of exorcising had diminished and yet the exorcist might be confronted with catechumens or Christians who were possessed.

---

[72] Mentioned by Firmilian of Cappadocia, c.235 (*apud* Cyprian, *Ep.* 75); Origen, c.240 (*Hom. Josh.* 24.1); Cyprian, 250s (*Epp.* 23, 69.15).

[73] Sulpicius Severus, *Life of Martin* 5.

[74] Paulinus of Nola, *Birthday 4 of Felix*.

[75] Qu. Woolley, *Exorcism*, 43.

*The value of exorcism*

Athanasius (c.296–373) declares that while non-Christians can drive out demons, only Christians can *thoroughly* banish them.[76] Those released from spirits who then believed in Christ, were baptised and joined the Church, would have experienced a new quality of life unobtainable elsewhere.

Sorensen asserts that the idea of demon possession as an illness is noticeably absent from the conventional healing tradition before the Christian era and plays no role in medicine or the healing cults.[77] He admits, however, that epilepsy was popularly viewed as possession by a god, and that the Greek gods Dionysus, Pan and Hecate (and we must add Apollo, at the oracle of Delphi and elsewhere) were said to 'enthuse' (Gk. *en* + *theos*, 'in god'), i.e. take possession of their devotees. In Greek tragedy the Olympian gods were said to possess and afflict those who offended them, but there was no exorcism; people could only offer sacrifices and petition the gods to desist.[78] Sorensen points out that possession was not attributed to lesser spirits like demons. But, as we have said above, the Church Fathers constantly reiterated that the 'gods' and inferior 'demons' were in fact one and the same. Exorcism demonstrated this perfectly. Cyprian drives the point home to the elderly pagan magistrate Demetrianus:

> You will see that we are entreated by those whom you entreat, that we are feared by those whom you fear, whom you adore. You will see that under our hands they stand bound, and tremble as captives, whom you look up to and venerate as lords: assuredly even thus you might be confounded in those errors of years, when you see and hear your gods, at once upon our interrogation betraying what they are [demons], and even in your presence unable to conceal those deceits and trickeries of theirs. (*Dem.* 5)

And so exorcism was valued as an apologetic weapon in the battle to win over the hearts and minds of the people of the Roman Empire.

---

[76] R.J.S. Barrett-Lennard points out that, in the former case, Athanasius uses weaker words for exorcism, *elaunō, apelaunō* ('drive away'), whilst for the latter words like *diōkō* ('pursue'), *Christian Healing after the New Testament: Some Approaches to Illness in the Second, Third and Fourth Centuries* (Lanham: University Press of America, 1994), ch. 6.

[77] *Possession*, 6.

[78] Ibid. 6, ch. 4.

As for Sorenson's contention that there was no apparent demand for exorcism before the Christian era,[79] the sheer number of those the second-century Fathers tell us were liberated by Christian exorcists suggests there was a great demand awaiting fulfilment.

## Conclusion

Surveying the evidence we have brought forward it is surely clear that from the start deliverance and exorcism played an important part in the life of the Early Church. Christians of that time believed emphatically in the reality of the demons, evil spirits out to afflict and subvert humanity, and found in faith, the sacraments, prayer, Bible reading, the sign of the cross, and virtuous living effective means to resist their ploys. In the acute case of spirit-possession commands in the name of Christ generally proved successful in evicting the intruders. Christians in the West today think little of demons and tend to regard temptations and afflictions as simply 'thrown at us by life'. But even so we need the same weapons as the early Christians to achieve stability and success. For those who through evil living or entanglement with the occult find themselves enslaved to dark forces, the power of Christ is still available to provide release and restoration, but the present-day exorcist needs careful discernment in each case as to whether medical, psychiatric, or spiritual means are the most appropriate for effective cure.

---

[79] *Possession*, 6.

Chapter 4

# Deliverance and Exorcism in the Twentieth Century

*James Collins*

The Devil is being resisted and he is forced to flee. For the first time we are seeing the backside of the Devil. It is a beautiful sight.

*Frank and Ida Hammond 1973*

**Abstract**

This chapter examines the course of deliverance ministry during the twentieth century focusing in particular upon its practice within Charismatic and Evangelical Fundamentalist circles. Deliverance was a marginal activity until the emergence of the Pentecostal movement which heightened spiritual immanency in both its advocates and its opponents. Nevertheless, deliverance remained only a secondary characteristic even of the emerging Pentecostal movement; it was not until the post-war healing evangelists with their love of and need for sensational spirituality that deliverance ministry became a more central activity. Its zenith came in the 1970s and 1980s during the peak of the Charismatic Renewal after which it has been embedded in an increasingly routinized form into the post-Charismatic spirituality of mainstream Evangelicalism.[1]

---

[1] This chapter comprises a brief summary of my PhD thesis. The full version is entitled *Exorcism and Deliverance in the 20th Century: An Analysis of the Practise and Theology of Exorcism in Modern Western Christianity* (Milton Keynes: Paternoster, 2009).

## Introduction[2]

In 1973, during the heyday of the Charismatic Renewal, Frank and Ida Hammond published Pigs in the Parlour, subtitled *A Practical Guide to Deliverance*.[3] In many respects it was typical of much of the popular theological material produced by Charismatic writers around this time, predominantly anecdotal, exegetically naïve and simplistic in outlook. It sold like hot cakes and proved profoundly influential. It, and others like it, fuelled the already burgeoning interest in the exorcism of evil spirits.

Exorcism, or as non-sacramentalist practitioners usually prefer, deliverance ministry, is a widely accepted though controversial practice. Many Christians continue to advocate this ministry to a greater or lesser extent. There exists a spectrum of alternative views on and methods of deliverance and exorcism. These include the traditional, sacramental, liturgical rite, Charismatic and Evangelical Fundamentalist strains of deliverance ministry and hybrids of these which emerged towards the end of the last century. In this chapter we will examine each of these in order to chart the progress of exorcism in the twentieth century.

## The Charismatic stream

### Early Pentecostalism

Exorcism/Deliverance was a persistent secondary feature of early Pentecostalism inherited from the pre-existing radical evangelical groups from which it emerged.[4] The practice of deliverance in this

---

[2] Please note that this chapter will focus on exorcism/deliverance within *Western* forms of Christianity. The prescribed length of this study precludes an examination of the function of this ministry within black majority churches, despite the fact that this is of great public interest and significance at the current time.

[3] F. & I. Hammond, *Pigs in the Parlour: A Practical Guide to Deliverance* (Kirkwood: Impact Books, 1973).

[4] Reference to the eviction of evil spirits is common in early Pentecostal journals such as *The Apostolic Faith Magazine* and *Confidence*. See also G. Wacker, *Heaven Below: Early Pentecostals and American Culture* (Cambridge: Harvard, 2003), 38f., 64, 65, 88 and 91–93. Cf. F. Bartleman, *Azusa Street* (New Kensington: Whittaker House, 1982), 66 and J.G. Lake, *John G. Lake: His Life, His Sermons, His Boldness of Faith* (Fort Worth: Kenneth Copeland, 1994), 149f.

setting was closely allied and ran parallel to physical healing due to a belief that at least some diseases were demonic in origin.[5]

The early Pentecostals held to a conservative demonology and frequently indulged in theological dualism envisaging the Christian life as a battle against Satan and his demonic powers.[6] In addition to physical disease, a range of other problems might be attributed to their pernicious activity. Nevertheless, the early Pentecostals held a very high view of the spiritual benefits of 'baptism in the Holy Spirit' and this insulated them from preoccupation with the demonic.

The early Pentecostals faced visceral criticism from their evangelical opponents. The latter commonly attributed Pentecostal 'manifestations' to the activity of demons. Consequently, the Pentecostals were understandably at great pains to dismiss the threat of demonic activity. Hence, they were keen to prove that they could evict demons from non-believers (usually as a component of conversion) and equally determined to demonstrate that demons were not able to possess a 'Spirit-filled' Christian.[7] This latter belief went on to become a tenet of most Pentecostal denominations.[8]

### The post-war Pentecostal healing revival[9]

The late 1940s and the 1950s witnessed a remarkable surge in the popularity of the itinerant Pentecostal healing evangelists. Whilst this was primarily an American phenomenon, several figures rose to international fame including (pre-eminently) Oral Roberts, William Branham and Tommy Lee Osborn.

It was within the earthy, enthusiastic and fervent atmosphere of the healing revival that popular attention was drawn towards the need for widespread deliverance ministry. A seed was planted in the Charismatic consciousness which took root and would eventually flower some decades later.

It is a relatively straightforward affair to demonstrate the significance of demonology and deliverance within the ministry of these

---

[5] Wacker, *Heaven*, 92. See Lake, *Lake*, 341–84.

[6] Wacker, *Heaven*, 24, 33, 35, 38, 59, 61, 63, 66 and particularly 91–92.

[7] These assertions are common place in the early Pentecostal journals.

[8] K. Warrington, 'Healing and Exorcism: The Path to Wholeness' in K. Warrington (ed.), *Pentecostal Perspectives* (Carlisle: Paternoster, 1998), 173.

[9] D E Harrell has penned by far the best studies of the post-War healing revival, including D.E. Harrell, *All Things are Possible* (Bloomington: Indianan University Press, 1975) and D.E. Harrell, *Oral Roberts: An American Life* (Bloomington: Indiana University Press, 1985).

itinerant healing evangelists. Both William Branham and Oral Roberts claimed to be able to detect the presence of demons via vibrations in their left and right hands respectively.[10] Healing, in particular, was often understood in terms of the expulsion of oppressing spirits.[11] Furthermore, the defeat and eviction of evil spirits was so central to their language and understanding that the term 'deliverance' was often used as shorthand for their entire ministry.

A.A. Allen was one of the more extreme figures within the post-War revival; if Branham was the pioneer of the revival and Roberts was its popular face, then Allen exemplifies its extreme sensationalism. Accordingly, Allen's ministry demonstrated a preoccupation with demons and ministry to those they afflicted.[12] He published numerous books and pamphlets on the subject of demon possession, deliverance, and other related topics.[13] Allen attributed a great deal of spiritual and physical problems (including mental illness) to demonic possession[14] and encouraged sufferers to attend one of his revival meetings or, failing that, to write to him for a specially anointed cloth.[15] He also suggested that sufferers should 'name the kind of demon from which you desire to be set free (if known).'[16] His preoccupation with the demonic led Allen to publish eighteen pictures of demons as seen and drawn by a demon possessed woman[17] and recordings of what Allen claimed to be a demon speaking and revealing important information.

A.A. Allen represents the most extreme end of the healing revival and indeed Charismatic Christianity in general. His example indicates

---

[10] F.F. Bosworth, *The Voice of Healing* (March 1950) cited by Harrell, *All*, 37. Cf. Harell, *All*, 50.

[11] Harrell, *Oral*, 453. Note also the comments of O.E. Sproull in Roberts' early and popular *If You Want Healing Do These Things* (Tulsa: Healing Waters, 1954 (but first published in 1947)), viff.

[12] Harrell, *All*, 88.

[13] Including, principally, A.A. Allen, *Demon Possession Today and How to be Free* (Miracle Valley: A.A. Allen, 1953). See also A.A. Allen, *Invasion from Hell* (Miracle Valley: A.A. Allen, 1953), A.A. Allen, *The Tormenting Demon of Fear* (no publication details available), A.A. Allen, *It Pays to Serve the Devil* (no publication details available), A.A. Allen, *Witchcraft, Wizards and Witches* (Miracle Valley: A.A. Allen, 1968).

[14] Allen, *Demon*, 36–41.

[15] Allen, *Demon*, 143–52.

[16] Harrell, *All*, 88.

[17] Harrell, *All*, 88.

how great a significance deliverance ministry may take on in excessive versions of Charismatic ministry. Its sensational and dramatic nature lends credibility to the practitioner where appeal is based upon charismatic endowment and spiritual authority.

Emphasis upon the demonic was a component in a general tendency towards the sensational which was part of the appeal of the evangelists. Moreover, the frequent relation of successful and spectacular power encounters certainly helped to establish the spiritual credentials of the evangelists when they were often under attack from critics outside the revival (most notably the established Christian, even Pentecostal, denominations) and even from one another. It seems likely therefore that emphasis upon deliverance ministry was driven in part by the competitive nature of the ministry during the revival which demanded continual evidence of the evangelists' elevated spiritual status and increasingly spectacular evidence of God's presence and power.

The healing revival of the late 1940s and 1950s 'stood at the cradle' of the birth of the Charismatic Movement. Hence the Charismatic Movement bears the stamp of the healing revivalists such as Branham, Allen, and Roberts including their key emphasis upon deliverance ministry and many aspects of their practice of it. The personal and indeed institutional channels of influence between the healing revivalists and the emerging Charismatic Movement should not be underestimated.

### The Charismatic movement

Writing in 1977, Colin Buchanan described exorcism as one of five 'minor incidentals' of Charismatic Worship:

> Exorcism is not necessarily, nor perhaps usually, performed in the context of worship. But charismatics have tended to associate the two . . . the Charismatic Movement has led to a vastly increased interest in demonology, a vastly increased diagnosing of invasion or possession by demons, and a vastly increased practice of exorcism. This may (in its more respectable practitioners) be compared to the ministry of healing.[18]

Buchanan may have been correct (at least at the time) to label exorcism as incidental to charismatic worship although the term seems a little weak. Nevertheless, this 'incidental' had a 'vast' impact, at least for a

---

[18] C. Buchanan, *Encountering Charismatic Worship* (Bramcote: grove, 1997), 20.

while. The Charismatic Movement provided clement conditions for deliverance ministry to become a common occurrence in churches of most mainline denominations. What follows is a cursory examination of Charismatic deliverance ministries and the response they provoked from prominent Charismatic leaders.

### Derek Prince, Don Basham, and the 'Fort Lauderdale Five'

Derek Prince was in many ways the most significant Charismatic practitioner of deliverance ministry. Most of the Charismatic deliverance 'experts' of the 1970s and 1980s acknowledge that he heavily influenced their understanding of deliverance. His impact lies not so much in the uniqueness of his teaching but in his stature as a mainline Pentecostal minister with impeccable intellectual credentials.

Prince was serving as a Pentecostal minister when, in 1953 (at the peak of the post-war healing revival!), he experienced a personal deliverance from a 'spirit of heaviness'. This left him with an immediate difficulty integrating this experience within a Pentecostal denomination that denied outright the possibility of Christian being demon possessed. Eventually this led Prince to leave the pastorate and adopt an itinerant ministry in which deliverance would play a prominent part.

Prince came to the conviction that the underlying need of many (even the majority) of Christians was to be set free from demons that had gained entrance into their person and a consequent degree of control. He concluded that without the practice of deliverance much Christian ministry is superficial since it does not grapple with the underlying problem, namely demons.

Throughout the early years of the Charismatic Movement Derek Prince was energetically practising deliverance ministry in the various locations he was invited to speak, often sponsored by the Full Gospel Business Men's Fellowship International (FGBMFI). This trailblazing Charismatic para-church organisation had close links with healing evangelists such as William Branham and Oral Roberts and self-consciously allowed scope for deliverance ministry where the mainline Pentecostal churches were usually not so favourable.

Perhaps the most contentious aspect of Prince's understanding was his perception of the scale of the problem. Compulsions, addictions, many illnesses and emotional disorders are all attributable to 'demonization'.[19] Although Prince did not explicitly make the claim, it is hard not to draw the conclusion that everyone is demonized to some extent. For example, Prince claimed that one in five people needed to be delivered from a demon of fear! Prince describes the person who is 'probably' demon-free as one 'who can maintain an attitude of serene composure in all the troubled circumstances of life. But there are not many such people.'[20]

Prince leaves one with the impression that we are all surrounded by an unseen spiritual ether, which is teeming with evil spirits longing to get inside the bodies of human beings. He compounds this alarming outlook with an exceedingly pessimistic view of the security of Christians from such demonic invasion. This view has been criticised by Andrew Walker who observed that it creates the perception of a 'paranoid universe.'[21] In any case, most orthodox Christians would find Prince's perspective neither biblical nor credible.

Despite its controversial nature, Prince successfully developed a high profile public ministry with a significant emphasis upon deliverance in the very earliest days of the Charismatic Movement. Because of the controversy surrounding this ministry his reputation was to a large extent built upon his practice of deliverance. Consequently, when at a later stage other Charismatics began to perceive the need for deliverance ministry it was natural that they should turn to Prince for guidance.

Among those influenced by Derek Prince was Don Basham. Basham was already a well-known Charismatic leader when he published *But Deliver Us From Evil* in 1972.[22] Having previously experienced great joy in his experience of baptism in the Holy Spirit,[23] Basham found himself in a new pastorate, feeling disillusioned and stressed, wondering where that joy had gone. The Charismatic experience that Basham had seen as the turning point in his Christian experience suddenly

---

[19]   In common with most subsequent practitioners of deliverance (and indeed some of his forebears) Prince eschewed the term 'demon possession' in favour of 'demonization'.

[20]   Prince, *Expel*, 177

[21]   A. Walker 'The Devil You Think You Know: Demonology and the Charismatic Movement' in T. Smail et al (eds.), *Charismatic Renewal* (London: SPCK, 1995), 88.

[22]   D. Basham, *But Deliver Us Form Evil* (London: Hodder and Stoughton, 1972).

[23]   Described in his previous book *Face Up With a Miracle*. D. Basham, *Face Up With a Miracle* (Northridge: Voice Christian Publications, 1967).

dissipated leaving him feeling hypocritical in that he was preaching up an experience he was no longer enjoying himself.[24] This sense of guilt was compounded by his persistent attacks of fear and depression.[25] Much later on when he was already deeply involved in deliverance ministry, Basham realised that these attacks were demonic and he delivered himself from a spirit of fear.[26]

Basham went on to join Prince, Charles Simpson, Ern Baxter, and Bob Mumford to form the controversial Fort Lauderdale group who pioneered the Shepherding/House Church Movement. At the time of writing *Deliver Us From Evil* the shepherding dimension was not at the forefront of this coming together. From Basham's perspective, he and Prince were to provide the expertise in deliverance ministry which was rapidly gaining acceptance within Charismatic circles. As a leading Charismatic figure, Basham's advocacy of deliverance ministry was an important link in its developing popularity within the movement as a whole.

### The Full Gospel Business Men's Fellowship International (FGBMFI)

The FGBMFI was an important Charismatic organisation that undoubtedly did much to encourage the popularity of deliverance ministry among Charismatics. Established by Demos Shakarian in 1951 it grew dramatically, organised into local chapters. The name of the organisation indicates its Pentecostal leanings and the speakers in the early days were frequently prominent healing evangelists; Oral Roberts was the speaker at the very first meeting. Later, the FGBMFI proved a receptive environment for the deliverance ministry of Prince and Basham among others.[27] Zielger notes that: 'The original vision of the FGBMFI was of a non-sectarian fellowship of laity who could come together to share what God had done in their lives without any apology – even if that testimony included healing or tongues or *deliverance from demonic forces.*'[28]

---

[24] Basham, *Deliver*, 251.

[25] Basham, *Deliver*, 23–33.

[26] Basham, *Deliver*, 104f.

[27] Later Shakarian and the FGBMFI fell out with Basham and Prince over their Shepherding teachings. S.D. Moore, *The Shepherding Movement* (London: SCM, 1996), 92.

[28] J.R. Ziegler, 'Full Gospel Business Men's Fellowship International (FGBM-FI)' in S.M. Burgess and E.M. Van Der Maas (eds.), *The New International Dictionary of Pentecostal and Charismatic Movements* (Grand Rapids: Zondervan, 2002), 92.

The FGBMFI is an extremely significant organisation for the development of deliverance ministry. It provided a broadly Pentecostal environment, free from the denominational controls that resisted the excesses of the itinerant healing evangelists, with added credibility due to its respectable, successful leaders and added capability due to their financial resources. When deliverance surfaced as the major theme in Prince's ministry the FGBMFI provided him with an immediate platform to communicate his message and practice his ministry.

### The unfolding of deliverance in the context of the Charismatic movement

Charismatic advocates of deliverance ministry included Francis MacNutt who did much to introduce the practice in the context of Roman Catholic Renewal, Frank and Ida Hammond, Bill Subritzky, Peter Horrobin who made deliverance ministry a central plank of his healing centre 'Ellel Grange' and John, Paula and Mark Sandford.[29]

It wasn't long before the major pioneers of the Charismatic Movement felt the need to respond to this emerging emphasis on deliverance ministry. Consequently, Cardinal Léon-Joseph Suenens, Michael Green, Michael Scanlan, Michael Harper among others wrote books aimed at grounding deliverance ministry in a more considered approach. John Richards wrote a well researched and influential contribution entitled *But Deliver Us From Evil*.[30]

### Third Wave

In the early 1980s a new, broadly Charismatic group surfaced referring to themselves as the 'Third Wave' (TW). This group typically hailed from evangelical backgrounds and perceived themselves to be sympathetic to, yet distinct from, the Charismatic Renewal. Peter Wagner identifies 'casting out demons' as a basic characteristic of the TW.[31] Whilst this is true as far as it goes, it is important to understand that deliverance ministry was only one component in the TW's stress

---

[29] Space precludes any further examination of the individual emphases each of these brought to bear.

[30] J. Richards, *But Deliver Us From Evil* (London: Darton, Longman and Todd, 1980).

[31] C.P. Wagner, 'Third wave' in S.M. Burgess and E.M. Van Der Maas (eds.), *The New International Dictionary of Pentecostal and Charismatic Movements* (Grand Rapids: Zondervan, 2002), 1141.

upon warfare with evil spirits, this stress itself being a key part of an overriding missiological methodology.

John Wimber was the dominant figure within the TW. He developed teachings regarding the Kingdom of God, founded on the systematic theology of George Eldon Ladd,[32] which emphasised the 'power encounter';[33] deliverance ministry was incorporated as a key component of this wider category. Wimber's ministry was characterised by these power encounters which often, but not always, took the form of encounters with demons oppressing the people to whom he ministered.

Wimber's approach to deliverance ministry is essentially a straightforward version of that of his Charismatic forebears. Simply, he asserted that demons are a reality and that many people (Christians and non-Christians alike) are under their influence. These demons, which cause various specific problems, may be cast out by a power encounter in which Christ evicts them.

Wimber did not prescribe a methodology for dealing with the demonic. What he did commit to paper is fairly simple and avoids many of the abstruse ideas so prevalent in the writings of the more colourful and fanciful Charismatics. He appears to have been less interested in the technique of achieving deliverance than in presenting such ministry as valid, essential even.

Whilst Wimber's approach to deliverance may not differ notably from that of other Charismatics, there is a key divergence in his judgement on the ministry's significance. Within his wider schema of power evangelism and power encounter, Wimber views deliverance as more than just pastorally desirable. Instead, he holds it (alongside other supernatural phenomena) to be essential inductive evidence of God's presence. Wimber's dualistic emphasis on power (which has been robustly critiqued by Martyn Percy)[34] includes an emphasis upon conflict; this conflict is focused on Satan who functions as a scapegoat for failure[35]

---

[32] J. Wimber and K. Springer, *Power Evangelism* (London: Hodder and Stoughton, 1985), 9.

[33] Wimber, *Evangelism*, 28–43.

[34] M. Percy, *Words, Wonders and Power* (London: SPCK, 1996). To balance Percy's very critical investigation see John White's more sympathetic (though lightweight) treatment: J. White, *When the Spirit Comes With Power* (London: Hodder and Stoughton, 1992).

[35] Wimber famously accused Satan of murdering David Watson when the latter failed to recover from cancer. M. Percy, *Words, Wonders and Power* (London: SPCK, 1996), 55; cf. D. Watson, *Fear no Evil* (London: Hodder and Stoughton, 1984).

(necessary since Wimber's stress on God's power to effect positive out-
comes would otherwise be vulnerable to contrary conditions) and
'places a great weight on the agents of power: demons or exorcists.'[36]

Consequently, deliverance in TW circles was practised in much the
same way as one would find in other Charismatic settings, however far
from being one Charismatic emphasis among many, for Wimber and
his followers it is an essential element of church life that supports and
is supported by the theology and *de facto* sociology of the TW movement.

The Third Wave's concept of 'power evangelism', the 'power
encounter' and Strategic Level Spiritual Warfare (SLSW) breathed new
life into Charismatic deliverance in the early 1980s. As a whole the
movement served to galvanise the ebbing Charismatic Movement in
the direction of mission, incorporating existing Charismatic spirituality into an evangelistic agenda. Hence deliverance took on new significance as a powerful and convincing demonstration of the in-breaking
Kingdom.

### Reflection on the Charismatic movement

The defining mark of Charismatic Renewal was the crisis experience of
'Baptism in the Holy Spirit.' Many claims were made regarding the
personal, psychological, and spiritual benefits of such an experience
which (with the benefit of hindsight) now appear exaggerated leaving
many Charismatics frustrated after their initial excitement faded. As a
result Charismatics were ready to adopt Deliverance Ministry as a further step towards the promised land of personal *shalom*.[37] Charismatic
spirituality was conducive to the practice of deliverance ministry and
therefore it was widely exercised within the movement and frequently
with an intensity bordering on hysteria. This in itself, along with evi-
dences of its misuse either through ignorance or, worse, outright
abuse, was enough to produce a powerful reaction against deliverance
among the more sober minded within and without the ranks of the

---

[36] Percy, *Words*, 93. It is therefore important for Wimber to present himself as
a successful exorcist in an analogous manner to that of post-War healing
revivalists: 'Wimber's anecdotes about healings and deliverance play a crucial part in affirming the body of believers.' Percy, *Words*, 108, cf, 118.

[37] In effect the idealism of the Charismatic Movement was a key component
in its vulnerability to novelty. In establishing unrealistic expectations
among its adherents it left them forever hankering after a final, decisive
pneumatic experience.

Charismatic Movement. Others sought to bring a more balanced perspective whilst still allowing for the practice of exorcism/deliverance. The progress of deliverance ministry continued, although somewhat arrested since the heady days of its peak popularity.

Charismatic Deliverance Ministry, an enduring secondary characteristic of Charismatic Christianity, briefly flared into prominence during the 1970s before gently receding into the background; nevertheless, Charismatic deliverance ministry still has its campaigners. Towards the end of the century it was incorporated into a subsequent fad for a much larger category, namely, Strategic Level Spiritual Warfare, or it was mutated or became routinized within more traditional categories of Christian spirituality.

## The Evangelical Fundamentalist stream

During the last century, a form of deliverance ministry (parallel to that practiced by Charismatics) emerged among groups that might be fairly termed Evangelical Fundamentalists (EF).[38] Evangelical Fundamentalists often frown on the emotionalism and sensationalism of their Charismatic counterparts and assume an air of intellectual superiority; nevertheless, they share many of the same characteristics. This is unsurprising since they share the same roots.

### The emergence of EF deliverance ministry

The beginning of the twentieth century witnessed a number of dynamic and extraordinary developments within evangelical Christianity. The Welsh Revival was of great importance but pales into comparative insignificance alongside the world changing events of the Azusa Street Revival in Los Angeles which is rightly seen as the crucible of Pentecostalism. These decisive moves towards a more emotional and

---

[38] 'Fundamentalism' is, of course, a contentious and ambiguous term. It is used here to highlight the 'oppositional' nature of the Evangelicals among whom Evangelical deliverance emerged in self-conscious distinction from Charismatic deliverance. (Partridge asserts that 'oppositionalism' is the 'fundamental theological feature of modern [religious] fundamentalisms.' C.H. Partridge, 'Pagan Fundamentalism?' in C.H. Partridge (ed.), *Fundamentalisms* (Carlisle: Paternoster, 2001), 156). For a general discussion regarding the term 'fundamentalist' see H.A. Harris, 'How Helpful Is The Term Fundamentalist?' in *Fundamentalisms* (Carlisle: Paternoster, 2001), 3–18.

dynamic Christian spirituality were not welcomed universally however. Some groups resisted them and indeed identified spiritual danger
in the emerging spiritualities. Specifically, German Evangelicals united
to assert that Pentecostal manifestations were 'from below'. A parallel
and significant development was the publication in 1912 of *War on the
Saints*[39] jointly authored by Jessie Penn-Lewis and Evan Roberts.

Evan Roberts had previously been the leading figure in the Welsh
Revival. Following a dazzling but short-lived ministry he sought
refuge with the Penn-Lewis family where he came to the opinion that
the Revival had in its inception been a work of the Holy Spirit but that
the deepened spirituality of those involved had also brought to the
surface demonic elements which were not being properly handled.
*War on the Saints* was written to address this situation.

*War on the Saints* was viewed as a dangerous book by early
Pentecostals since it attributed at least some of their ecstatic experiences to demonic sources; conversely, it exerted a good deal of influence over the explicitly non-Charismatic EF forms of deliverance
ministry that emerged in mid-century. The first notable examples of EF
deliverance ministries are those of Kurt Koch and Merril Unger. Unlike
Penn-Lewis, their deliverance ministry was not motivated *primarily* by
a reaction against the Charismatic; it came out of an EF mileu that
inherited her antagonism to Charismatic praxis and yet, like Penn-
Lewis, at many points (including the practice of deliverance) closely
resembled the praxis of the movement it demonised.

Kurt Koch became well known among EFs for his deliverance ministry in the 1970s although he was actually practicing deliverance for
many years prior to this.[40] Koch's writings reveal his experience in the
area of what he calls 'occult bondage' and a serious attempt to interact
with sympathetic members of the medical profession in dealing with
it.[41] He stresses Christ's power to overcome the power of Satan: 'The

---

[39] J. Penn-Lewis and E. Roberts, *War on the Saints* (Leicester: Excelsior, 1912).

[40] Koch's books were published in the late 1960s and early 1970s and it was
these that brought his ministry to international attention. Koch's books
in the area of demonology and deliverance ministry are as follows: K.
Koch, *Between Christ and Satan* (Berghausen, Evangelisation, 1972), K. Koch,
*Occult Bondage and Deliverance* (Berghausen: Evangelization, 1970), K. Koch,
*The Devil's Alphabet* (Grand Rapids: Kregel, 1971), K. Koch, *Demonology, Past
and Present* (Grand Rapids: Kregel, 1973).

[41] Koch, *Occult*, 71–81. The second half of this book is actually written by
Alfred Lechler, a Christian psychiatrist who supported Koch's approach to
demonology and deliverance ministry.

only real method of defense against the supernatural is Christ . . . Christ leads us in triumph with all the defeated powers of the Evil One following in His train.'[42] Koch's interest in deliverance appears to have been stimulated by his experience in overseas missions although he also quotes some European case studies. His influence was very significant; almost all of the American EFs quote him as a source.

Merill Unger was already a well-known evangelical theologian when he began to write on the subject of demonology and deliverance ministry. At first he held tightly to the view that a Christian believer is immune from demonization.[43] His later position (based on a tri-partite anthropology) was that demons might wreak havoc in a believer's body and soul but may not affect the spirit, which is eternally secure.[44] This systematic argument is the foundation of his concept of the danger of progressive demonization of Christians if they capitulate to demonic influence via sin. In the worst cases God may even allow demons to kill a Christian but never to divest him or her of salvation.[45]

Unger was concerned to outline a Christian approach to dealing with the demonic and to highlight the dangers of extreme Charismatic experientialism that he clearly deplored. Hence his work should be seen as a response not only to the problem of the demonic itself, but also to his frustration with his perception of confusion and spiritual naiveté within the Pentecostal/Charismatic movement.

---

[42] Koch, *Devil's*, 132.

[43] M. Unger, *Biblical Demonology* (Grand Rapids: Kregel, 1994), 100.

[44] M. Unger, *What Demons can do to Saints* (Wheaton: Tyndale, 1971), 76f. This development was apparently due to the overwhelming evidence of 'numbers of letters and reports of cases of demon invasion of believers.' Unger, *Saints*, 69. Dickason claims that Unger's change of heart was largely driven by the experience of overseas missionaries C.F. Dickason, *Angels: Elect and Evil* (Chicago: Moody, 1975), 205. Moody actually published a compendium of such experiences from overseas in 1960; Various Authors, *Demon Experiences in Many Lands* (Chicago: Moody Press, 1960). Unger's U-turn made a considerable impact upon the Evangelical world. M. Cuneo, *American Exorcism* (London: Bantam, 2001), 246, cf. C. Arnold *Spiritual Warfare* (London: Marshall Pickering, 1997), 77f.

[45] Unger, *Saints*, 86–98. Unger's Calvinistic emphasis upon God's sovereignty in the 'perseverance of the saints' surfaces here as it becomes apparent that demons are only operating in those areas that God allows them to and, despite their malevolent intentions, their actions ultimately serve to further God's ends.

The influence of Koch and Unger was great and a good number of EF theologians went on to develop ministries and publish books in the field of deliverance, most notably Mark Bubeck, Fred Dickason and Hal Lindsay. There is a considerable irony in the fact that this school of deliverance ministry developed in parallel to that of the Charismatics and yet was antagonistic to the latter and found its roots in the early EF rejection and demonization of the emerging Pentecostal movement.

### Late-century deliverance ministry

Deliverance Ministry peaked in popularity during the 1970s and 1980s. During the last final fifteen years or so of the twentieth century it was still practiced in some Charismatic circles although there is much evidence to suggest it frequently became routinized. Furthermore the boundaries between Charismatic and EF deliverance ministry have been breached. The popular ministry of Neil Anderson emerged out of the Third Wave and represents a wider return to more orthodox and thoughtful Evangelical forms of confronting the demonic oppression. Other practitioners that exemplify a return towards less contentious and more inclusive forms of deliverance include Ed Murphy and Neil Lozano.

## Conclusion

After the explosion of deliverance ministry marked by assertive and mutually exclusive Charismatic and EF approaches the rite began to bed down, integrating the various perspectives into a more moderate, less contentious version. Herein lies the simultaneous victory and defeat of exorcism/deliverance. Like countless aspects of Christian spirituality that surf a wave of enthusiasm and achieve brief prominence, exorcism/deliverance was by the 1990s largely washed up on the beach in a somewhat more acceptable form having had many of its hard edges worn away during its brief but turbulent ride. It may have enjoyed an exhilarating voyage, drawn great attention to itself and earned the right to be taken more seriously on the broader Christian scene. Nevertheless, the metaphor holds; by the late 1990s enthusiastic deliverance/exorcism was to a large extent washed up in the church settings under examination here.

## Chapter 5

# Deliverance and Exorcism in Majority World Pentecostalism

## *Allan Anderson*

**Abstract**
Majority World Pentecostal Christianity responds to the problems arising out of a belief in a pervading and dangerous spirit world, offering its solutions to the religious market. It thereby attains an indigenous character eluding many older, western forms of Christianity by realistically penetrating the old, indigenous worldviews and creating the new. In the process, the old religion is reintegrated into Christianity through the confrontation with 'Satan'. It is this synthesising character of Pentecostalism that makes it an attractive alternative both to older forms of Christianity and to pre-Christian religions. What is clear is that deliverance and exorcism is a most important part of Pentecostal ministry in the Majority World, whatever one may think about its overemphasis or the sometimes bizarre practices involved. These practices suggest that there are questions raised in these continents for which traditional western forms of Christianity have no adequate answers. The practices are evidence of problems that face people in daily life for which religious solutions are coveted. Pentecostal Christianity responds to these particular problems arising in the real fear of evil spirits, and thereby attains a contextual character. At least part of the reason for the remarkable growth of Pentecostalism in the Majority World has to do with its appeal to the popular world of spirits that dominates in these areas – its message of 'deliverance from evil' is a powerful message in the face of constant fear of serious harm caused by this ever-present spirit world.

## Introduction

I will use the term 'Majority World' geographically here to refer to the 'global South', the continents of Africa, Asia, and Latin America and the surrounding islands. These regions of the world are where the majority of people live; they are also where the vast majority of Pentecostals and Charismatics live. There is a remarkable similarity across this region with regard to discussions about the topics of evil spirits, demons, deliverance, and exorcism; for there is a shared worldview that makes abundant provision for spirits – and of course, this is also a worldview with parallels in that of the biblical writers. It is what social scientists have described as an 'enchanted universe' that dominates in the Majority World's popular religions. Pentecostalism is one of the most significant expressions of Christianity in the Majority World today and probably the most rapidly expanding form, not only in its thousands of denominational forms but also in its effects upon older churches. It is not surprising that Pentecostalism's sharing the worldview of an enchanted universe is one of the reasons for its success in the Majority World. In highly debatable, annually published statistics, it was estimated that there were 68 million 'Pentecostals/Charismatics/NeoCharismatics' in the world in 1970. Thirty years later this figure had risen exponentially to 505 million, and by 2008, just eight years later, another 100 million were added to make a total of 601 million, about a quarter of the world's Christians. This figure is projected to rise to almost 800 million by 2025.[1]

Whatever one may think about the accuracy of these numbers, at least they illustrate that something remarkable has happened in the recent history of Christianity. The rapid rate of growth of Pentecostalism and its associated movements accelerated dramatically in the last quarter of the twentieth century and especially in the Majority World.[2] But however we define Pentecostalism (this task is by no means easy and probably unnecessary), its many varieties have contributed to the transformation of the demographics of global religion itself. This has enormous implications for understanding both

---

[1] David B. Barrett, Todd M. Johnson & Peter F. Crossing, 'Missiometrics 2008: Reality Checks for Christian World Communions', *International Bulletin of Missionary Research* 32:1 (Jan 2008), 27–31. See p. 30.

[2] The figures are considerably inflated by including such large movements as African and Chinese independent churches and Catholic Charismatics. These movements, although having a 'Spirit' focus, do not consider themselves 'Pentecostal' and in many cases eschew such identification.

Christianity and its encounter with other faiths, and particularly in its relationship with the spirit world of popular religions in the global South. The future of Christianity and the nature of global religion are affected by this seismic change in the character of the Christian faith. There are other studies pointing to this global proliferation. In the Pew Forum's *Spirit and Power: A 10-Country Survey of Pentecostals*, conducted in 2006, it was discovered that in all ten of the countries surveyed,[3] Pentecostalism constituted a very significant percentage of Christianity. It was, declared the summary, 'one of the fastest-growing segments of world Christianity', and was defined as those Christian churches that 'emphasize such spiritually renewing "gifts of the Holy Spirit" as speaking in tongues, divine healing, and prophesying.' Although the proportion varied from country to country, in six of the countries, Pentecostals and Charismatics were over 60% of all Protestants.[4]

In this paper I will consider this message from the perspective of Latin America, Africa, and Asia, with somewhat more detail in Africa, the continent I know best. Pentecostals throughout the world share a New Testament belief in the possibility of demonic influence in human behaviour. Some will call this 'demon possession', 'oppression', or 'demonization', but the net result is that the persons suffering from this form of affliction need 'deliverance' (the preferred term among Pentecostals) or 'exorcism'. This has always been a prominent part of Pentecostal and Charismatic practice, often conducted in inner rooms and private counselling sessions of churches and exhibiting a wide variety of procedures. Most Pentecostals and Charismatics also believe in the biblical position of a personal devil (Satan) and his messengers known as demons or evil spirits. The corresponding experience of a foreboding spirit world for millions of people and the need for there to be a Christian solution of liberation from it is particularly important in the Majority World, where these unseen forces of evil are believed to be so prevalent. Exorcism or 'deliverance' is regarded as a continuation of the New Testament tradition and was a feature of the ministry of healing evangelists and those regarded as having a special gift of 'deliverance ministry'. Although its incidence

---

[3] United States; Brazil, Chile and Guatemala in Latin America; Kenya, Nigeria and South Africa in Africa; and India, the Philippines and South Korea in Asia.

[4] http://pewforum.org/surveys/Pentecostal/published 5 October 2006, accessed 5 September 2008.

in western Pentecostalism has probably declined in recent years (see chapter 4), in some parts of the world it has become a very prominent activity.

## Deliverance and exorcism in Latin America

The Majority World continent most influenced by western and European culture is Latin America, where the rapid growth of evangelicalism in the second half of the twentieth century prompted David Stoll to ask whether the continent was turning Protestant.[5] But the popular religious world of Latin America is quite different and often more akin to Africa and Asia than to the West. In some countries of this region Pentecostals and Charismatics are close to outnumbering Catholics and at least in Guatemala, they have become half of the total population. The Pew survey states that Pentecostalism has grown from 4% of the total population of Latin America in 1970 to 28% in 2005.[6] Brazil has the largest population of Pentecostals in the world; they are even found in the national legislature and consist of some tenth of its members. Even in those Latin American countries where Pentecostalism is less than 10% of the population, Pentecostalism is now growing rapidly.[7] They have become catalysts of social change and are already becoming instruments of political and public clout. Guatemala has had two Pentecostal presidents, and Brazil and Nicaragua also have political parties initiated by Pentecostals. Whether Pentecostals proactively oppose reactionary structures or bolster the forces of conservativism remains to be seen.[8] Deliverance from demons is one of the main preoccupations of some Latin American and Caribbean Pentecostals. The world of popular religions in this region varies from country to country. Some countries are more influenced by a West African spirit world than others, but throughout Latin America a religious universe has been influenced by African religions, the religions

[5] David Stoll, *Is Latin America Turning Protestant?* (Los Angeles: University of California Press, 1990).

[6] http://pewforum.org/surveys/Pentecostal/latinamerica/ published 5 October 2006, accessed 5 September 2008.

[7] Paul Freston, 'Contours of Latin American Pentecostalism', in Donald M. Lewis (ed.), *Christianity Reborn: The Global Expansion of Evangelicalism in the Twentieth Century* (Grand Rapids: Eerdmans, 2004), 221–70.

[8] Allan Anderson, *An Introduction to Pentecostalism: Global Charismatic Christianity* (Cambridge: CUP, 2004), 63–82.

of the indigenous peoples, and popular Catholicism. In some areas the distinctions between these different influences are not easily discerned. Pentecostalism in Latin America has entered into this popular religious world with a message of deliverance from all evil forces and spirits that bind people.

Brazilian Pentecostalism has specially devoted services to deliverance, especially from the demons of African Brazilian popular religions such as Macumba, Candomblé and Umbanda. The Igreja Pentecostal Deus É Amor (God is Love Pentecostal Church) practises congregational exorcisms of African Brazilian spirits that have become a main attraction in its services. One of Brazil's fastest growing churches is the Universal Church of the Kingdom of God, led by Bishop Edir Macedo, which selectively draws elements from classical Pentecostalism, African Brazilian religions, and mass media culture, and promotes a prosperity theology. The UCKG practices reflect a society permeated by the belief and fear of spirits and consequently exorcism is the most frequent practice. Once again, during congregational prayer and in a state of high emotion, the whole community exorcises the 'demons' present in the service and disturbing ecstatic manifestations occur, resulting in the leader of the service performing highly dramatic exorcisms on the stage.[9] These and similar practices have been exported from Brazil into other parts of Latin America with varying success. Alcoholism is also seen as a 'demon' from which a person needs deliverance in Latin American Pentecostalism.[10] Cecília Loreto Mariz points out that by offering 'deliverance from evil', Pentecostalism 'enables the believer to perceive himself or herself as an individual, with a certain degree of autonomy and freedom of choice, and to reject any self-conception that restricts individuals to traditionally prescribed roles and denies them the capacity to choose their own destiny'.[11] Mariz suggests that Pentecostalism has the ability to conjoin 'enchanted or magical elements with ethical ones', and that alcoholism is seen as a manifestation of human imprisonment to evil spirits from which deliverance is offered. Pentecostals do not, she

---

[9] R. Andrew Chesnut, *Born Again in Brazil: The Pentecostal boom and the pathogens of poverty* (New Brunswick: Rutgers University Press, 1997), 38–39, 45–47.

[10] Cecília Loreto Mariz, 'Deliverance and Ethics: An Analysis of the Discourse of Pentecostals who have recovered from alcoholism', in Barbara Boudewijnse, André Droogers & Frans Kamsteeg (eds.), *More than Opium: An Anthropological Approach to Latin American and Caribbean Pentecostal Praxis* (Lanham: Scarecrow Press, 1998), 203–23. See p. 216.

[11] Mariz, 'Deliverance and Ethics', 205.

points out, 're-enchant' their worldview – for the belief in a world of spirits is already there – but they see their individual disorders and moral failures as 'caused by the absence of God and manifesting the presence of the devil'.[12] The Pentecostal church community becomes an effective place where deliverance from 'the devil' and ongoing support is offered.

Deliverance has also been the emphasis of some of Argentina's best known Pentecostal leaders, like Omar Cabrera, Carlos Annacondia, and Claudio Freidzon, who exorcise demons in public confrontations at the end of their services. Annacondia in particular has influenced Pentecostal churches in their ritual practices of deliverance.[13] Wilma Wells Davies in her research into the relationship between popular religion and Pentecostalism in an urban barrio in Buenos Aires shows that there are various spheres of spirit beings in the Argentine popular religious world. The bottom sphere, and that furthest from God, is the abode of evil spirits and Satan. Argentine Pentecostalism has elaborated on these ideas and has relegated popular spirits to the category of demons. African Brazilian religions have also affected Argentina, and Pentecostal exorcisms include battles against Macumba and Umbanda spirits. Demonic attack is directed primarily against individuals but also against the church community. Deliverance is accomplished during special times of prayer, sometimes using shouting, singing, stomping, and kicking actions.[14] Through the concept of 'liberación' (liberation), converts to Pentecostalism are set free from a host of complaints thought to be the work of occupying demons, always after they have converted. A particular procedure is followed in dealing with converts needing deliverance, and involves prayer for personal cleansing and protection, an interview in which past associations with the occult are explored, and then rebuking the spirits in the name of Christ. The person being prayed for, usually in a private session, may manifest the demon and sometimes it takes many hours of 'spiritual warfare' and intense prayer to get rid of the offending demon. Sometimes past practices are renounced and religious artefacts destroyed.[15]

---

[12] Mariz, 'Deliverance and Ethics', 204, 216, 218.

[13] Wilma Wells Davies, 'The Embattled but Empowered Community: Comparing Understandings of Spiritual Power in Argentine Popular and Pentecostal Cosmologies' (PhD thesis, University of Birmingham, 2007), 94–97, 159.

[14] Davies, 'Embattled but Empowered', 111–12, 127–28, 132–36.

[15] Davies, 'Embattled but Empowered', 157–59, 189–91.

## Deliverance and exorcism in Africa

'African Pentecostalism' is constituted by three main types: (1) classical Pentecostals, with origins in North American and Western Europe at the beginning of the 20th Century and established from 1908 onwards; (2) independent Charismatics, mostly black-led, that have arisen since the 1980s and are influenced by western Pentecostalism; and (3) the majority of African independent 'Spirit' churches, known throughout Africa as 'churches of the Spirit', with origins in the 1910s and 1920s. These three groups influence and permeate each other, and cannot be easily distinguished in theology and praxis. African Pentecostalism began with the independent Spirit church movement in the second decade of the twentieth century. In West Africa, prophets and healers such as William Wade Harris, Garrick Sokari Braide and Peter Anim heralded in a new form of spiritual African Christianity that was paralleled simultaneously in South Africa by Edward Lion, Elias Mahlangu, Elias Letwaba, and Engenas Lekganyane, among many others. The 'Spirit church' movements they founded and influenced together form a prominent part of African Christianity today.[16]

These early roots paved the way for other African initiatives in Pentecostalism that interacted with western forms to make Africa one of the most vibrant areas of Pentecostalism today. It is now one of the most prominent forms of Christianity and this has also profoundly affected older mission churches that have become 'Pentecostalized' as a result. The independent 'Zionist' and 'Apostolic' churches in South Africa together form the largest grouping of Christians in the country today and the Zion Christian Church is the country's largest denomination. Although these independent churches may no longer be described as 'Pentecostal' without further qualification, the most characteristic features of their theology and praxis is overwhelmingly Pentecostal and, in the case of South Africa, was also influenced by the Zionist movement of John Alexander Dowie in Illinois. Healing, deliverance, prophecy, speaking in tongues, baptism by immersion, and even the rejection of medicine and of the eating of pork, are some of these features that remain among these African churches. Whatever their motivation might have been, Pentecostal missions in Africa were unwittingly catalysts for a much larger movement of the Spirit that was to dominate African Christianity for the remainder of the twentieth century.

---

[16] Allan Anderson, *Spreading Fires: The Missionary Nature of Early Pentecostalism* (London: SCM & Maryknoll: Orbis, 2007), 161–81.

During the last quarter of the twentieth century, new Pentecostal and Charismatic churches have become a major expression of Christianity, emerging all over Africa with services that are usually emotional, enthusiastic, and loud, especially as most make use of electronic musical instruments. Benson Idahosa (1938–98) in Benin City, Nigeria was one of the earliest leaders of this new African Pentecostalism propagating a prosperity gospel. Some of the largest Pentecostal churches in the world and the largest Christian gatherings are found in Nigeria today, especially in its south-western region. Zambia has had two Pentecostal presidents. This new form of Pentecostalism has spread throughout Africa and into Europe and North America in the wake of African migration. The largest congregation in Britain and the largest in Europe (in Kiev, Ukraine) are led by Nigerians. Megachurches in African cities that make judicious use of the media and electronic music play a prominent role in public life and attract many thousands, especially young people. It is among these churches that a new emphasis on deliverance is to be found in Africa. With some it could be said that deliverance ministry is a preoccupation.

Traditionally Africa had a myriad of spirit beings believed to be omnipresent. In West Africa they form a complex hierarchy of power, derived ultimately from God. The African spirit world infiltrates the whole of life and the fear of witchcraft is overwhelming. The same essential experience permeates everywhere and is not easily verbalised. All things are saturated with religious meaning. Any religion that only caters for one portion of African experience – which portion in isolation does not have any real meaning or even existence – will often appear inadequate. African religious phenomena such as these encounters with the spirit world should be evaluated in the light of scholarly research and similar manifestations in Pentecostal and Charismatic churches worldwide. When a Christian transformation takes place in African Pentecostalism, it often meets needs more substantially than does either its traditional 'counterpart' or the theology imported to Africa in western philosophical garb. The old types of spirit possession, divination as practised by traditional healers, the ancestors, and traditional medicines and charms are rejected and replaced by an African Christian transformation. Deliverance and exorcism are an integral and essential part of this transformation.[17]

---

[17] Allan Anderson, *Zion and Pentecost: The Spirituality and Experience of African Pentecostal and Zionist/Apostolic Churches in South Africa* (Pretoria: University of South Africa Press, 2000), 196.

Opoku Onyinah coined the term 'witchdemonology' to refer to the process of exorcism among Akan Pentecostals in Ghana. He says that the focus of Akan religious activity is *abisa*, or divinatory consultation, based on the fundamental desire to know the supernatural causes of problems. Pentecostal exorcism is based on the same religious framework.[18] This fundamental question is found throughout Africa, and the consequence of this is that most African Pentecostal deliverances are preceded by a period of consultation. Sometimes this is formalised by the setting up of 'prayer camps' and consultation rooms by people who are regarded as 'prophets'.[19] In these centres and during the public ministries of preachers and specialists of 'deliverance' witchcraft, evil spirits, and 'ancestral curses' are identified everywhere as the cause of 'bondage' of all sorts of sickness, affliction and aberrant practice, and this is declared roundly to be the work of Satan. During two trips to Ghana in 2002–3, I visited three such camps, where 'patients' (usually women) who were considered possessed by demons were prayed for exorcism by a team of people (usually men) presided over by a prophet, or in one case by a prophetess, during deliverance services that might last a whole day. Onyinah found that although some Church of Pentecost members had 'traditional [western] Christian belief' that demons were 'fallen angels', many linked them with African deities and natural phenomena. He also did extensive research among the 'prayer camps' of his denomination, and found that the method of giving counsel followed by prolonged prayer for 'deliverance' was 'just like' *abisa*.[20] There is no question but that 'deliverance' is a prominent product of the African religious market.

It is quite normal for there to be a confrontational approach to African religious practices among Pentecostals just as there are in Latin America; and people who have been involved in these practices are regarded as needing 'deliverance' from demons. 'Witchcraft' and 'demons' are virtually interchangeable and synonymous terms.[21] Birgit Meyer refers to the transfer of local religious concepts into Christian parlance as 'translating the devil'. She describes Pentecostalism as giving place for people to experience spirit possession while denouncing

---

18 Opoku Onyinah, 'Akan Witchcraft and the Concept of Exorcism in the Church of Pentecost' (PhD thesis, University of Birmingham, 2002), 115, 231.

19 Onyinah, 'Akan Witchcraft,' 196–204, 252–93; Paul Gifford, *Ghana's New Christianity: Pentecostalism in a Globalising African Economy* (Bloomington: Indiana University Press, 2004), 86.

20 Onyinah, 'Akan Witchcraft,' 238, 252.

21 Onyinah, Akan Witchcraft, 236.

it as 'Satanic' and subservient to Christianity. However, it must be remembered that the introduction of the terms 'Satan' and 'demon' or 'devil' into religious terminology in Africa not only represents 're-labelling' of old practices but also marks the strict boundary between Christianity and 'paganism' in the minds of the users.[22]

Anthropologists see the increase in demonic beliefs today as part of a reaction to modernity. Behrend and Luig write of the international proliferation of spirit possession cults and declare that 'the disappearance of spirits, as foretold by Westerners, has not taken place.' Instead, in Africa and throughout the world 'many spirits and their mediums are part of local as well as global or transglobal culture.'[23] They see this as a manifestation of modernity, and not as a return to a premodern or 'traditional' past. The missionaries, they say, created these 'enemies' against which this Christian God would be victorious and in effect made the African spirit world an essential part of understanding Christianity.[24] Birgit Meyer goes along with this interpretation and writes of the 'translation' of ancient gods and spirits in Ghana so that 'the image of Satan offers a discourse with which to approach these powers as "Christian" demons.'[25] She found that this discourse, which had translated many 'heathen' terms, appeared most frequently in Pentecostal churches. The spirits and gods of Africa have been reinterpreted from a Christian perspective into demons that can be exorcised.

Although the practice of 'deliverance' has origins in African Christian 'prophets' and 'spiritual churches' of the early twentieth century, the new Charismatic churches were stimulated especially by the ministry of Benson Idahosa, whose training college was the centre out of which new Charismatic churches and 'ministries' sprang up throughout West Africa. Idahosa had formal ties with other new Pentecostal and Charismatic groups throughout Africa, especially in Ghana, where he held his first crusade in Accra in 1978. Through the influence of Idahosa and his protégés in Ghana, the subsequent visit

---

[22] Birgit Meyer, *Translating the Devil: Religion and Modernity among the Ewe in Ghana* (Edinburgh: Edinburgh University Press, 1999), 149; Gifford, Ghana's New Christianity, 93.

[23] Heike Behrend & Ute Luig, 'Introduction' in Heike Behrend & Ute Luig (eds.) *Spirit Possession: Modernity and Power in Africa* (Oxford: James Currey, 1999), xiii.

[24] Heike Behrend, 'Power to Heal, Power to Kill: Spirit Possession and War in Northern Uganda 1986–1994', in Behrend and Luig, *Spirit Possession*, 22.

[25] Meyer, *Translating the Devil*, xvii.

(in 1987) of English Charismatic and deliverance guru Derek Prince,[26] and the many booklets of Nigerian 'specialists' like Emmanuel Eni, the deliverance ministry has become a prominent, if controversial part of West African Pentecostalism.

Eni in particular wrote an elaborate account of his affair with a witch who could change her body into a snake, and his later intimate involvement with the 'Queen of the Coast', a mermaid-like water deity called Maami Wata, who would take him to a city under the sea and give him the power to change into an animal. He became a very powerful wizard until he was converted to Pentecostal Christianity in 1985.[27] Eni himself has travelled all over Africa with his story, coming twice to South Africa in 1992 and 1993 and preaching in the Praise Tabernacle Church in Soshanguve near Pretoria, on which two occasions I was present. Not only did his testimony of intimate relations with evil spiritual powers as a priest of the water goddess fascinate African Pentecostals, but his high-powered preaching and exuberant dancing were welcome in a society where such religious enthusiasm was commonplace.

Not all African Pentecostals would identify with the extremities of Eni's account, but demonology is certainly an important feature of Pentecostalism in West Africa. There is widespread belief in the power of witchcraft throughout West Africa, including among educated people.[28] The many large Charismatic churches there have teams of people who specialise in deliverance ministry and this has also become a feature in many of the older Protestant and Catholic churches.

In many ways the procedures used are similar to those employed by western specialists in 'deliverance ministry' like Prince, but the cases treated are given a fundamentally African orientation. West African religion has a complex pantheon of gods, ancestors, and spirits often related to natural phenomena, and in Pentecostal Christian discourse these have been transferred or 'translated' to the realm of 'demons'. So when a person is prayed for deliverance, what is exorcised is a reconfigured African spirit. The relevance of the deliverance from 'demons' for the people suffering affliction is obvious and those delivered will testify to their freedom from African psychic symptoms, ancestral curses and other similar disturbances. Of course, the

---

[26] Onyinah, 'Akan Witchcraft,' 220–23.

[27] Emmanuel Eni, *Delivered from the Powers of Darkness*, Ibadan, Nigeria: Scripture Union, 1988.

[28] Onyinah, 'Akan Witchcraft,' 234–35.

identification of the work of demons is by no means limited to 'traditional' spirit beings, as modernity and globalisation has resulted in a host of new threats to Christians living a holy life, including temptations in the modern market economy. These too are often ascribed to the work of demons.

Richard Burgess points out that 'deliverance' theology with its focus on liberation from the influence of evil spirits, although resonating with traditional religion, is 'elaborated in forms that are consistent with global Pentecostal culture'.[29] The way it is expressed is influenced by western deliverance specialists, whose books are readily available across Africa, and of course, it has also developed a life of its own with African specialists in deliverance in abundance. An example highlighted by Burgess is the Mountain of Fire and Miracles founded by former scientist Dr Daniel Kolawole Olukoya, now one of the largest Pentecostal churches in Nigeria with congregations in the West. This church, Burgess says, has 'an elaborate liturgy of prayers designed to liberate Christians from demonic powers and remove obstacles to individual progress and prosperity'.

Deliverance theology is popular not only because of the dire economic context of Africa, but also because of 'its close affinity to biblical cosmology'.[30] In all these cases the ultimate purpose of deliverance ministry is ethical, to change the behaviour of people feeling the need for spiritual power above that of the ancestors, the witches, and the spirits causing trouble of various kinds.

Asamoah-Gyadu points out that for Ghanaian Pentecostals 'deliverance' is an all-encompassing term, meaning much more than 'exorcism', the casting out of demons. It refers to the whole process of freedom from the obstacles of life, from sin and Satan. 'Deliverance ministries' exist in which a ritual procedure includes making a 'diagnosis' through a detailed questionnaire. Visiting 'Spirit' churches or traditional healers and receiving ritual objects are particularly thought of as evil and needing deliverance. The demons are then identified, 'bound', and cast out to hell, to the bottom of the sea, or even to the Sahara desert. The religious paraphernalia considered evil (including those associated with 'Spirit' churches) are destroyed.[31]

---

[29] Richard Burgess, 'Freedom from the Past and Faith for the Future: Nigerian Pentecostal Theology in Global Perspective', *PentecoStudies* (2008), http://www.glopent.net/pentecostudies; Gifford, *Ghana's New Christianity*, 89.

[30] Burgess, 'Freedom from the Past'.

[31] J. Kwabena Asamoah-Gyadu, *African Charismatics: Current Developments within Indigenous Pentecostalism in Ghana* (Leiden: Brill, 2005), 167, 185–88.

In my research in a South African township, I considered Pentecostal responses to and encounters with the African spirit world, drawing upon fieldwork conducted in Soshanguve in the 1990s, in north Gauteng, the most populous province in the country.[32] In Southern Africa the ancestors play a more important role in popular religion and spirits are not as prominent here as they are in West Africa. But evil spirits have also reappeared in Southern African Pentecostalism in abundance, and the exorcism of evil spirits is a regular part of pastoral ministry in Pentecostal churches. Sometimes evil spirits are associated with bad dreams, and Pentecostals will seek help from a pastor, a prophet, or another church leader.

Exorcism plays a major role in the activities of Pentecostal and independent churches, even though the 'theory' behind exorcism is unknown to many members and only a few could say much about it.[33] Nevertheless, exorcism is 'considered to be of importance to the pastoral ministry in the African context'.[34] In this regard, in spite of personal misgivings about methods used, I identify with those who emphasise the 'liberating value' of a ministry of exorcism, 'which appears to confront the existential needs and fears of people in a ritually understandable and therefore psychologically and religiously satisfying manner'.[35]

Exorcism is practised among Pentecostals to varying degrees. In some churches it is seldom seen, while in others it is a fairly common occurrence. A person may be demonised in various ways. Usually the manifestations occur when prayer is being offered. These manifestations include shouting and screaming, unkempt or unwashed appearance, restlessness, violent contortions of the body (often accompanied by extraordinary strength), jumping, falling to the ground, and running around a room. Pastors and people specialising in 'deliverance' will sometimes pray for demonised people for a long time until the demons are subdued and exorcised. Pentecostal churches often have members whose special ministry it is to cast out demons. They must not only deal with the problem in the church services, but they

---

[32] Anderson, *Zion and Pentecost*, 175–98.

[33] This discussion is based on Anderson, *Zion and Pentecost*, 266–71.

[34] Gerhardus C. Oosthuizen, 'The interpretation of and reaction to demonic powers in indigenous churches', in PGR de Villiers (ed.), *Like a Roaring Lion: Essays on the Bible, the Church and Demonic Powers* (Pretoria: University of South Africa Press, 1987), 77.

[35] M.L. Daneel, 'Exorcism as a means of combating wizardry: liberation or enslavement?' in *Missionalia* 18:1 (April 1990), 220.

must also follow up the people for some time until they are established. One of the independent Pentecostal churches in Soshanguve with which I am very familiar makes exorcism one of the most important and prominent features of its Sunday prayer time, with many 'deliverances' taking place every week.

Exorcism becomes a very important feature in pastoral therapy.[36] One cannot reflect on the descriptions of these 'deliverances' without honestly acknowledging the reality of the help that was received, despite the strange and exotic nature of the encounters to western eyes. To suggest that the exorcisms reinforced the sufferer's preoccupation with the African spirit world and the fear of evil spirits, as some have done, ignores the fact that for many Africans exorcism provides certain relief from psychological stress.[37] It thus becomes a major incentive for conversion to Pentecostal Christianity. It is also apparent that for most Pentecostals, demon possession and 'ancestor possession' were the same things, and for many members the 'ancestor' was in fact a demon impersonating departed relatives. It needed to be exorcised in the name of Jesus Christ and by the power of the Holy Spirit. The exorcisms therefore pointed to a confrontation between the Holy Spirit and the so-called 'ancestors'.

It is clearly important for African Pentecostals to respond somehow to the ancestors, traditionally believed to be the guardians and protectors of their surviving families, and still commemorated by most southern Africans. Ancestors are believed to bring harm to those who ignore or neglect their instructions, given through dreams or through diviners. Their sanctions have a certain fearful control over people's lives and most African people seem to practise the ancestor rituals in order to be rid of disturbing visitations. Pentecostal churches have responded to the reality of the ancestors in two contrasting and antithetical ways. The first and most frequent response is that of confrontation. The weight of evidence points to the fact that for most members of these churches, the commemoration of ancestors is rejected. The 'ancestors', they believe, are not ancestors at all, but demon spirits impersonating them that need to be confronted and exorcised – for they only lead to further misery. They believe they have no power over Christians, because Christians have the greater power of the Holy Spirit within them to overcome all of Satan's power. The prophets diagnosing sicknesses and other problems

---

[36]  Daneel, 'Exorcism', 220.

[37]  Aylward Shorter, *Jesus and the Witchdoctor: An Approach to Healing and Wholeness* (Maryknoll: Orbis, 1985), 197.

as being caused by ancestors or sorcery exhibit the orientation towards the popular worldview. But in contrast to the traditional diviner, instead of accommodating the ancestor, the manifestation is branded a demon, its claims rejected, and the evil spirit exorcised.[38]

But a second and opposite response was one of accommodation and concession. For a significant minority in the 'Spirit' churches, ancestors still played an important role and were to be respected and obeyed. They were seen as the mediators of God who sometimes revealed the will of God to people, and who sometimes inspired the prophets. The traditional function of ancestors as protectors and benefactors of their progeny was preserved by those who held this view. This more tolerant and ambivalent attitude to the ancestors confirms what other researchers have found – but this was not the predominant reaction to the ancestors among members of these churches. A confrontation with ancestors represented by ministries of deliverance has replaced traditional beliefs with a relevant Christian alternative.[39] Far from being a resurgence of ancestor possession, once the forms of the Spirit phenomena have been separated from their meaning, the revelations of the Spirit in African Pentecostalism throughout the sub-Sahara point to both a dialogue and a confrontation between the new, 'powerful' Christian faith and the old beliefs in spirits and ancestors.

## Deliverance and exorcism in Asia

Asia is the world's largest and most diverse continent, and to generalise about cultures and religions in particular can be very misleading. Having said that, there is no doubt that across Asia, as in the other two continents, there exist forms of popular religion in which a spirit world is very prominent. Malaysian Methodist bishop Hwa Yung supported the position of Raymond Fung, who deplored the 'invoking the spirits' that took place at the World Council of Churches assembly in Canberra in 1991. He writes that Asians understand and take seriously the realities of the spirit world and that their theologies should take this world into account. He points out that 'charismatic' forms of Christianity exist throughout Asia, whose

---

[38] M.L. Daneel, *Old and New in Southern Shona Independent Churches*, Vol 1 (The Hague: Mouton, 1971), 462; id, *Quest for Belonging* (Gweru, Zimbabwe: Mambo Press, 1987), 233, 261.

[39] Anderson, *Zion and Pentecost*, 196–98.

origins stem not from western Pentecostalism but rather from Asian movements that often predate it, and that these movements often have 'signs and wonders' and 'power encounters' with evil spirits among their main characteristics.[40] This was a characteristic of famous Chinese Christians like pastor Hsi Shengmo (1836–96) in Shansi province in China, who operated opium refuges in which his own Chinese medicines were used for the treatment of opium addiction; and he emphasised casting out demons and healing the sick through prayer.[41] Although our information on this Chinese Christian healer is miniscule, he is an example of other preachers in Asia and elsewhere in the Majority World for whom divine healing and deliverance from demons was an essential part of Christian ministry in the late nineteenth century.

The 'Korean Pentecost' of 1907–8 commenced at a convention in Pyongyang under the Presbyterian elder Sun Ju Kil and, like those revivals in Wales and India, was part of the international holiness revivals characterized by emotional repentance with loud weeping and simultaneous prayer.[42] Hundreds of Korean preachers went out with these revival fires. This was a specifically Korean revival, whose features still characterize both Protestant and Pentecostal churches in Korea today: prayer meetings held daily in the early morning, all-night prayer meetings, vocal simultaneous prayer, Bible study, and an emphasis on evangelism and missions. But beyond these features are other Pentecostal practices like Spirit baptism, healing the sick, miracles, and casting out demons. As was the case in India, national evangelists, especially the Presbyterian pastor Ik Du Kim, who was famous for his healing and deliverance ministry, probably took the revival movement into a more 'Pentecostal' direction than the western missionaries were comfortable with. Overseas Pentecostal papers also reported on the Korean revival, one noting its 'extraordinary manifestation of power'.[43] John Sung (1901–44), considered by many to be the greatest Chinese evangelist of the twentieth century, was another example of the 'power encounters' experienced in Asian Christianity, travelling far and wide throughout east and south-east Asia with his

---

[40] Hwa Yung, *Mangoes or Bananas? The Quest for an Authentic Asian Christian Theology* (Oxford: Regnum, 1997), 74–75, 238–39.

[41] Geraldine Taylor, *Pastor Hsi: A Struggle for Chinese Christianity* (Singapore: Overseas Missionary Fellowship, 1900, 1949, 1997), 164–65, 191.

[42] William N. Blair & Bruce Hunt, *The Korean Pentecost and the Sufferings which Followed* (Edinburgh: The Banner of Truth Trust, 1977), 71, 75.

[43] The Bridegroom's Messenger 7 (1 Feb 1908), p. 1.

message of healing and deliverance from demons.[44] Deliverance from demons in Asia, as in other parts of the Majority World is often called for when people have been associated with pre-Christian practices that are condemned. This was also a characteristic of the Indonesian Revival in the 1960s, when preachers like Mel Tari testified to deliverances from demons and healings, the former usually associated with traditional religious practices.[45] These revivals also provided opportunities for 'translating the devil'.

Pentecostalism has expanded remarkably in many parts of Asia. In India, vigorous missionary and church planting activities characterise Pentecostal churches, especially in and from South India. In these churches, deliverance from evil and from the myriads of gods and demons in popular Hinduism are frequent messages, bringing them into severe confrontation with Hindu fundamentalists. Evangelist and healer D.G.S. Dhinakharan (1935–2008) took a message of healing and deliverance to millions of South Indians in tent and open air stadium meetings all over south India. Chinese Christianity is growing rapidly and is also dominated by a Pentecostal type of spirituality that began in Hong Kong, Beijing, and Shanghai in the first decade of the twentieth century. Greater freedom of religion in this country since the 1989 tragedy of Beijing's Tiananmen Square has resulted in the proliferation of unregistered Pentecostal and Pentecostal-like independent churches, which probably constitute the majority of Christians and have an uneasy relationship with both the Communist Party and the officially-recognized China Christian Council. South Korea has had the largest Protestant churches in the world, including the Yoido Full Gospel Church founded by David Yonggi Cho in 1958 in a slum area of Seoul, reputed to be the largest congregation in the world by 1990 with 700,000 members. Somewhat surprisingly, Yonggi Cho in his many writings and published sermons does not say a lot about deliverance and exorcism. He does, however, identify 'the devil' as the source of sin, sickness and poverty, teaching that casting out an 'unclean spirit' or 'deliverance' must be followed by being filled with the Holy Spirit, so that evil spirits cannot return.[46] There are now several large Charismatic churches in Seoul with memberships exceeding twenty

---

[44] John Sung, tr. Stephen L. Sheng, *The Diaries of John Sung: An Autobiography* (np: Brighton, MI, 1995).

[45] Mel Tari, *Like a Mighty Wind* (London: Coverdale House, 1973).

[46] David Yonggi Cho, *Salvation, Health & Prosperity: Out Threefold Blessings in Christ* (Altamonte Springs, FL: Creation House, 1987), 155.

thousand. Some of them have a much more elaborate 'deliverance ministry' than Cho's. During my first visit to Korea in 1998 I visited the Sungrak Baptist Church in Seoul led by controversial pastor Dr Ki Dong Kim, who has been declared a 'heretic' by the main Presbyterian churches and shunned by most others because of his particular approach to deliverance and demons. His church is (or used to be) the largest Baptist church in the world and is Charismatic, with a particular emphasis on casting out demons. The source of the controversy around Kim stems from his approach to demonology, found in his published popular literature and consisting of his belief that demons are the spirits of unbelievers who have died. These can enter human beings and cause a multitude of troubles, the most common of which is sickness. The cause of sickness is invasion by these unclean spirits of dead unbelievers, or in Kim's view, demons.[47] Here we have an interesting example of someone who has continued the traditional Korean shamanistic view of sickness and affliction of every kind being the work of the spirits of the dead. But Kim has 'demonised' these spirits with Christian language, so that they are demons to be cast out through the ministry of deliverance. In my view, this is not very different from what happens all over the Majority World, where local religion has been appropriated by Pentecostals and then is confronted by the use of new Christian terminology setting the old spirits against the new Christian revelation. In Africa the same happens with regard to the ancestors who are declared to be demons from which people need deliverance. The end result in both cases is that relief and liberation is offered as part of the Pentecostal message that attracts suffering and fearful people.

## Conclusion

Pentecostal Christianity responds to these perplexing problems arising out of a belief in a pervading and dangerous spirit world, offering its solutions to the religious market in the Majority World, and thereby attaining an indigenous character eluding many older, western forms of Christianity by realistically penetrating the old and creating the new. In the process, the old religion is reintegrated into Christianity through the confrontation with 'Satan'. It is this synthesising character of Pentecostalism that makes it an attractive alternative both to older

---

[47] Ki Dong Kim, *Demonology* (Seoul: Berea Press, 1997), 23, 163–68, 209.

forms of Christianity and to pre-Christian religions. What is clear is that deliverance and exorcism is a most important part of Pentecostal ministry in the Majority World, whatever one may think about its overemphasis or the sometimes bizarre practices involved. These practices suggest that there are questions raised in these continents for which traditional western forms of Christianity have no adequate answers. The practices are evidence of problems that face people in daily life for which religious solutions are coveted. Pentecostal Christianity responds to these particular problems arising in the real fear of evil spirits, and thereby attains a contextual character. We should not therefore be surprised if the result is widespread conversion to Pentecostalism. At least part of the reason for the remarkable growth of Pentecostalism in the Majority World has to do with its appeal to the popular world of spirits that dominates in these areas – its message of 'deliverance from evil' is a powerful message in the face of constant fear of serious harm caused by this ever-present spirit world.

## Chapter 6

# Deliverance and Exorcism in Anthropological Perspective

*Peter Versteeg*

**Abstract**

Spirit possession has always been a favourite topic of anthropologists studying religion and anthropologists studying health and healing in a cultural comparative way. Exorcism has also drawn the attention of anthropologists, although until recently to a far lesser extent. What particular insight can we glean from anthropological studies of possession and exorcism? In this article we will take a look at several approaches in the anthropology of religion that have focused on the theme of spirit beliefs and spirit experiences. Because these beliefs and experiences are part of a particular construction of the self we argue that possession and exorcism should be studied together. The different anthropological approaches described in this article, demonstrate the major ideas about the function and meaning of exorcism. In the different approaches we will see how researchers on the one hand have placed possession phenomena in an ambitious theoretical framework of sociological evolution, whereas on the other hand researchers have been looking for meaning, focusing more on the internal logic of these beliefs. Recent studies position exorcism practices within the emergence of new forms of Christianity, especially in the Global South, as a way to handle processes of modernisation and the formation of modern identities.

## Introduction

Despite its interest in spirit possession and representations of evil, the anthropological study of exorcism is a marginal pursuit in the anthropology of religion. Interest in exorcism from an anthropological perspective basically comes from two research angles: first, the study of cultural practices and ideologies of healing and well-being, and second, inquiry into the ways in which societies have dealt with evil. Although studies on this topic certainly overlap and cannot neatly be distinguished, we could say that the first category of studies is primarily focused on the construction of knowledge about reality, whereas the second category is a comparative philosophy of how the experience of suffering and wrong-doing is contemplated and subsequently acted upon.[1] The majority of studies, however, fall into the first category, and they are to be considered a part of the broader fields of anthropology of religion and medical anthropology, sub-disciplines which sometimes overlap.

Central to the anthropological approach is the methodological principle which makes no moral distinctions between practices but sees them as ways of living that can be studied comparatively. In other words, the anthropological approach is *normatively indifferent* towards the phenomena it studies. I think it is important to bring this to the attention of the reader given the heated discussions in Christian circles that often arise in relation to the reality of the specific experience of evil that we call exorcism. So, it is common in anthropology to compare religious practices from different traditions; for example, a comparison between exorcism in a Singhalese Buddhist context and in an American Catholic Charismatic context. Anthropology will thus also take the term exorcism as an analytical, so-called 'etic' term, to describe similar cultural practices cross-culturally.[2]

In what follows we are *not* considering 'possession' and 'exorcism' in terms internal to Christian theology but in cross-cultural terms. The idea that possession is the opposite of deliverance betrays a perspective *internal* to Christian theology, in which spiritual freedom and wholeness are defined as a state of de-possession. Although the language in which the relation between the Spirit of God and believers is described has overtones of possession (and this has been a central

---

[1] See the classic volume edited by David Parkin, *The Anthropology of Evil* (Oxford: Blackwell, 1985).

[2] The 'emic' term, on the other hand, refers to the contextual language of religious insiders. In this case the 'emic' Christian term for exorcism would be 'deliverance'. The emic approach deals with the insider's view of the culture, usually by those born to it. On the other hand 'etic' is the researcher's view, that is, the outsider's view from someone who is not the part of that culture.

analytical point in certain studies of Christian movements),[3] the language of possession has been reserved, for the most part, for negative experiences of possession by malevolent spirits.[4]

Obviously, as religious phenomena possession and exorcism denote different states of being and self; the first speaks of spiritual entrance into the self; the second describes the spiritual ousting or exiting of the self. However, the reality of possession, that is, its experiential reality within a particular cultural context, is more complex than being the mere opposite of exorcism. Possession often signifies a longer process of affliction and healing through (voluntary) possession. Many historic and contemporary examples throughout the world abound which show that possession religions form groups of people involved in healing, bonding, and empowerment. Therefore, if we look at the aim of both possession and exorcism and the mediumistic methods that are used in both phenomena, we should rather see them as mirror images of each other. In both, practices of healing and restoration play an important role.

In this respect, it is interesting to note that within singular religious healing complexes, possession cult and exorcism can exist side by side, although not without animosity. The belief in spirits makes various conflicting practices regarding spirits possible in a single context. Examples from the world religions testify to this.[5] While spirits may be revered or appeased in one situation, they may be driven out in the next. In the

---

[3] For example in the work of Felicitas Goodman, who analyses phenomena such as speaking in tongues as 'trance possession' (see paragraph 2). Psychological anthropologist Erika Bourguignon speaks of the infilling of the Holy Spirit as the 'positive side of possession belief in Christianity': E. Bourguignon, *Possession* (San Francisco: Chandler & Sharp, 1976), 55.

[4] A few notable exceptions in this respect are the Montanist movement and the Shakers. As a fieldworker I have witnessed myself how some Pentecostal preachers, associated with 1990s renewal movements such as 'Toronto Blessing', literally referred to their experiences as *possession* with the Holy Spirit.

[5] See e.g. for Sinhala Buddhism: B. Kapferer, *A Celebration of Demons: Exorcism and Healing in Sri Lanka* (Washington, DC: Smithsonian Institute Press, 1991); see for Sudanese Islam: J. Boddy, *Wombs and Alien Spirits: Women, Men, and the Zar Cult in Northern Sudan* (Madison: University of Wisconsin Press, 1989); see for Afro-Brazilian spirit possession vis-à-vis a plural (Christian) context: E. Pressel, 'Umbanda, Trance and Possession in São Paulo, Brazil', in F.D. Goodman, J.H. Henney and E. Pressel (eds.), *Trance, Healing, and Hallucination: Three Field Studies in Religious Experience* (New York etc.: John Wiley and Sons, 1974), 113–225.

latter case, we see how instrumental and effective the personification of evil is. Personification is clearly a way to control, contain and eventually combat something that is feared for its unknown power or inherent malicious nature.[6] Interestingly, and although not easy to comprehend from the more dualistic outlook of, for example, the Christian tradition, personification also brings up the possibility of negotiation, which, in turn, makes it possible to see spirits not as wholly evil but to experience them as ambivalent tricksters. In the milieu of the possession cult these tricksters can even become good companions. Indeed, the career of the member of a possession cult – whether it is called *zar*, *umbanda* or *vodou* – shows this process of negotiation very nicely; spirits are the disease and the cure at the same time.

From an anthropological point of view it thus does not make sense to talk about exorcism without addressing spirit possession. Every cultural belief in possession seems to know of negative forms of spirit involvement which have to be neutralised one way or the other. People all over the world have found many cultural ways to deal with these influences and afflictions, 'deliverance' being one specific example.

In the following pages I will show more of this spectrum of the spirits, ranging from spirit possession to exorcism. More importantly, I will describe some key approaches from anthropology to understand the cultural, i.e. lived religious reality of the relationship between human beings and spirits. In the study of spirit possession, anthropology and psychology cannot always be separated, and in fact in this field both disciplines often fruitfully converge. However, because the psychological approach of exorcism is the subject of another chapter in this volume I will focus more on the 'strictly' anthropological side. This leads me to the purpose of this chapter, namely to demonstrate that the experience of spirits, no matter how it is valued from a certain religious position, is bound to the social and cultural context in which people live.

### Altered states of consciousness

The approach that is perhaps most commonly associated with the anthropological study of spirits and possession is the Altered States of Consciousness theory (ASC). This psychology-influenced school became well known through the work of Erika Bourguignon (1924).

---

[6] Cf. D. Parkin, *Anthropology of Evil*, 19.

Before we introduce the 'altered states of consciousness' approach to spirit possession, we will first make some defining remarks about forms of religious ecstasy.

An important distinction, first of all, must be made between possession belief and possession trance. Possession *belief* means that within a certain context people *believe* that a person's behaviour is changed because of the interference of a spirit that is different from that person's self or soul. Possession *trance*, in turn, is a belief that attributes 'alterations or discontinuity in consciousness' to the presence of a spirit.[7] Thus in certain cultural contexts a particular state of being indicates that spirits are present in somebody's life. This can be the case, for example, with rude behaviour or sickness.[8] In East African societies the association of female sterility and spirit possession is common.[9] But possession never automatically includes an altered state of consciousness. Possession trance, on the other hand, is observable, out-of-the-ordinary behaviour, expressing loss of mental, physical and emotional control.[10]

Bourguignon shows an interest in patterns of altered states of consciousness (ASC) in relation to the evolution of societies. As such, Bourguignon's ASC approach is a form of psychological anthropology.[11] Bourguignon tries to explain how possession and trance behaviour are distributed in various societies. The crux of her argument is that there is a correlation between the complexity of societies and the different forms of altered states of consciousness that exist in these societies. Bourguignon distinguishes between possession and trance possession. Societies with an emphasis on possession tend to be less

---

[7] E. Bourguignon, *Possession*, 7–8. Note that there is also trance, in religious and other contexts, without possession.

[8] E. Bourguignon, *Possession*, 7. Bourguignon mentions the examples from the New Testament where physical affliction was attributed to possession with 'unclean spirits'.

[9] J. Boddy, *Women and Alien Spirits*; see for an interesting case study from Kenya: E.C. Orchardson-Mazrui, 'Jangamizi: Spirit and Sculpture', *African Languages and Cultures* 6.2 (1993), 147–60.

[10] For an insightful anthropological description of the sudden and persuasive out-of-the-ordinary nature of spirit possession see: M. Van de Port, 'Circling around the Really Real: Spirit Possession Ceremonies and the Search for Authenticity in Bahian Candomblé', *Ethos* 33.2 (2005), 149–79.

[11] E. Bourguignon, *Psychological Anthropology: An Introduction to Human Nature and Cultural Differences* (New York: Holt, Reinhart and Winston, 1979).

complex, whereas societies in which some experience trance possession show more social stratification, in the form of class, age, and gender. The less complex society is perhaps best associated with hunter-gatherer groups where certain people are qualified by the spirits, and acknowledged as such by a community, to be in touch with spirits of various natures. The common label for this type of spirit mediator is shaman.[12] In the other, more stratified type of society, a no less dramatic performance of possession is found. Here possession belief is displayed in trance, when people are 'mounted' by the spirit, to borrow the phrase from Haitian *vodou*. The specialist is a spirit medium rather than a spirit mediator, which means that the specialist herself will become inhabited in trance by a spirit. According to Bourguignon possession trance is an indication of societies which emphasize 'compliance' toward the powerful, whether they are humans or spirits. Indeed, possession ceremonies dramatically testify to an idea of being overpowered. At the same time, ecstasy allows the individual to experiment with roles that are sometimes not available in real life.[13] Non-trance possession, on the other hand, coincides with a society in which 'assertion' is dominant. In these societies the belief that a person is possessed indicates a lifelong change of the person who is recognized as having a special charisma to sustain the social and spiritual order but as a *primus inter pares*.

One of the students who was to continue the interest in the relation between social order, personality, and possession, was Felicitas Goodman, a pupil of Bourguignon. Goodman studied trance phenomena, specifically dissociation accompanying 'speaking in tongues', among indigenous Guatemalan Pentecostals.[14] With her book *How*

---

[12] Although Bourguignon does not really employ the shaman typology, the spirit communicator type of religious specialist is recognized as such in the study of religion. Although the shaman can go into trance, generally speaking she will rarely incorporate the spirits she encounters.

[13] Bourguignon, *Possession*, 23.

[14] F.D. Goodman, 'Apostolics of Yucatan: A Case Study of a Religious Movement in E. Bourguignon (ed.), *Religion, Altered States of Consciousness, and Social Change* (Columbus: Ohio University Press, 1973), 185–90. The question whether the 'gifts of the Spirit' were 'received' in a trance-like state is a controversial topic among Pentecostal/Charismatic Christians. Some fear that this kind of interpretations trivializes religious experiences as mere psychological phenomena. But the controversy perhaps also shows how Christians 'domesticate' these religious experiences, denying any resemblance with unruly religious behaviour, in particular when it reminds of behaviour from other religious traditions.

*about the Demons?* the topic of ASC in religion left its scientific confines and found a broader audience with a more general, if not popularized, interest in the subject.[15] At a later stage Goodman's research moved even more in the direction of insider-research. Her research interest shifted to the physiological side of trance, following the assumption that the ecstatic experience was the result of certain types of body postures, which she claimed were found worldwide and throughout history. In experiments these shamanic journeys were reproduced.[16]

In general one could ask what the value is of ASC approaches. People everywhere in the world go into altered states of consciousness but what does that say? This is not always made clear in psychological anthropology. Trance in itself does not tell us anything besides one very crucial thing, namely that there is an experience of receiving the trance as a 'gift', as a bonding with, and an affirmation of, a transempirical reality. As we will see below, other approaches have been more imaginative and relevant in exploring this important existential dimension of trance.

It is not surprising that the practice of exorcism is not a matter of special interest to the ASC approach, because within this school it is seen as just a particular form of possession belief. One of the reasons for this view is that psychological-anthropological studies of possession rarely were focused on religions where the expelling of spirits was

---

[15] F.D. Goodman, *How about Demons? Possession and Exorcism in the Modern World* (Bloomington & Indianapolis: Indiana University Press, 1988).

[16] F.D. Goodman, 'Body Posture and the Religious Altered State of Consciousness: An Experimental Investigation', *Journal of Humanistic Psychology*, 26.3 (1986), 81–118; F.D. Goodman, *Where the Spirits Ride the Wind: Trance Journeys and Other Ecstatic Experiences* (Bloomington & Indianapolis: Indiana University Press, 1990). Goodman was not the first social scientist who became involved in the topic of possession as a practitioner. Well-known in this respect is the anthropologist Michael Harner who started shamanistic workshops in the 1970s; M. Harner, *The Way of the Shaman: A Guide to Power and Healing* (New York: Harper & Row Publishers, 1980). Broadcasting website Youtube.com has a short clip about Michael Harner's work (search terms: 'michael harner', 'shamanism'). It is interesting to observe that several anthropologists have been influential in the emergence of neo-shamanism within the alternative spiritual milieu in the last three decades, albeit most of them not as (personally and/or experientially) involved as Harner or Goodman. See for a critical view of the construction of these and other 'shamanisms': A.B. Kehoe, *Shamans and Religion: An Anthropological Exploration in Critical Thinking* (Long Grove: Waveland Press, 2000).

central. What can be deduced from psychological anthropology is that the exorcising of spirits indicates a spiritual limitation to the kinds of roles and identities a single person can perform within his or her social context.


## A sociology of spirit possession

ASC approaches are clearly a combination of psychological and anthropological theories and methods, in particular where they try to show relations between society and self. A different approach from anthropology, which more fundamentally looks into the social dimensions of spirit possession in an appealing generalizing way, was developed by the British anthropologist I.M. Lewis. Different from ASC approaches, Lewis wants to build a sociology of ecstasy through understanding possession-behaviour as intrinsically linked with processes of power and powerlessness in society.

In his classic work *Ecstatic Religion*, Lewis complains about the lack of analytical comparison in the study of religion after several decades of modern anthropology.[17] More important, Lewis states that anthropologists have left emotions and experience too much to the disciplines of medicine and psychology, whereas the sensational domain of religion would be seen by many religious traditions and believers as central to their religious praxis.[18] Hence his effort to construct a sociological framework that would be able to compare cross-culturally a rampant religious experience, namely possession. He achieves this by introducing a simple and plausible differentiation of central and marginal cults within religious traditions. According to Lewis every society knows a central religious expression that is linked to the political power of that society, a cult in which the distribution of power is affirmed and sustained through a claim of privileged access to the sacred, for example, a priest being the voice of the ancestors. Often, however, within these societies there are other religious practices that are more or less rivals to the central cult. These practices often show a preference for marginal spirits. An important aspect of these spirits is that they can possess people.

---

[17] I.M. Lewis, *Ecstatic Religion: A Study of Shamanism and Spirit Possession* (London & New York: Routledge, 1989 [1971]).

[18] Although I think we should not make the mistake of projecting a (current) Western preoccupation with religious experience onto other religions.

In these marginal cults, power is distributed differently than in the central religion, namely not through central rituals and symbols but through that which is on the margins or outside society. Marginality can thus be taken quite literally in situations where spirits represent a different order than the dominant social structure. They are the spirits of the outside and the outsiders; spirits of the uncultivated land (wilderness), 'evil' tricksters, or spirits of foreigners.

Writing in the same period, the work of Lewis was not unlike that of another influential British anthropologist, Victor Turner. In Lewis' idea of central and peripheral we detect a resonance with Turner's thoughts of structure and anti-structure in societies. In the anti-structure of society we see the power of the marginal in which the building blocks of the social structure are temporarily taken apart, subverted, and re-arranged.[19] From this broader perspective on religion in societies we can now begin to see why marginal religious practices can contain the experience of possession. According to Lewis the marginal cult attracts mainly women and the less powerful men in a society. In his view, marginal people are often susceptible to spirit possession because it offers them an alternative and unique kind of empowerment that bypasses the dominant power distribution in a society. Cult members are 'chosen' by the spirits, and by taking part in the spirit cult, members learn to deal with spirits and learn to control the unruly aspects of possession. Eventually they may learn to use their mediumistic abilities to contribute to other people's well-being through healing and counselling.[20] If in such a situation exorcism exists, it is from the

---

[19] See V. Turner, *The Ritual Process: Structure and Anti-Structure* (Chicago: Aldine, 1969). In Turner's ideas the dichotomy is more complex because he sees anti-structure as a processual dimension of social structure, which is played out mostly in liminal ('threshold') situations, such as rituals. Important in his theory is that in the ritual process the status of participants is transformed. The liturgy of deliverance shows a very clear example of this, often tri-partite, ritual process: (1) The participant is recognized as afflicted and in need of healing; (2) the participant becomes part of a spiritual struggle of release from 'evil'; (3) the participant receives a healed and renewed status.

[20] The fact is that some peripheral cults indeed help to advance people who are denied offices and power in dominant religions. But Lewis' theory also received critique on his alleged gender-bias represented in his model. There would have been too little attention for women's religious creativity and leadership, granting cults of women only a status as deprivation religion. See e.g.: J. Boddy, 'Spirit Possession Revisited: Beyond Instrumentality', *Annual Review of Anthropology* 23 (1994), 407–34.

perspective of this model a controlling mechanism of the central cult, meant to restore power and rule out alternative sources of power.

The central/peripheral model has been applied wider, e.g. in the context of new religious movements in relation to established churches. An example is the case of bishop Milingo, former Roman Catholic Archbishop of Zambia, as described by Gerrie ter Haar.[21] Her book is an analysis of the rise and fall of Milingo's successful but, in the eyes of several parties, controversial, healing ministry. Ter Haar interprets Milingo's practice of healing as a peripheral cult vis a vis the official Roman Catholic church. Crucial here is that the theological view and motivation of Milingo's healing ministry was that Christianity had to handle the spiritual life-world of Zambians and, more importantly, had to address the spiritual affliction of parishioners. The official church was not capable of doing so, according to Milingo, and people did not receive adequate pastoral care that would take into account the understanding of reality by many Zambians. In other words, deliverance was a method that would be of importance to a local, enculturated pastoral care.

The application of Lewis' model by Ter Haar is intriguing because Milingo's ministry involved deliverance rather than possession as a method of healing. Ter Haar clearly sees the Holy Spirit as having the role of possessing entity here, which indirectly points to a common opinion among charismatic Christians, who state that the Spirit of God is indeed peripheral to the dominant theological-practical system of the established church. One of the interesting things about this case is that Milingo on the one hand affiliated himself with the worldwide Charismatic Renewal in the Roman Catholic Church, whilst on the other hand pursuing a more enculturated Zambian theology. This has been aptly called 'a simultaneous "indigenization" of Charismatic healing and a "Charismatization" of a distinctly African form of Christian healing.'[22] An unintended, but nevertheless problematic aspect of Ter Haar's interpretation is that the use of the centre/periphery model to a large extent affirms the

[21] G. Ter Haar, *Spirit of Africa: The Healing Ministry of Archbishop Milingo of Zambia* (London: Hurst and Co., 1992).

[22] T.J. Csordas, 'Oxymorons and Short-Circuits in the Re-Enchantment of the World: The Case of the Catholic Charismatic Renewal', *Etnofoor* 8.1 (1995), 5–26; 17.

presentations by media and church officials of Milingo as a kind of witch doctor.[23]

Lewis' academic concern with spirit possession led him to the formulation of a general 'social epidemiology' of religious ecstasy. A crucial question in this respect is always what possession has to say about the social order in a particular society. Similar to the ASC approach we observe that exorcism is not explicitly mentioned. We can see, however, how in the differentiation between central and peripheral rites, the marginal is always the category that needs to be controlled or even extinguished. Those with less power are looked upon with anxiety and this anxiety of the powerful often culminates in fantasies of hidden spiritual power.[24] Following Turner's idea of liminality, we see that the margins, the places of passage, contain the things that people fear the most. The spirits of the margins, therefore, should be kept at bay. In modern Christian contexts, for example, the margins are often related to the ways in which believers and groups of believers draw their identity boundaries. In other words, most danger can be found in the areas where belief is discerned from unbelief and sin from redemption. If a Christian group has possession beliefs it is most likely that they will refer to these kind of boundaries.[25]

## The meaning of possession

One of the striking things in the aforementioned approaches is that they both have little to say about the meaning of spirit affliction, let alone the meaning for the people whom it concerns. Although both theoretical paradigms are able to show important social-cultural mechanisms regarding possession, they tend to neglect meaning or view

---

[23] Milingo eventually was transferred to Rome where he was assigned a post in the Vatican Pontifical Commission for Migration and Tourism. While in Rome he started a healing ministry again, which became very popular among Italian Catholics. For several reasons, Milingo remained a controversial figure and was excommunicated from the Roman Catholic Church in 2006. He appears to be still active as a priest, however.

[24] An example is how African diaspora religions, such as *vodou*, are often spectacularly depicted as 'black magic'.

[25] See for an interpretation of deliverance as a practice of boundary maintenance in British neo-Pentecostal groups: S. Hunt, 'Managing the Demonic: Some Aspects of the Neo-Pentecostal Deliverance Ministry', *Journal of Contemporary Religion* 13.2 (1998), 215–30.

meaning as something that is inclusive to their sociological explanations and therefore needs no further attention. Yet from the 1970s onward anthropologists working from a more interpretive paradigm started to look explicitly for ways to look into the meaning of possession. The analytical change of route meant very clearly that spirit belief, possession, and exorcism were explicitly treated as other ways to view and approach reality. Spirit possession became increasingly conceptualised as a system of meanings that could be analysed as such. A landmark in this approach is *Case Studies in Spirit Possession*, a very rich collection of contextual interpretations of possession.[26] Interestingly, these more hermeneutically oriented researchers often combined insights from symbolic anthropology with psychology, in which they showed that they were inspired by the anthropologist Clifford Geertz, who in his famous article 'Religion as a Cultural System' argued that religious meanings induce powerful moods and motivations in people.[27] An example of this interpretive approach is the cultural-psychological 'exegesis' that is developed by the Sri Lankan anthropologist Gananath Obeyesekere, who has written extensively on how cultural symbols, such as possession and exorcism, are used by people to articulate illness and social problems.[28] Hermeneutic anthropologists thus moved further in understanding possession and exorcism as a specific language through which people within certain religious contexts could think and talk about themselves and their society, and perhaps furthermore, as a way to ponder the human condition.

One anthropologist who has pursued this line in an original manner is Thomas Csordas. Csordas not only pursues the idea of deliverance as part of an interdependent system of religious meanings but his aim is to show how such meanings are in fact grounded in human experience. In this he points to the so-called embodied nature of meaning and experience. He has argued this point, interestingly, in a long-term study of the religious life-world of American Catholic Charismatics.[29]

---

[26] V. Crapanzano, & V. Garrison (eds.) *Case Studies in Spirit Possession* (New York etc.: John Wiley and Sons, 1977).

[27] C. Geertz, *The Interpretation of Cultures* (New York: Basic, 1973).

[28] See e.g. G. Obeyesekere, 'Psychocultural Exegesis of a Case of Spirit Possession in Sri Lanka' in V. Crapanzano and V. Garrison (eds.), *Case Studies in Spirit Possession* (New York etc.: John Wiley & Sons, 1977), 235–94.

[29] T.J. Csordas, *The Sacred Self: A Cultural Phenomenology of Charismatic Healing* (Berkeley: University of California Press, 1994); *Language, Charisma, and Creativity: The Ritual Life of a Religious Movement* (Berkeley etc.: University of California Press, 1997).

According to Csordas, in a now famous essay, meanings start with experience, and experience starts in the body.[30] He subsequently takes this idea to a specific context of healing and deliverance. In this context there already is a meaning, an object, namely the evil spirit as it is objectified within a particular contemporary demonology. The specific demonic objectification describes an evil spirit as having certain characteristics, such as intelligence, the possibility to interact with humans and an appetite for destruction. More characteristics will be described, if necessary, for example, the ability of spirits to transgress the bodily boundaries of interior and exterior, and, as a consequence of this metaphor, there is a need to 'cast out'.[31] Csordas notes that these traits are all part of a process of cultural objectification. 'Persons do not perceive a demon inside themselves; they sense a particular thought, behaviour, or emotion as outside their control. It is the healer, specialist in cultural objectifications, who typically "discerns" whether a supplicant's problem is of demonic origin.'[32] It is important, says Csordas, to see how demons as cultural objects should be distinguished from their 'experiential manifestations as concrete self-objectifications in religious participants'. In other words, the demon may be an object within a system of meanings, in this case American charismatic Catholicism. This in itself does not tell us how people actually *experience* these demons, i.e. have feelings that are identified as caused by evil spirits. According to Csordas self-objectification of demonization occurs where a particular thought or emotion is experienced as being out of bounds: '[the] expressive moment that constitutes this form of self-objectification as healing is the embodied image that accompanies the casting out of the spirit.' This image has a multiple signification: 'I have no control over this – it has control over me – I am being released.'[33] This signification phrases an experience which is deeply cultural, as Csordas shows. Both the experience and diagnosis of demonic possession and the method of 'release' through deliverance show the theme of control that is pervasive in North American culture, and, we may add, in other western societies as well.

The elegance of Csordas' theory is thus that it takes the world of possession and exorcism – a world that is so strange to those that inhabit a

---

[30] T.J. Csordas, 'Embodiment as a Paradigm for Anthropology', *Ethos* 18 (1990), 5–47. Csordas 'embodiment paradigm' is for the most part inspired by the phenomenology of Merleau-Ponty.

[31] T.J. Csordas, 'Embodiment', 13.

[32] T.J. Csordas, 'Embodiment', 14.

[33] T.J. Csordas, 'Embodiment', 16.

secular worldview – and translates it into a structure of feeling that most of us can identify with, whilst at the same time showing that this basic experience is in fact embedded within cultural patterns. Important to note is that this interpretation goes further than approaches, popular and academic, which see possession in relation to medical diagnosis – simply as different language fields working with different labels. In the end this would be a form of reducing experiences to a common denominator in which the cultural distinctions, i.e. between religion and therapy as different fields of cultural knowledge, become redundant.[34]

## Appeasing the evils of modernization

More recently, the study of exorcism has become more prominent in anthropology. A major reason for this increased interest is the attention of anthropologists for the emergence of Christian movements in the current age. In particular the spectacular growth of Pentecostal Christianity in its many varieties has become a topic of study, in particular in its relation to processes of modernization in Africa, Latin America, and Southeast (and part of East) Asia. In Pentecostalism a semi-dualistic belief in a struggle between real entities of darkness and light is common and normative. When studying Pentecostal churches one is therefore likely to come across these beliefs and practices as well.

Several authors have directed their attention to the social transformations that accompany the rise of Pentecostal Christianity in several parts of the Southern hemisphere. Rijk Van Dijk writes about the social transformations that result from exorcism as a part of a healing repertoire in Ghanaian Pentecostal Churches.[35] Deliverance in Ghanaian

---

[34] In a very interesting and elaborate case study Csordas has shown how different types of language in possession diagnosis have different consequences for the process of healing. See: T.J. Csordas, 'The Affliction of Martin: Religious, Clinical, and Phenomenological Meaning in a Case of Demonic Oppression', in A.D. Gaines (ed.) *Ethnopsychiatry: The Cultural Construction of Professional and Folk Psychiatries* (Albany: SUNY Press, 1992), 125–70. On the relation between exorcism and language, see also: P.G.A. Versteeg and A.F. Droogers, 'A Typology of Domestication in Exorcism', *Culture and Religion* 8.1 (2007), 15–32.

[35] R. Van Dijk, 'Time and Transcultural Technologies of the Self in the Ghanaian Diaspora', in A. Corten and R. Marshall-Fratani (eds.) *Between Bable and Pentecost: Transnational Pentecostalism in Africa and Latin America* (London: Hurst & Companion, 2001), 216–34.

Pentecostal churches often involves the severing of family ties which hold, in the eyes of believers, demonic bonds and obligations. The past of the client represents that bondage and people are therefore urged to completely 'break with the past', to use the words of Birgit Meyer, another researcher of Pentecostalism in Ghana.[36]

Some forms of Pentecostal healing ministry, such as the so-called prayer camps described by Van Dijk, although criticized by the Pentecostal churches, have placed deliverance and breaking with ancestors at the centre of their practices. People come to these prayer camps to be healed from specific problems such as misfortunes, illness or witchcraft – problems which are often related to the stress and frustration of migration to Europe.[37] Deliverance in these cases means very literally releasing people from family obligations and bonds, thereby enabling a detached individual identity to be created, empowering the person to become a successful migrant. Van Dijk thus observes that the prayer camps have a close relationship with the Ghanaian diaspora, whereas the Pentecostal churches in Ghana see the prayer camps as controversial.[38]

In an earlier study on Malawi, Van Dijk has studied how young 'born again' preachers resist the authority of older generations, focusing on the religious legitimation of that authority, and using a discourse that is strongly iconoclastic. The purpose is to do away with the traditions of former generations and to offer a 'puritan' evangelical religion as an alternative. Here too, we see a strategy that in its tone and language bears a strong resemblance with deliverance. In the religious purging of society 'deliverance' from tradition becomes a self-evident metaphor.[39] We should bear in mind that the imagery of exorcism is in itself violent and can be uncomfortably linked to the oppression and even destruction of people.[40]

---

[36] B. Meyer, '"Make a Complete Break with the Past": Memory and Post-Colonial Modernity in Ghanaian Pentecostalist Discourse', *Journal of Religion in Africa* 27.3 (1988), 316–49.

[37] R. Van Dijk, 'Time and Transcultural Technologies', 224.

[38] R. Van Dijk, 'Time and Transcultural Technologies', 223.

[39] R. Van Dijk, *Young Malawian Puritans: Young Puritan Preachers in a Present-day African Urban Environment* (Utrecht: ISOR, 1992). It is easy to extend this metaphor of deliverance to the purging efforts of contemporary 'puritan' iconoclastic movements in different world religions (i.e. Christian, Hindu, Buddhist, and Islamic).

[40] Although in European history the rise of exorcism in the early modern period can perhaps be seen as a pacified version of the violent persecution

The work by these authors writing on West African Pentecostalism shows that breaking with the past is much more than just a theological shift.[41] In particular the imagery of evil and redemption and deliverance make clear that in fact culture – as a sinful tradition – is transformed as it is incorporated in the individual, moving the person toward a new life that is severed from blood ties through the 'blood of Christ'. More important, however, is how Pentecostal strategies deal with the ambivalence of modernity, as it is associated with power, money, and desire. Deliverance serves as an attempt to cleanse modernity of its more fearful aspects. Whether this is always successful remains to be seen. The fact is that, at least in Ghana, the Pentecostal imagery of evil and deliverance is so strong that it has been able to spill over into popular culture to a great extent.[42]

It is interesting to observe that the study of exorcism gained more importance at the moment that anthropologists started researching contemporary Christianity, whether in mission situations or in contexts closer to the Western regions. This is not just an indication that exorcism is a performance that fits best in a (semi-)dualist religion such as Christianity; it shows first and foremost that present movements in Christianity increasingly emphasize dualistic views on the world, history and human beings. These views clearly are products of a conflicting communication between Western mission Christianity and historical practices in missionized countries. Where mission Christianity often failed to understand these traditional views, other movements have successfully incorporated them.[43] Pentecostal Christianity, moreover, has translated and embodied these views in a way that makes it very attractive to upwardly mobile people in the Southern hemisphere.

In the context of a Malagasy migrant town, Leslie Sharp has written how newer forms of Christianity of a Pentecostal variety compete with forms of local spirit mediumship – and in a certain way with psychiatry

---

(cont.) of groups that were seen as deviant by Catholic and Protestant authorities, i.e. heretics, Jews, and people identified as witches.

[41] See: B. Meyer, *Translating the Devil: Religion and Modernity among the Ewe in Ghana* (Edinburgh: Edinburgh University Press, 1999).

[42] B. Meyer, 'Praise the Lord: Popular Cinema and Pentecostalite Style in Ghana's New Public Sphere', *American Ethnologist* 31.1 (2004), 92–110.

[43] L. A. Sharp, *The Possessed and the Dispossessed: Spirits, Identity, and Power in a Madagascar Migrant Town* (Berkeley etc.: University of California Press, 1993).

too.[44] Different from earlier mission churches, evangelical Christians affirm the subjective reality of spirits and mediums. However, their purpose is to convert that reality or rather subvert it.[45] Sharp notes how Anglican clergy start training in exorcism to better understand the religious life-world of their parishioners, and also how modern conservative Islamic movements model their exorcistic practices after the evangelical example.[46] In this case from Madagascar in which spirit possession and mediumship form such an important part of the social fabric and of identity processes, that exorcism can only be seen as a necessary part of a process of conversion, which not in the last instance means a radical redefining of cultural identity. Clearly, from the perspective of modernization theories, contemporary exorcistic movements are at the frontline of a culture war.

## Conclusion

The theoretical detour in this chapter shows different trends and schools in anthropological analysis. But that is not our primary concern. What does concern us is the question what these specific theories teach us about exorcism and deliverance.

From the ASC perspective we can deduce how deliverance of evil spirits can function as a way to correct individual deviant behaviour. Exorcism can be an aspect of a psycho-cultural arrangement. In that case it is a dimension of certain folk psychologies in which relations between human and spirit are normal or sometimes normative, although not necessarily common. The approach by Lewis shows that this folk psychology involves political relations too. What is seen as good, evil, or ambivalent is the outcome of a power struggle, a struggle about who has the right to define and describe. Lewis shows how deliverance works as a power mechanism to rule out unwanted forms of inspiration, here literally a controversial form of spirit intrusion that is dangerous to the status quo in a given society. In turn, the interpretive approach aims to understand exorcism as a cultural objectification of psychological problems, or, in the inspiring and more radical phenomenological view of Csordas, as the objectification of an experience

---

[44] L.A. Sharp, *Possessed and Dispossessed*, 269–71.

[45] L.A. Sharp, *Possessed and Dispossessed*, 309, note 8; 254–55.

[46] Cf. I.M. Lewis, *Ecstatic Religion*, 184. See J. Boddy, 'Spirit Possession Revisited', 414.

which has its own irreducible efficacy. Lastly, modernization approaches in anthropology see deliverance foremost as a practice that signifies and accompanies the individual's passage to modernity, understood as a 'complete break with the past'. It is the closing off of an old world, deemed evil in the eyes of the born-again, which at the same time opens a door to the new, cleansed world of modernity's blessings. An important insight that the modernization perspective gives us is that exorcism as a method goes beyond the healing of individual affliction and in fact includes a radical transformation of life worlds.

What is there to learn from anthropology? Perhaps the most important thing: that phenomena such as deliverance in a contemporary Christian context clearly have a family resemblance with practices and experiences of ecstatic religion in other times and places. I started this article by stating that in anthropology we cannot talk about exorcism without talking about spirit possession as well. Otherwise, we would ignore the contextual nature of practices toward the 'world of the spirits'. By trying to see these diverse phenomena, we also begin to see the contextual and contingent nature of a certain religious experience and method, namely that beliefs about possession are specific ways of seeing and dealing with the indeterminacy of life, in particular when this involves pain and suffering. In a cultural and religious sense, consolation and coping with these difficulties can be worked out in many different ways. In the current age we see many different forms of spirit-beliefs emerging, including reinvented forms that are often called 'neo-shamanism'. At the same time, we see a heightened interest in Christian circles in a more experiential and practical faith, often inspired by Pentecostal/charismatic praxis. More often than not this Christian variety includes explicit ideas and practices about spiritual warfare and deliverance.

What reinvented spirit possession and Christian deliverance have in common is the promise of having immediate access to sacred reality. Ioan Lewis, on the last page of his classic work, somewhat critically describes the way in which Christianity has shut off the roads to immediate divine inspiration, but perhaps the current interest in immediate experiences in Christianity in fact is a sign that the 'shaman' still is an implicit religious role model. What spirit possession has offered people, and still offers them, is the possibility of taking up and experimenting with different roles. Contra a psychopathological reduction of possession as a loss of self, anthropologists have always been interested in the idea that being possessed actually is an expansion of the self. The so-called world religions, Christianity being certainly no exception, have been keen to simplify (spiritual) roles by putting them into neat good/evil and pure/unclean categories. This way of looking at and acting upon the transcendent can entail the danger of repression, which may easily lead to the demonization or even exclusion of people. A religion that strives to bring peace and healing to humanity and creation should be cautious in its evaluation of unfamiliar spiritual creativity.

Chapter 7

# Deliverance and Exorcism in Psychological Perspective

## William K. Kay

The term rationalisation, as distinct from reasoning, seems to have come from psycho-analysis. As soon as the Freudians had developed their special terminology of motives, they felt the need of a term to characterise non-Freudian terminologies of motives. Thus, if a man who had been trained, implicitly and explicitly, in the psychological nomenclature fostered by the Church were to explain his actions by the use of this Church vocabulary, the Freudians signified a difference between his terms and their terms by calling theirs 'analysis' and his 'rationalisation'.

*Kenneth Burke*[1]

**Abstract**
After surveying relevant aspects of the work of William James, Sigmund Freud, and Carl Jung this chapter considers more recent investigations of demon possession or multiple personality. It concludes that three basic positions have historically been taken by psychologists and psychiatrists: one that works in harmony with theological explanations, one that rules out theological explanations, and one that questions elements of previous explanatory models.

---

[1] Quoted by R.E. Turner and C.K. Edgley, '"The Devil Made Me Do It!" Popular culture and religious vocabularies of motives' in *The Journal of Popular Culture*, 8:1 (2004), 28–34.

## Introduction

Once we move from the discourse of theology to the discourse of social sciences, we cross an epistemological divide. We move from discourses where the existence of God and spiritual beings are taken for granted, or least respected, to discourses where such non-material entities are viewed with scepticism, if not rank incredulity. The contention of this chapter is that both theological and psychological/psychiatric discourses address the same phenomenon when they speak about spirit possession but that they describe it, analyse it, and explain it very differently.[2] Moreover, the social sciences divide up into various schools of thought with the result that they do not speak with a single voice. For simplicity's sake, this chapter deals with psychological accounts in a generally chronological sequence.

## William James (1842–1910)

William James' massive tome *The Principles of Psychology* was completed in 1890 after more than 12 years of intense labour. During the period of his writing James had held posts in physiology, psychology, and philosophy and his great work reflects these diverse interests.[3] In an extensive chapter dealing with consciousness of the self, James examines the options. The difficulty of describing what exactly the self is, and how it might relate to the soul and the ego, is both philosophical and practical. The self is concerned with consciousness of objects but also with reflections upon its own operations. The self appears to maintain continuity over the course of time so that personal identity is retained. It is related to the body and this leads James by way of a lengthy discussion to propose that:

---

[2] At least one Roman Catholic scholar makes a distinction between exorcism and deliverance along these lines, 'In exorcism we address the Devil in person so as to force him to leave a situation or release a person who is in his power . . . In the rite of deliverance on the other hand we call upon Christ or God to order the devil to depart.' See John Cornwell, *Powers of Light: Powers of Darkness* (London: Viking, 1991), 347. I see the distinction differently. I see exorcism as commanding an evil spirit to leave a person and deliverance as the completion of the task of rescuing the unfortunate individual, perhaps by further counselling and ministry.

[3] George Miller, 'Introduction' p. xiii in the 1983 Harvard edition of *William James The Principles of Psychology* (Cambridge, MA: Harvard University Press, 1890).

The consciousness of self involves a stream of thought, each part of which as 'I' can 1) remember those which went before, and know things they knew; and 2) emphasise and care paramountly for certain ones among them as 'me', and *appropriate to these* the rest. The nucleus of the 'me' is always the bodily existence felt to be present at the time . . . the same brain may subserve many conscious selves, either alternate or coexisting; but by what modifications in its action, or whether ultra-cerebral conditions may intervene, are questions which cannot now be answered (original italics).[4]

For our purposes it is sufficient to note that James does not rule out the possibility of multiple selves within the same body and, indeed, in a discussion of mutations of the self, considers delusions produced by cerebral disease, alternating selves based upon lapses of memory, hyp-nosis, the removal of inhibitions and trances and, as a third category, mediumship or spirit possession.[5] In a lengthy description of spirit possession, James appears to hold a basically agnostic position regard-ing the reality of spirits, sometimes veering towards belief in them and at other times veering away.[6] He points out that the brain of the individual under the condition of possession must be 'capable of suc-cessively changing all its modes of action, and abandoning the use for the time being of whole sets of well organised association-paths'.[7] In other words the brain of the individual during the period of possession must change gear in some way (his metaphor) because, in all these things, there is continuity of the body whatever else may be happening to the self.

In 1901–02 James gave the Gifford lectures which were published under the title *The Varieties of Religious Experience: a study in human nature*. The 20 lectures quoted extensive personal narratives and testi-monies to map out the contours of religious experience. James made sense of them by a formulating a distinction between a religion of healthy-mindedness associated with optimism, reasonableness, medi-tation, and relaxation and the contrasting 'sick soul' associated with

---

[4] William James, *The Principles of Psychology* (Cambridge, MA: Harvard University Press, 1890), 378–79.

[5] In this James was not alone. 'Double consciousness' had been identified earlier by Jean-Martin Charcot (1825–93) and his student Pierre Janet (1859–1947).

[6] His later Expériences d'un Psychiste published in 1909 add up to a defence of the validity of mediumship.

[7] James, *Principles*, 377.

morbidity, pessimism, melancholy, fear, and antagonism to healthy-mindedness. The sick soul is cured by conversion – and he instances Bunyan and other evangelical conversions – which unites the divided self and generates emotional excitements and new centres of personal energy. Conversion works because it integrates the whole being and creates harmony between the self and associated emotions.

While James does not deal with spirit possession in these lectures, his conception of a self that is ill or maladjusted because it is disorganised, unbalanced, and divided is in line with his *Principles of Psychology* and, as we shall see, has been followed with variations by later writers on the subject.

## Sigmund Freud (1856–1939)

Like William James, Freud was a gifted and intellectually restless individual who took a long time to reach his ultimate professional destination. Freud's Jewish ancestry bulked large in his latent understanding of himself, particularly because anti-Semitism was found in Catholic-dominated Austria where Freud grew up.[8] Freud's early studies were physiological and, because he imbibed post-Darwinian and materialistic ideas derived from Hermann Helmholtz, he at first came to understand mental illness by reference to physical causes. His studies of hysteria, in which he became interested after qualifying as a doctor in 1881 and visiting Paris in 1885, made use of hypnosis and free-association. He came to believe in a mechanism whereby the conscious mind was capable of repressing undesirable thoughts and emotions and burying them in the unconscious and, conversely, the bursting out from the unconscious of apparently irrational emotionally-toned behaviours that required medical help to unravel.

The mind or 'psychical apparatus' was composed of three provinces or agencies.[9] The first is the *id* which springs from the instincts that originate in the body. The id is the dark basement of the mind full of unsatisfied desires and impulses. Above this is the *ego* which is

---

[8]  A.M. McGlashan and C.J. Reeve, *Freud: founder of psychoanalysis* (London: Rupert Hart-Davis Educational Publications, 1970).

[9]  S. Freud, *The Standard and Complete Psychological Works of Sigmund Freud* (2001), includes 'An Outline of Psycho-Analysis' which was published in English in 1940, p 144. J. Rickman, ed., A General Selection from the Works of Sigmund Freud (London: Hogarth Press, 1937). Rickman's selection contains extracts from an earlier set of lectures given in 1909 at Clark University by Freud in which he outlined his psychoanalytic theories and their origins.

connected with sense perception, muscular action and voluntary movement. It becomes aware of incoming stimuli and ought to act rationally in relation to reality. It decides whether to grant the wishes of the id or not. Above the ego is the *super-ego* which incorporates parental influences, racial and national traditions, teachers, and admired social ideals. This also impinges upon the ego which must negotiate its way between the demands of the two other agencies. It is noticeable that both the id and the super-ego represent the influences of the past whereas the ego is determined by contemporary events.

Among his earliest publications Freud wrote *The Interpretation of Dreams* (1900) in which he argued that neurosis (or emotional distress) results from the repression of impulses that are, in dreams, expressed as a fulfilled wish. Dreams allow the unconscious to manifest itself without censorship by the ego though, in many instances, these expressions are symbolic and therefore require interpretation. Throughout these years Freud subjected himself to intense analysis so as to re-understand his childhood, his relationship with his father and his mother, and the urges and wishes that resulted from these relationships. His nanny had been a Roman Catholic who had taken him to church and impressed upon him a particularly punitive form of Catholicism. The humiliations of the Jewish people at the hands of Catholics bred in him a desire for revenge rather parallel to that of the admirable semitic Hannibal who took vengeance upon the Roman Empire.[10] Freud's own passing and unfulfilled sexual desire for his mother had instilled in him the view that sexual drives begin in childhood and are at the root of many later mental processes. During childhood the child hates the father because of his sexual success with the mother and, at the same time, loves him to the point of emulation: the father is both a rival and a role model.

Freud's life was too long and his literary output too extensive to allow us to consider every aspect of what he wrote. In essence his account of religion, even the Jewish religion which his father had lightly held, was hostile. His *Interpretation of Dreams* drew upon biblical material and in later life he wrote *Moses and Monotheism* (1938) in which interpreted the wrath of God as a displaced version of Moses' own anger. In *The Future of an Illusion* (1927), he delivered a comprehensive dismissal of religion. He had already argued for the similarity between religious ritual and neurotic behaviour and in his later works religion becomes a universal neurosis, a convenient illusion, whose

---

[10] McGlashan and Reeve, *Freud*, 64.

miracles and symbols can be explained by reference to the perennial patterns of psychological development caused by child-rearing and family life.[11] In 1923 Freud published the paper 'A neurosis of demoniacal possession in the 17th century' which illustrates both his reduction of religion to psychological terms and his understanding of demon possession and deliverance.[12]

The paper tells the story of Christoph Haitzmann, a Bavarian painter, who had first undergone terrible convulsions while in church on August 29th, 1677. The unfortunate man had been sent to the Abbott of Mariazell and St Lambert where a miraculous cure is reported to have been effected on September 12th, 1677. The documentation of the case on which Freud based his reconstruction and interpretation of events was compiled some time after 1714. The document is made up of a deposition given by the clerics involved in the cure, some paintings of his visions of the devil made by Haitzman, and Haitzman's diary.

The narrative of events is as follows: after his initial convulsions the painter goes to the shrine to seek help. While he was there, he is taken into the church by the clerics and a deliverance process is begun. At some point he breaks free from the clerics and rushes into a corner of the church where he has a vision of the devil. In this vision the devil hands back to him a copy of a pact signed in blood that he made with the devil nine years earlier. The painter then returns to normal life and lives with his married sister for a while but, shortly afterwards, the convulsions and torments return and the painter goes back to receive further ministry. A second document is produced, this one signed in black ink, and a more or less permanent cure has now been secured. The painter is admitted to a monastery and serves out the rest of his days as a monk until he dies in peace about 20 years later.

Freud deduces that the man made a pact with the devil soon after his father had died. The devil is enjoined to protect the painter for a period of nine years and it is at the end of this period, when the painter has to submit to the devil, that the convulsions begin. Freud argues that the man takes the devil as a father-substitute. He argues this on the basis of the pictures that are included within the documentation. The first picture of the devil shows 'an honest old burger with a flowing brown beard, dressed in red mantle with a black hat' but later pictures

---

[11] 'Obsessive acts and religious practices' (1907) is included in S. Freud, *Collected Papers*, volume 2, (London: The Hogarth Press, 1948), 25–35.

[12] S. Freud, *Collected Papers*, volume 4, 436–72.

show the devil as having two pairs of breasts.[13] Freud interprets these events as indicating that the painter deeply loved his father and depended inordinately upon him. When his father died, the painter was melancholic and looked for protection to the devil. If it seems odd that the beloved father of the painter should be transformed into the devil, Freud argues that the earthly father is the source of both divine and devilish beliefs. As we have seen earlier, the father is both a rival and a role model, both loved and hated. Freud considers that the account of Lucifer as at first an angel of light and then, after the fall, as the Prince of Darkness as indicative of the dual nature of this authoritative being.

The period of nine years during which the bond with the devil was in force is, so far as Freud is concerned, symbolic of a period of nine months and therefore of fertility. The painter expresses his dependence upon the devil by viewing himself as feminine in relation to the devil's masculinity. The painter struggles against his own feminine attitude to his father and so generates a contrasting fantasy in which the father is turned into a woman and the painter remains male. Thus the devil-figure may be both masculine (so that the painter can be dependent and feminine) and feminine (so that the painter can turn the tables and also express his own tenderness towards this protecting figure).

If these speculations appear obtuse – and Freud admits that criticisms of psychoanalysis have been made along these lines – the other features of the analysis are very hard-headed. The painter goes to the church carrying a copy of the bond which he produces while concealed in a corner. The second bond is invented by the painter to account for the temptations he receives while staying with his sister and in order to prepare the way for his own final deliverance and admission to the monastery.

The account of the deliverance of the painter had been preserved by the Catholic Church as evidence of a genuine miracle. What Freud's analysis does is to remove the miraculous and to reduce it to the level of the natural and, perhaps it is not too much to say, enables him to gain revenge on his old Catholic nanny.

## Carl Jung (1875–1961)

The son of a cold marriage between an unhappy Swiss pastor and a depressive, mediumistic mother, he was born in 1875 and grew up as a

---

[13] S. Freud, *Collected Papers*, volume 4, 449.

gifted and introverted child, speaking German and French, learning English, Latin and Greek, with a capacity for self-analysis that early manifested itself by an interest in dreams and their symbolic meaning. He believed himself to be possessed of two personalities, one pointing towards science and the other towards pantheism and the arts.

This background was ripe for an experience of séances with a young cousin who claimed to be able to communicate with Jung's paternal and maternal grandparents, a claim Jung, while training as a physician, explained by reference to the unconscious mind. Perhaps inevitably, then, he gravitated towards the world of mental illness and worked for several years at the Burghölzli hospital under the distinguished Eugen Bleuler treating schizophrenics, alcoholics, neurotics, amnesiacs, and manic depressives. In the exciting and mysterious world of abnormal mental states, he was able to develop the notion of a *complex* or dynamic cluster of ideas that functioned as a sub-personality which could be brought into the open by the use of word association tests because the reaction to the stimulus word was either unusual or unusually delayed.

The complex, analysed in this way, was close to the Freudian notion of *repression*, probed by interpreting a patient's dreams. In 1906 Jung wrote to Freud and the two met in Vienna the following year. They talked non-stop for thirteen hours and the outcome of that and subsequent meetings was Freud's view that Jung should become the 'crown prince' of psychoanalysis, the person destined to take over leadership of the new movement after Freud (Freud was 19 years older than Jung), and the 'apostle to the Gentiles' the man during Freud's life who would take the 'gospel' of psychoanalysis to the Gentiles while the 'master' worked with the Jewish community.

Jung was becoming uneasy about Freud's insistence on the all-importance of infantile sexuality while Freud worried about Jung's mystical tendencies. Jung later wrote:

> Above all, Freud's attitude towards the spirit seemed to me highly questionable. Wherever, in a person or in a work of art, an expression of spirituality (in the intellectual, not the supernatural sense) came to light, he suspected it, and insinuated that it was repressed sexuality . . . I can still recall vividly how Freud said to me, 'My dear Jung, promise me that you will never abandon the sexual theory. That is the most essential thing of all. You see, we must make a dogma of it, an unshakeable bulwark' . . . in some astonishment I asked him, 'a bulwark – against what?' To which

he replied, 'against the black tide of mud' – and there he hesitated for a moment, then added – 'of occultism'.[14]

Relations were worsened when Sabina Spielrein, probably one of Jung's mistresses, became a Freudian, and they finally broke down in 1914 as Jung engaged in a bitter Oedipal struggle with Freud. As a consequence Jung withdrew from medical practice, battled with mental illness over a period of about four years, desperately analysed his own dreams and engaged in long conversations with the imaginary Philemon, a figure who emerged from his own unconscious and whom he considered to be an *archetype*. That Jung experienced or survived schizophrenia seems to be without question, and his cure was found in reconciling the opposites he discovered within himself, a motif that was to recur in subsequent writings. Its first outcome, however, led him to propose a theory of mind that he set up in contradistinction to Freud's.

In *Psychological Types* (published in 1921, English translation 1923) Jung contended that human beings were either primarily extravert (directed towards the outer world of people) or introvert (directed towards the inner world of feelings or ideas) and that psychological functions operated in two pairs, thinking or feeling and sensation or intuition. This results in eight basic personality types: extravert-thinking, extravert-feeling, extravert-sensation, and extravert-intuitive that are matched by the corresponding introvert equivalents. Archetypes are a crucial part of the Jungian thesis. They are mental images into which collective and personal meaning is poured and are analogous to Platonic forms by which we identify specific instances. Archetypes typically manifest themselves as ancestral figures – ancient sages, wise old women, priests, medicine men, and even animals. The common themes among archetypes are explicable by the fact that they derive from the collective unconscious as opposed to the individual unconscious. In the Jungian account of life's pilgrimage there is a quest for individuation, for the finding of the *Self*, the archetype of archetypes. Yet this *Self* is closely identified with God so that individuation paradoxically occurs by interaction with the greater whole. This said, the Self is by no means the same as the *ego* with which it must remain in balance.[15]

---

[14] C.G. *Jung, Memories, Dreams, Reflections* (London: Fontana Press, 1961 /1995), 172, 173.

[15] F. McLynn, *Carl Gustav Jung* (London: Transworld Publishers, 1996), 308, 309.

Jung's battle with mental illness – his hearing of voices and conversations with imaginary beings – involved long discussions with his spirit-guide, Philemon. In later life Jung insisted upon attempts to reconcile opposites, especially good and evil, as a means by which individuation could be achieved.[16] Or, to put this another way, spirits possessing a person on the verge of insanity must be overcome and incorporated into the totality of the personality: it is not a matter of deliverance but of conquest. None of this prevented Jung believing in the other psychic phenomena. He thought there were connections between the inner life of the mind and the outer world, either in the form of unexpected coincidences or the appearance of ghosts and poltergeists. On one occasion when Jung had compulsively written down all his conversations with Philemon, his eldest daughter saw a ghost, his son drew a symbolic picture, and the doorbell rang when nobody was there.[17] This line of thinking leads Sperber to argue that Jung would have attributed the convulsions of Haitzmann to his rejection of the 'trickster archetype' (who is related to the shape-changing devil) which is then externalised in the form of a hallucination.[18]

## Clinical practice and research

We move now into a different discussion that is not based exclusively round the work of any individual figure. Rather we are concerned with the conclusions of medical practitioners or academic researchers using a variety of classification systems but, in the main, sticking to empirical methods.[19] P.M. Yap (1960), a consultant to the Child Guidance Centre in Hong Kong University and a lecturer in psychiatry, was concerned to investigate 'the possession syndrome' by comparing the findings of French scholars and his own drawn from a population in

---

[16] R.A. Segal, 'A Jungian view of evil', *Zygon*, 20.1 (1985), 83–89. Segal writes, 'because the shadow is composed of antisocial, Freudian-like drives which oppose the persona archetype, or public image, it corresponds to what Jung . . . call(s) human's evil side,' 85.

[17] F. McLynn, *Carl Gustav Jung* (London: Transworld Publishers, 1996), 242.

[18] M. Sperber, 'The daimonic: Freudian, Jungian and existential perspectives', *Journal of Analytical Psychology*, 20.1 (1975), 41–49.

[19] I have refrained from comment on R.K. McAll, 'Demonosis or the possession syndrome', *International Journal of Social Psychiatry*, 17 (1971), 150–58, since it is (a) a very confused piece of writing and (b) where it does make sense it appears to say many of the things said better by Yap.

Hong Kong.[20] Reviewing the literature back to 1930 he noted that Leroy and Portier (1930) divided cases of spirit possession following spiritualism into acute and curable, chronic and incurable cases.[21] Vinchon (1931) distinguished three types of possession: obsessions connected with the associated processes; anxiety nightmares due to sexual conflict; hysteria conditioned by excessive imagination.[22] Delay (1945) referred to findings of possession connected with melancholia whereas Mars (1946), studying cases in Haiti, took possession to be connected with schizoid and mystical conditions.[23] Aubin (1952) distinguished cases of 'pseudo-possession' in which there is 'no true doubling of the personality but only a morbid transformation'.[24] Pidoux (1955) reported on ritual possessions in Africans which they considered normal within the cultural context.[25]

The more extensive work of Lhermitte (1944, 1946, 1955, 1956) is rather different in that he was an orthodox Catholic psychiatrist working in cooperation with exorcists.[26] Lhermitte (1955) distinguishes between true and false possession. True possession cannot be adequately explained by psychiatric means whereas false possession can be. This distinction, however, is not widely held by French psychiatrists. The difficulty of diagnosis for psychiatrists arises from the penumbra of mental health issues that surround possession: anyone

---

[20] P.M. Yap, 'The Possession syndrome: a comparison of Hong Kong and French Findings', in the *Journal of Mental Science*, 106 (442), (1960), 114–37.

[21] J. Leroy and C. Portier, 'Délirer systématisé de persecution et de possession démoniaque consécutif à des practiques spirites', *Ann. Méd. Psychol.*, 88 (1930), 217–32.

[22] J. Vinchon, 'The Possession Syndrome: A Comparison of Hong Kong and French Findings', chapter 6 in M. Laignel-Lavastine, *Concentric Method in the Diagnosis of Psychoneurotics*, International Library of Psychology, Philosophy, and Scientific Method (London: Kegan Paul, 1931, 1st edition in English).

[23] J. Delay, 'Délirer de possession diabolique', *Press Méd*, 11 (March 17, 1945), 143; L. Mars, *La Crise de Possession dans le Vaudou* (Porte-au-Prince: Imprimerie de L'Etat, 1946).

[24] H. Aubin, *L'Homme et la Magie* (Paris, Desclée de Brouwer, 1952), 76.

[25] C. Pidoux, 'Les états de possession rituelle chez les Mélano-Africains', *L'Evolution Psychiat.*, 26, (1955), 271–83.

[26] J. Lhermitte, 'Les psychoses de possession diabolique', *Rev. Méd. Franc.*, No. 4 (April, 1944), 51–54. J. Lhermitte, 'Essai sur les phénomènes de possession démoniaque', *Encephale*, 10 (1946–7), 261–82. J. Lhermitte, 'Les démonopathiese engenderées par l'encéphalite epidémique (lethargique)', *Prog. Med.*, 83 (1955), 115–16. J. Lhermitte, *Vrais et Faux Possédés*, chap. 1, (Paris: A. Fayard, 1956).

suffering from a genuine demon possession is also likely to have mental problems as a consequence of possession. It is very difficult to disentangle mental problems that present themselves with all the symptoms of demon possession from demon possession that induces mental problems. In addition to these difficulties is the further problem caused by the different degrees of possession that appear to exist: some cases are associated with clouding of consciousness while, in others, the patient is lucid and able to give an account of the physical or psychological aspects of his or her condition. On top of all these complications, it is also true that demon possession is diagnosed differently in Japanese and Chinese cultures, in some cases standard psychological or psychiatric terms are used (often deriving from German) and in others the condition is described in an oriental language.

Yap investigated 66 men and women admitted to the Hong Kong Mental Hospital between 1954 and 1956. Of the sample 50 cases were female and 16 male with ages from 16 to 60. The diagnosis of these cases made by psychiatrists ranged between hysteria (44%), schizophrenia (24%) and depression with hysterical features (12%); and the rest with a series of vaguer designations. These possessions were assessed by degree. Only seven of the cases, all women, were thought to be completely possessed, with clouded consciousness, changed voice, and amnesia; just under half (47%) were partly possessed with reduced symptoms; and a third were more characterised by attention-seeking mannerisms like giggling.

In the first instance Yap believes that most of the cases that he studied could be traced to hysterical dissociation[27] and mental automatism and what he calls 'mythopoeic' thinking that helps the individual grasp a life-situation holistically. The second approach to the study of possession goes back to Jungian theory in which the personality is reorganising itself through inner struggles. He accepts Jung's distinction between the personal unconscious and the collective unconscious. The personal unconscious may be connected with the soul whereas the collective unconscious may be connected with ghosts and spirits. As he points out, 'Jung's explanation of the development of subsidiary personalities emphasises the spontaneous evolution of complexes in the unconscious.' At any rate there is a division within the self, which

---

[27] See S. Freud, 'The origin of psycho-analysis' in J. Rickman, ed., *A General Selection from the works of Sigmund Freud* (London: Hogarth Press, 1937), 11, where 'hysterical dissociation' is described as 'the splitting of consciousness'.

clearly harks back to the thinking of William James. In Yap's view normal personalities alter by the gradual penetration of new values whereas in cases of possession a new sub-personality will be disconnected from full awareness and then suddenly overcome some part of the self. But this does not answer the question of the manifestation of negative possession, minions of Satan, and vengeful spirits. In Yap's view the devil is a personification of undesirable aspects of the unconscious projected onto the cultural environment and, in some cases, the individual who manifests these negative characteristics may obtain a secondary gain at a superficial level by being able to pass the blame for guilt onto the devil.

Swanson, also using empirical methods, considers trance and possession but his notion of possession is much lighter and less pathological than Yap.[28] He attributes possession, or 'feeling ourselves moved from within by purposes that are not merely our own' to the immersion by members in collective currents and interests. In other words, individuals who are most deeply immersed in collective life are more likely to be, in his sense, possessed. This does not take us very far beyond alerting us to the fact that there may be social elements inducing susceptibility to possession.

A more persuasive and relevant set of arguments is presented by Ward and Beaubrun who carried out interviews with 'possessed individuals in contemporary Trinidadian society'.[29] They make a distinction between demon possession (the focus of their study), bewitchment as a result of a spell or charm, and ritual possession by sympathetic spirits that is usually voluntary and reversible. The cultural background of Trinidad, although it is located in the West Indies, draws upon the Nigerian Yoruba tribe who comprise 43% of the total population. Consultation with fortune tellers is commonplace despite the Christian nature of Trinidadian society.

Four individuals, all attending a local Pentecostal Church, are the subjects of case studies. The first, a Black woman suffering from headaches, stomach pains, and suicidal tendencies attributes her problems to demons that she believes come at night to engage in sexual intercourse with her. She has attempted to find relief from her disorders in various forms of folk healing. Her demon attacks first occurred

---

[28] G.E. Swanson, 'Trance and Possession: studies of charismatic influence', *Review of Religious Research*, 19.3 (1978), 253–78.

[29] C.A. Ward and M.H. Beaubrun, 'The psychodynamics of demon possession', *Journal for the Social Scientific Study of Religion*, 19.2 (1980), 201–7.

when she was about 16 years of age when a boyfriend with whom she had had sexual relations and who had promised marriage rejected her. After refusing to marry as her mother had planned, she moved into her uncle's residence to help with the housework and attend his sick wife. She eventually became involved in sexual relations with the uncle, became pregnant by him and was forced to have an abortion. After experiencing abdominal swelling she believed herself to be under attack from the demons desiring intercourse with her. Over the last year the woman has reported 32 exorcisms within the Pentecostal Church and is currently cohabiting with a married man.

The other cases also involve sexual relations and domestic stress. In another case a woman was, at the age of 15, married against her will to a partner she disliked and suffered the disapproval of her father-in-law. In one case a woman engaged in sexual relations that her parents did not approve and was forced to separate from her boyfriend. She suffers headaches and depression and believes she is demon possessed. After receiving a proposal of marriage from another man she believes herself to be possessed by a demon who desires to seduce her and who is jealous of the new boyfriend. Again exorcisms have been performed by the Pentecostal church.

Ward and Beaubrun conclude 'the women experience intense guilt over the incestuous or illicit love affairs . . . further compounded by an unwanted abortion.' While their symptoms may differ, the individuals share similar situations. Possession, unlike any other psychological defence, is 'ideally suited to coping with their conflicts'. This is because possession offers escape from an unpleasant reality *and* the reduction of guilt by projecting blame 'onto an intruding agent'. The possessed individual is not liable to guilt and, in the context of a Pentecostal church, 'possession-individuals are treated with deference and concern.' The conclusion of the researchers avoids a discussion about the reality or otherwise of the demon spirits. Rather they note the supporting cultural environment that predisposes individuals to consider themselves to be possessed, and the advantages that accrue to be an individual of possession and the further advantages that accrue as a result of going through a process of exorcism, in one case many times.

Since 1980 attempts at dealing with the demon possession have been made by the creation of new disease categories. Given the presumptions and protocols under which most clinicians work (i.e. that there are no non-material entities like spirits and angels), mental health professionals have found it necessary to advance other explanations for the phenomena than those within popular culture or theology.[30] Essentially where more than one recognisable personality is seen within a single individual this is thought to have been brought about by protective mechanisms within the psyche, often in response to child abuse or trauma of this kind. Such a diagnosis must first of all rule out physical causes for the multiple personalities, however. The criteria by which psychiatrists identify mental illnesses known as DSM-IV have renamed what was formerly called Multiple Personality Disorder with the new term Dissociative Identity Disorder and provided guidelines for diagnosis and treatment.[31] Treatment may be by psychotherapy or drugs, with the aim of combining the personalities into one coherent or dominant whole.

The diagnostic features of Dissociative Identity Disorder are: (a) two or more distinct identities or personality states (b) that currently take control of behaviour so that there is (c) an inability to recall important personal information which (d) is not due to any direct physiological effects. Individuals with this disorder experience memory gaps. The more passive identities have more sketchy memories whereas the more hostile identities have more complete memories. Some of the memory loss and may be extended to the period of childhood or adolescence and transitions between the identities may be triggered by psychosocial stress. According to clinicians about half reported cases included individuals with 10 or fewer identities. Moreover the diagnosis of this condition is complicated by overlapping symptoms with schizophrenia and other psychotic disorders.[32]

The medicalization of personality disorders triggered professional debate and the appearance of a group of patients calling themselves Speaking For Our Selves who publicly attacked sceptical doctors.[33] In

---

[30] One of the most famous accounts of mental treatment is given in the 1957 film *The Three Faces of Eve* in which a woman with three personalities is eventually cured by Dr Luther, her psychiatrist, who traces her condition to a childhood trauma.

[31] 'DSM' refers to the Diagnostic and Statistical Manual of Mental Disorders by which the American Psychiatric Association classifies symptoms. SSDPP Project, http://www.fortea.us/english/psiquiatria/history.htm (accessed 8 August 2008).

[32] *Diagnostic and Statistical Manual of Mental Disorders: DSM-IV-TR*, 4th edition, (Washington, DC: American Psychiatric Association, 2000), 526–29.

[33] All the information in this paragraph is taken from Roland Littlewood, *Pathologies of the West: an anthropology of mental illness in Europe and America* (London: Continuum, 2002), 165–81.

the face of patient anger sympathetic professionals legitimated the claims of the patients so that in 1988 the largely supportive journal *Dissociation* was launched. Disputes among health professionals polarised opinion. Some medical experts argued that as many as 10% of psychiatric patients had multiple personalities and popular manuals suggested up to half the female American population had been sexually abused and were therefore *latent multiples*. As a result of further debate 'the preferred therapeutic option is now to keep all the personalities in play, establishing explicit therapeutic contracts with each' with the aim of reaching 'co-consciousness'.[34] Sexual abuse is routinely seen as the cause of multiple personalities and general dissociative disorders and some American psychiatrists ratcheted up the strangeness of the entire debate by blaming abuse on extra terrestrials. Not surprisingly sceptical therapists have countered by advancing the notion of 'false memory syndrome' i.e. completely unreliable evidence from patients. One questionnaire in the 1980s appeared to provide evidence that up to 15 million Americans had been abducted, sexually interfered with, and then returned to give birth to hybrids though, in many cases, they were re-abducted for the actual process of giving birth. In other cases sexual abuse is being attributed to Satanic practices but police investigations, in Britain at least, have not led to prosecutions.[35] Indeed one British doctor, contrasting British scepticism with what appears to be American credulity, argues that any suggestion that there are two or three personalities in one individual should simply be replaced by saying that each personality has more than two or three aspects.

## Conclusion

The literature shows that there are psychiatric and psychological confrontations with phenomena which, in a theological context, might be attributed to demon possession.[36] A survey of psychiatric and psychological literature suggest three basic positions might be taken. First, the apparently demonic phenomena are explicable in terms of materialist models of the universe, models that presume human beings are entirely

---

[34] Littlewood, *Pathologies*, 167.

[35] http://news.bbc.co.uk/1/hi/uk/636302.stm (accessed 25th October 2008).

[36] Jean La Fontaine (ed.), *The Devil's Children: From Spirit Possession to Witchcraft, New Allegations That Affect Children* (Aldershot: Ashgate, 2009).

physical entities. Second, the phenomena may be addressed by accepting the equal expertise of both medical personnel and theologically-informed exorcists.[37] Third, there is a debate among health professionals as to the validity of evidence given by patients with Dissociative Identity Disorder (Multiple Personality Disorder). This means that the multiple personalities are accepted by some health professionals and not by others. Consequently, while some health professionals build upon double consciousness and the work of James, Freud and Jung, others wish to start the debate all over again on quite different grounds.

---

[37] John White for instance would accept both perspectives. See John White, *The Masks of Melancholy* (Leicester: Inter-Varsity Press, 1982).

Chapter 8

# Deliverance and Exorcism in Philosophical Perspective

*Phillip H. Wiebe*

There are two equal and opposite errors into which our race can fall about the devils. One is to disbelieve in their existence. The other is to believe, and to feel an excessive and unhealthy interest in them. They themselves are equally pleased by both errors and hail a materialist or a magician with the same delight.

*C.S. Lewis*[1]

**Abstract**
This chapter attempts to sketch a philosophical case for the reality of demonic possession. In contemporary western culture a belief in evil spirits is usually dismissed as primitive and irrational for a number of reasons. Contemporary philosophy, when not silent on the subject, is similarly rejectionist. However, it is commonly accepted by scientists and philosophers that an argument to the best explanation can be used to postulate unobserved entities on the basis of observed phenomena that do not plausibly yield to alternative explanations. This article considers specific features of certain ancient and modern accounts of exorcism that seem very hard to account for on naturalistic assumptions but which make perfect sense if one postulates the existence of evil 'spirits'. Thus one has the foundations of a case for the rationality of postulating demonic possession as an explanation of certain events.

---

[1] *The Screwtape Letters* (London: Geoffrey Bles, 1942), 3.

## Introduction

The existence of evil spirits is so vigorously repudiated now by educated people in western civilization that the prevalence of the opposing belief in earlier eras is something of a mystery. During the medieval era both evil and good spirits, belonging to three hierarchical orders each having three tiers, were thought to be located in a cosmos of hollow and transparent globes.[2] The medieval world also considered other creatures to exist, variously known as fairies, elves, gnomes, trolls, hags, nymphs, and by other terms,[3] but modernity's influences have virtually eliminated beliefs in them.[4] Social anthropologist, Sir James Frazer (1854–1941), poetically observed more than a century ago that 'the army of spirits, once so near, has been receding farther and farther from us, banished by the magic wand of science from hearth and home, from . . . haunted glade and lonely mere, from the riven murky cloud that belches forth the lightning, and from those fairer clouds that pillow the silver moon or fret with flakes of burning red the golden eve.'[5] Although the academy continues to debate the existence of the Supreme Deity, it rarely given serious attention to the existence of lesser beings known as demons and angels, and by other names. The work of Emma Heathcote-James from the University of Birmingham on recent encounters with angels is an exception to this trend, but she also backs away from endorsing their reality, maintaining that her interests are not those of philosophers.[6] Several significant philosophers in the 20th century either contribute to this decline or give firm expression to it.

Paul Carus (1852–1919), philosopher and theologian, published *The History of the Devil* in 1900, remarking that the possibility of a demonic

---

[2] C.S. Lewis, *The Discarded Image: An Introduction to Medieval and Renaissance Literature* (Cambridge: Cambridge University Press, 1964), 70f, describes (Pseudo)-Dionysius as having had more influence than any other author in bringing the medieval frame of mind into being; cf. the 6th century texts, *The Mystical Theology* and *The Celestial Hierarchies*.

[3] Lewis discusses the various views held in the medieval world about this group of beings, *Discarded Image*, ch. 6.

[4] For a recent defense of their reality see Janet Bord, *Fairies: Real Encounters with Little People* (New York: Dell, 1997).

[5] J. Frazer, *The Golden Bough* (ed.), (London: Oxford University Press, 1994; orig. 1890), 546.

[6] Emma Heathcote-James, *Seeing Angels: True Contemporary Accounts of Hundreds of Angelic Experiences* (London: John Blake 2002), 232, ch. 13; she has collected more than 800 first-hand accounts.

reality was already widely neglected and overlooked in his time. Carus articulated a monistic philosophy that was predicated on the belief that nature is one and indivisible, and on the assumption that the methods of research found in science are applicable to all of life, including religion.[7] Carus's monism appears to derive from such beliefs that without heat we would not understand cold, without darkness we would not understand light, without goodness we would not understand evil, and so on. He describes his God as 'the norm of existence, that factor which conditions the cosmic order and is formulated by naturalists as laws of nature.'[8] This cosmic order includes a moral order, which allows Carus to identify the Devil as the contrast to the 'ideal embodiment of all goodness.'[9] Claiming that God would cease to be God if there were no Devil, Carus considers 'God' and 'Devil' to be relative terms. He consequently describes the Devil as 'the father of all misunderstood geniuses,'[10] 'the rebel of the cosmos, the independent in the empire of a tyrant, . . . the individualising tendency, [and] the craving for originality, which bodily upsets the ordinances of God.'[11] Carus thought that scientific developments would allow these complementary beliefs about God and the Devil to be approached rationally, but he asserted that 'the idea of a personal Devil is as imaginary as a fairy, or an elf, or a hobgoblin.'[12] Carus established *The Monist* as a journal, and published seventy-five books and 1500 articles in his lifetime, making him an important influence on Euro-American religious thought during the 20th century.

Philosopher-mathematician, Alfred North Whitehead (1861–1947), is known for his wide-ranging work in a number of fields of philosophy, including collaborating with Bertrand Russell in developing symbolic logic. Their *Principia Mathematica*, which was the result of more than ten years of collaboration, is an effort to give a compact description of the structure of rational thought and of the universe itself. Whitehead's metaphysical ideas, expressed in various writings, make *relations* between unique objects, rather than objects and their properties, the basis for understanding the world, while granting that our views could vary about what these objects might be. His *Process and Reality* is the outworking of his Gifford Lectures (1927–28), the

---

[7] *The History of the Devil and the Idea of Evil from the Earliest Times to the Present Day* (La Salle, IL: Open Court, 1974).

[8] Carus, *History of the Devil*, 465.

[9] Carus, *History of the Devil*, 468.

[10] Carus, *History of the Devil*, 487

[11] Carus, *History of the Devil*, 482.

[12] Carus, *History of the Devil*, 454.

presentation of which remains one of the most prestigious awards for advances in philosophical theology. In it he asserts that belief in evil spirits is both primitive and in need of elimination,[13] which suggests that he did not consider the belief in evil spirits to have been completely obliterated at the time. I surmise that his influence in the development of process theology has contributed to the impression that such beings do not exist.

T.K. Oesterreich (1880–1949), a philosophy professor at Tübingen University from 1910 until his removal by the Nazis in 1933 for expressing democratic and anti-militaristic views, wrote an impressive book on demon possession titled, *Possession: Demoniacal and Other*. In it he documents states of mind widely described as possession in various historical eras and in diverse places of the world. He observes that the belief in possession varies inversely with the degree to which Enlightenment views have penetrated human society, noting that in the Europe of his day, Russia was most likely to be the place where possession could still be encountered.[14] He makes extensive use of psychological accounts of mental illness in order to offer an alternative view to that of classical demonic possession, and generally exhibits little sympathy for traditional views about how demons (or spirits of the dead) seemingly possess and act through living persons. He hesitates to rule out the possibility of possession completely, however, observing that the trance states typically cultivated in spiritualist circles exhibit the essential factor in possession, namely, 'the transformation of the personality.'[15] Oesterreich deplores the prejudices not only of spiritualists against science, but also of psychologists concerning spiritualism, and holds out some hope that further information might be forthcoming that would decide the debate about the reality of possession.

Richard Rorty (1931–2007), well known for his philosophical achievements while occupying academic positions at Princeton University, the University of Virginia, and finally Stanford University, began his career as an analytic philosopher, but later became one of its outspoken critics. Analytic philosophy focuses upon close analysis of philosophical claims and upon critical assessment of related arguments, including

---

[13] Alfred North Whitehead, *Process and Reality* (Cambridge: Cambridge University Press, 1929), 150.

[14] T. K. Oesterreich, *Possession: Demoniacal & Other among Primitive Races, in Antiquity, the Middle Ages, and Modern Times*, D. Ibberson (tr.), (New York: University Books, 1966), 203.

[15] Oesterreich, *Possession*, 366.

arguments for and against both Christian theism and general theism. This movement grew out of logical positivism, which has earned it a reputation for being opposed to Christian faith, but analytic philosophy cannot be so narrowly characterized, since some of its proponents are advocates of natural theology, and others are open to the possibility of revelatory events. Rorty published an influential paper in the mid-sixties that had a bearing then upon the discussion of the nature of mind. Philosophers of a materialist persuasion were exploring the possibility that everything characterizing our mental lives would be found to be much more comprehensively described in some future development of neurophysiology. Rorty advances a variation on this view by arguing that supposed references in ordinary language to mental phenomena would be *eliminated*, much as the theory of demons, he remarked, had been successfully eliminated in Western thought.[16] His paper portrays the theory of demons as having been advanced primarily to explain illness and certain kinds of apparitions, even though many other kinds of phenomena have been understood as explained by the existence of demons.[17] He probably spoke for many educated people when he construed the theory as already having been discarded. No reply to Rorty's claim concerning the theory of demons ever occurred, to my knowledge, and silence on the topic has probably reinforced the impression that the theory has no rational standing.

In the Boyles Lectures for 1965, Eric Mascall, historical theologian at the University of London, spoke about the warfare between angels of light and the powers of darkness, and its implications for human life. He courageously dismissed the objection that some would likely write him off as pre-Copernican or antediluvian for endorsing the reality of these beings, and gave explicit witness in these remarks to prevailing attitudes at the time of these lectures. His defensive tone is indicative of the hesitancy that had been created around the topic of (generally) invisible beings. Peter Kreeft, philosophy professor at Boston College,

---

[16] Rorty, Richard, 'Mind-Body Identity, Privacy, and Categories', in David M. Rosenthal (ed.), *Materialism and the Mind-Body Problem* (Englewood Cliffs, NJ: Prentice-Hall, 1971), 174–99.

[17] Heinrich Kramer and James Sprenger, *Malleus Maleficarum*, Montague Summers (tr.) (New York: Dover, 1971; orig. ca. 1486), identify more than seventy phenomena attributed to evil spirits in medieval times. This document, first published *circa* 1486, is perhaps the most influential document on the subject in Western history, and served as an authoritative document in courts for several centuries.

has recently advanced the traditional Christian view of demons and angels, acknowledging that his position is based on the assumption that the Bible expresses the revelation of God.[18] His occasionally strident tone suggests that he is weary of the contempt now publicly exhibited toward this aspect of traditional Christian beliefs. Representative of common opinion is the recent remark of Dan O'Brien, philosopher at the University of Birmingham, 'Certainly, at one end, ontologies such as those concerning demons or phlogiston should be eliminated.'[19]

The basis for the dismissal of spirits is a subject for some conjecture, and the following developments strike me as especially significant:

1. Western culture has dismissed the authority of the Christian Church (or any religion) to advance ontological claims, in favour of scientific investigation, even though scientific discovery is limited by the assumptions that are intrinsic to its method. Moreover, biblical criticism of various kinds – genre, source, redaction, historical, and so on – has undermined the credibility of the Bible's portrayal of the universe. Its reference to evil spirits is often considered an antiquated way of understanding mental illness[20] and the causes of physical ailments.
2. The modern era has made *experimental* evidence the most important basis for advancing any theory, so that *experiential* evidence, which was once virtually the only basis for knowledge about the world, is relegated to a subordinate place, if it is given one at all.
3. The sharp ontological distinction between matter and spirit, which characterizes most theorizing in the history of Western thought, is now widely thought obsolete, primarily because of its dubious capacity to illuminate mental phenomena in human

---

[18] Peter Kreeft, Angels and Demons: *What do we Really Know about Them?* (San Francisco: Ignatius, 1995), 28, 43, and 105.

[19] 'Review of *The Emergence of Consciousness*', *Human Nature Review* 2 (2002), 249–252. Website: http://www.human-nature.com/nibbs/02/ obrien.html (accessed on Sept. 1, 2008). Phlogiston is the material in substances once postulated to exist in order to account for oxidation, calcification, rusting, and other well known chemical changes. Its nonexistence became apparent upon the discovery of oxygen and other elements, and the term 'phlogiston' has become a byword among philosophers for things once mistakenly postulated to exist.

[20] For an example see Myers, David, and Malcolm Jeeves, *Psychology Through the Eyes of Faith* (San Francisco: Harper & Row, 1987), 41.

experience. The disappearance of this distinction appears to be viewed by naturalists, as well as some Christians, as having eliminated the feasibility of the view that pure spirit, devoid of a material body, can exist.

4. The theory postulating spirits as discrete causal agents is incapable of having its limits clearly circumscribed, and virtually any phenomenon is interpretable as subject to the influence of spirits. This theory consequently appears to be imposed upon observations, rather than a theory that attempts to provide limited causal accounts of selective phenomena. Theorists who expect rational theories to be marked by their susceptibility to falsification generally view claims about evil spirits with suspicion. Karl Popper, a prominent Viennese post-war philosopher at the University of London, maintained that scientific (or 'rational') claims need to be susceptible to falsification, and even though this view limits what can count as science, it continues to enjoy considerable respect.

5. The modern era is marked by a penchant for descriptions and explanations that are capable of mathematical expression, and theories postulating spirits are inimical to these objectives. Also, the proclivity for simplicity in modern theorizing has brought theories into prominence that postulate as few objects, properties, or relations as possible, and spirits are considered superfluous in describing or explaining phenomena.

6. The horrors undertaken in the Inquisition and in the 'witch trials' of Europe and America have left the impression that claims related to demonic oppression are too irresponsible to entertain seriously.

7. The study of abnormal behaviour undertaken by psychology and psychiatry seemingly leaves little or no place for spirits as the unique causes of particular kinds of behaviour. The study of malicious behaviour undertaken by Carl Goldberg in *Speaking with the Devil*, for example, pointedly dispenses with spirits in explaining malevolence.[21] Such a position is characteristic of much modern psychology.

Modernity appears to have put claims about evil spirits, or good ones, for that matter, in a desperate position, so that we might wonder

---

[21] By contrast, psychiatrist Scott Peck allows for the possibility of a supernatural evil presence as a causal influence in five percent of the disorders he has treated, in *People of the Lie: The Hope for Healing Human Evil* (New York: Simon & Schuster, 1983), 195ff, esp. 209.

whether a rational basis exists for advancing their reality apart from an appeal to the authority of Christian tradition or its scriptures. An important methodological development for understanding scientific theories, however, provides a reason for re-examining common beliefs about evil spirits.


## Existence of evil spirits

With the demise of logical positivism as a reigning paradigm in Anglo-American philosophy, according to which all meaningful claims need to be established by observation, interest has become directed toward theories that postulate unobservable objects, processes, or events. Prominent examples of such theories from the 19th and early 20th centuries include the following: the theory of chemical elements summarized in the periodic table, as first advanced by Dmitri Mendeleev; the theory of 'inheritance factors,' now known as genes, advanced by Gregor Mendel; the model of evolutionary theory by way of natural selection of the fittest organisms advanced by Charles Darwin; the theory of atomic structures proposed by John Galton, and modified by Amedeo Avogadro and many subsequent physicists; and the psychoanalytic theory of Sigmund Freud that isolates 'elements' of the human personality and attempts to explain human behaviours, including behavioural disorders. These theories consist of well integrated conceptual sub-domains in which a limited number of phenomena are described and explained, often using a unique vocabulary that originally was parasitic upon the language of commonsense but has since acquired relative independence. The capacity of theories postulating unobservables to be slightly modified or substantially altered suggests that the methodology implicit in their use is rational, although the interpretation of 'rational' employed here might not be fully definable. The prominent American philosopher-scientist of a century ago, Charles Saunders Peirce (1839–1914), called the methodology 'abduction' or 'retroduction,'[22] in order to distinguish it from deduction, whose structure is quite well defined, as well as from induction, whose structure is under continued scrutiny. The study of induction includes on-going attempts to define confirming evidence, and to explicate the

---

[22] Charles Saunders Peirce, *Collected Papers of Charles Saunders Peirce*, Charles Hartshorne and Paul Weiss (eds.), *Pragmatism and Pragmaticism* (Cambridge, MA: Harvard University Press, 1934), vol. 5, bk. 1, lec. 6 and 7.

many interpretations of the term 'probable',[23] so abduction – also some-times known as inference to the best explanation,[24] or as inference to the most probable cause[25] – might be subsumable under induction, but I will treat it here as having its own distinctive character.

Abductive reasoning involves advancing conjectures about an observed event, inasmuch as no known explanation for that event is available. A significant recent example is found in the work of astronomer and geophysicist, Alfred Wegener (1880–1930), who was struck in 1910 by the fact that the shapes of Earth's continents could be fitted together to form a coherent whole, and conjectured that the con-tinents had slowly drifted to the positions they now have.[26] Although he conducted no research on the conjecture at the time, he soon after discovered that similar fossils could be found in similar geological for-mations that were oceans apart. He took this as corroborative of his theory, but several decades of criticism and discoveries dependent upon numerous technological innovations span the time before the theory was accepted. Abduction is sometimes described as "regressive reasoning" inasmuch as it begins with observed data and probes back-wards (temporally) into possible explanations. It is consistent with the view that much about the cosmos awaits our discovery, as opposed to the outlook widely expressed in the early part of the 20th century according to which the fundamental laws for understanding the uni-verse had been discovered.

Some critics of abduction assert that this strategy for obtaining pos-sible explanations for phenomena is too open ended, and that many different conjectures could be advanced, perhaps more than we have the time and resources to examine. Moreover, since some conjectures are more susceptible to empirical corroboration than others, and for that reason might be preferred to those for which corroboration is dif-ficult to obtain, the factors that enter into choosing between competing alternatives might include pragmatic considerations, not just the truth

---

[23] At least six are known to philosophers; cf. Richard Swinburne, *Epistemic Justification* (Oxford: Clarendon, 2001), esp. ch. 3. Moreover, some of these six have competing interpretations.

[24] G. H. Harman, 'Inference to the Best Explanation', *Philosophical Review* 74 (1965), 88–95 introduced this phrase in this article.

[25] Thus Nancy Cartwright, 'The Reality of Causes in a World of Instrumental Laws,' in R. Boyd, P. Gasper, and J. D. Trout (eds.), *The Philosophy of Science* (Cambridge, MA: MIT Press, 1993), 379–86.

[26] Alfred Wegener, *The Origin of Continents and Oceans*, trans. John Biram (New York: Courier Dover, 1966), 1.

or plausibility of a conjecture based on evidence. Critics of abduction consequently see it as advancing a dubious methodological principle. Writing in defence of abduction, philosopher Douglas Walton says that if a conjecture decisively surpasses any of its competitors, and if the alternative explanations have been thoroughly examined and none appears satisfactory, the proposed explanation becomes plausible.[27] In addition to these considerations advanced by Walton, we might also look at the degree to which known causal patterns are allowed to influence the kinds of conjectures that are entertained, so that a conjecture might be more than 'a shot in the dark'. This cautious principle in the use of abductive argument suggests that a broad background of existing knowledge about numerous phenomena guides us in the conjectures we might initially propose and then choose to examine. Selecting conjectures that reflect known causal patterns found elsewhere in nature could be said to satisfy a principle of conservativeness, inasmuch as we are supposing that an explanatory hypothesis in a new context might resemble previous hypotheses that have proved successful. This principle is used for evaluating scientific theories favourably, as is the principle that simpler conjectures have greater chance than complex ones for being adequate explanations of inexplicable phenomena (Occam's Razor), notwithstanding disputes about criteria of simplicity. Other usual criteria in evaluating theories are relevant, such as their susceptibility to being falsified by evidence, and their use in predicting future events. Related to the matter of predicting events is the matter of the scope of the events that might be predicted on the basis of the conjecture. Studies in the last century of how science proceeds have brought to light many methodological principles in actual use in science, and philosophers are now more loath to rule on what kinds of exact inquiry are rational than they were during the period of logical positivism. This does not mean that philosophy has lost its critical edge, however.

Another illustration of the abductive method comes from particle physics, where baryon-II was first postulated to exist in order to interpret tracks on a photographic plate in a cloud chamber.[28] The photographic plate featured a point of collision of known particles, followed

---

[27] See Douglas Walton, *Ethical Argumentation* (Lanham, MA: Lexington Books, 2003), 94–101.

[28] A comparable account of k-mesons is found in M.R. Wehr, James A. Richards Jr., and Thomas W. Adair III, *Physics of the Atom* (Reading, MA: Addison-Wesley, 1979), 450f.

by a straight line, then a blank, and finally a V-branch in the trajectory of the straight line (see below). The markings indicate that the collision first produced a charged particle, which quickly decayed to produce a particle that had no charge (baryon-II), which in turn also quickly decayed to produce two particles having the same charge – the V-branch indicates that they are repelling each other. Baryon-II is postulated to exist in order to account for the blank on the photographic plate, and the causal sequence of events in which baryon-II is implicated provide its contextual definition, even though it is unobservable.

The argumentation used here gives a conjectural result, inasmuch as subsequent experimental work can show either that objects once postulated to exist might not, or that objects speculated to have certain properties might have different ones. However, although the result might be conjectural and subject to change, postulating the existence of baryon-II is rational, since the probability (in some sense) that it exists is greater after the experimental finding is obtained than before it was. Moreover, previous experience with objects in general, including objects belonging to the domain of subatomic physics, suggested to theorists that sequences of caused events have a continuity to them, so that an object does not simply disappear in one place and then reappear in another, especially when significant distances are involved. Still, the conjecture is open to modification and even rejection, on the basis of further evidence. The application of the abductive methodology, vital in all branches of science, has an important result when it is applied to particular kinds of religious experience.

Consider the strange event described in the synoptic gospels in which Jesus is said to have performed an exorcism where 'evil spirits' passed from men to swine.[29] According to the account in *The Gospel of St Matthew*,[30] certain men in the region of the Gadarenes were so fierce that they threatened anyone coming near, and were forced to live in

---

[29] I have explored other aspects of this case in 'Finite Spirits as Theoretical Entities', and more fully explored possession and exorcism in my book *God and Other Spirits: Intimations of Transcendence in Christian Faith* (New York: Oxford University Press, 2004), ch. 1.

[30] Matt 8. Mark 5 and Luke 8 say of seemingly the same event that there was only one demoniac, but I will ignore this difference.

tombs outside the community. When Jesus came near they addressed him, surprisingly, as the Son of God, and when he told the supposed evil spirits in the men to leave, 'they' begged to be sent into a herd of swine feeding nearby. When Jesus gave the spirits leave to enter the swine, the herd rushed down into the sea and were drowned, and the men began to behave normally.

The first explanation a naturalist is likely to consider for the strange greeting of the men from the Gadarenes is some psychopathology, such as dissociative identity disorder (DID), which is a protective natural mechanism in which the self 'divides' in order to cope with severe trauma, sometimes resulting in strange speech patterns that reflect fragments of the divided self. While the strange greeting can be explained, hearing that the 'voices'[31] ask to be sent into a herd of swine, which actually are feeding nearby, and observing that when the 'voices' are commanded to go the swine immediately (implied) behave in a manner consistent with the destructive behaviour in the men, which simultaneously disappears, the earlier understanding of the greeting needs to be reconsidered. A defender of DID must conclude that this theory cannot account for everything about this case. This disorder is attributed to *individuals* because of certain behaviours, including peculiar verbal behaviour, but it does not explain seem-ingly connected events such as the termination of destructive behaviours in one followed by the immediate onset of similar behaviours in another that happens to have been just named. A theorist familiar with the use of abduction in scientific methodology can plausibly postulate the existence of *something-we-know-not-what* – we could call it a 'spirit'[32] – that has passed from the men to the herd of swine, which is also considered to be malevolent because of its apparent effect on the men (and swine). Background information that shapes this conjecture is that speech that is both intelligible and appropriate for a given situation is indicative of a sentient being having powers of perception and verbal expression. Philosopher Anthony Quinton once observed that if we were to hear intelligent speech emanate from a knot-hole in a tree, we would consider the

---

[31] No sense can be made of the men asking to leave themselves, so the description of this event presupposes the existence of the evil spirits that the theory postulates, which involves in an especially marked way the fact that descriptions are theory-laden.

[32] I will assume that a single spirit is postulated here as a theoretical entity. The grounds in experience for considering spirits to be more than one are curious in their own right, but are not uppermost in this example.

tree to be a person.[33] No specific religious commitments are required or presupposed in theorizing about the observed phenomena, although the event has implications for ontology.

The reference of the term 'spirit' is secured in this context (primarily)[34] by the causal role that the postulated entity plays in relation to behaviours, particularly in the transfer of a causal power from men to swine. The spatial and temporal proximity of the relevant events – they do not occur far apart in either time or space[35] – contributes to a plausible assessment of the events as causally related. The term 'spirit' need not be interpreted as denoting a non-material substance in order for its postulation to make sense, and here I break with tradition. The term simply purports to denote that which accounts for the destructive behaviours in two kinds of living things. This approach allows a concept vital to religious belief-systems to be introduced without getting caught up in intractable problems concerning ultimate substances. Spirits that are thus postulated might be immaterial or incorporeal, but nothing about the method proposed here requires asserting so, and subsequent investigation could even indicate a link to neuropsychological structures. A similar approach can also be used for viewing the extraordinary abilities operating through Jesus in removing the malevolent influences in the demoniac(s) – which he is once said to have described as 'the finger of God' – inasmuch as normal human abilities are seemingly incapable of achieving this result. The traditional approach to defining God by means of superlative properties that distinguish God from the finite natural order is not inconsistent with the contextual definition that I am suggesting here, but it is neither suggested in the event that is described, nor is it required for examining the event and conjecturing about the beings (or forces) that are implicated. Neither is my strategy for 'defining' God inconsistent with the Thomistic approach, following Aristotle, of refusing to place God in a genus, consequently

---

[33] Anthony Quinton, 'The Soul', *The Journal of Philosophy* 59 (1962), 408.

[34] The precise way in which postulated entities acquire their 'status' is unclear, and other links to things whose existence is not in doubt, e.g., spatio-temporal or species-genus links, seemingly serve some role; cf. Robert Nola, 'Fixing the Reference of Theoretical Terms', *Philosophy of Science* 47 (1980), 505–31, and Berent Enc, 'Reference of Theoretical Terms', *Nous* 10 (1976), 261–82, for discussion.

[35] Biblical accounts are often remarkably terse, and poorly serve contemporary theorizing, which prefers thick description.

refusing to attempt a definition using genus and differentium, and then using analogies to describe God.

The methodology of abductive argumentation shows us that if physics is possible, metaphysics is possible, thus overturning a philosophic tradition that goes back to David Hume. Rudolf Carnap, a prominent philosopher of the positivistic persuasion, once described metaphysicians as 'musicians without musical ability,'[36] and the impossibility of metaphysics has also been championed by Friedrich Nietzsche and Martin Heidegger,[37] philosophers who are widely associated with postmodernity. Rorty recently asserted that 'empirical evidence is irrelevant to talk about God,' remarking that this viewpoint applies equally to theism and atheism.[38] In saying so he gave expression to an opinion that is now widely held, even in the Church. The position I am advancing here is just the opposite of these, and although it should not be interpreted as *proving* that God and evil spirits exist, it offers evidence for these claims – proof is another matter, and eludes science at the theoretical level just as it eludes religion. The strategy I have advanced here is adapted from that developed for mental states several decades ago by various philosophers, including David Lewis, professor of philosophy at Princeton University for many years. Lewis argues that mental terms in the language of ordinary language users – often described as the language of 'folk psychology' – can be defined by the causal role that their postulated referents typically play, and that the question whether mind might be non-material is irrelevant to the question whether mental terms have reference.[39] Other prominent philosophers involved in advancing the interpretation of mind as an entity-postulating theory include American philosophers Wilfrid

---

[36] Rudolph Carnap, 'The elimination of metaphysics through logical analysis of language', in A. J. Ayer (ed.), *Logical Positivism* (New York: Free Press, 1959), 60–81.

[37] Wolfhart Pannenberg, *Metaphysics and the Idea of God*, Philip Clayton (tr.), (Grand Rapids, MI: Eerdmans, 1990), 3f; he also remarks that the only theologians now willing to deal with questions of metaphysics tend to belong to the Catholic Church.

[38] Richard Rorty, and Gianni Vattimo, *The Future of Religion*, Santiago Zabala (ed.), (New York: Columbia University Press, 2004), 33.

[39] 'Psychophysical and Theoretical Identifications', 250f. Lewis also addressed these and related issues in 'An Argument for the Identity Theory', *The Journal of Philosophy* 63 (1966), 17–25 and 'How to Define Theoretical Terms', *The Journal of Philosophy* 67 (1970), 427–46.

Sellars,[40] Jerry Fodor,[41] and Hilary Putnam,[42] as well as Australian philosophers J.J.C. Smart[43] and David Armstrong.[44] This theoretical development concerning mind has allowed cognitive science to flourish as an academic discipline.

No other exorcism cases in the New Testament exhibit the features of the Gadarene exorcism case, and few of the exorcisms alleged to occur by those who accept them at face value seemingly involve a transfer of 'something' from one being to another;[45] they only involve the termination of unusual behaviours in an individual.[46] The 1st century historian Josephus reports that Jewish exorcism in his day included an instruction to the exorcised demon to overturn a basin of water in order to prove to onlookers that it had indeed left.[47] Josephus says that he saw methods of exorcism attributed in Jewish tradition to King Solomon used in his own day in the presence of Vespasian, the Roman emperor, but he does not say whether the 'basin-test' was included. If a basin of water were indeed to be overturned at the appropriate moment in such a ritual, this would corroborate the claim that an invisible agent had been present, and would be comparable to the transfer of causal powers in the case of the Gadarenes discussed above. Of course, we would want assurance that the basin was not turned over by some natural cause, for example, a gust of wind or an earth tremor. The fact that this test for a successful exorcism was present in Jewish culture suggests that among its 'theorists' were those who construed

---

[40] See esp. his essay, 'Empiricism and the Philosophy of Mind', *Science, Perception and Reality* (London: Routledge & Kegan Paul, 1963), 127–96.

[41] Jerry Fodor, *Psychological Explanation* (New York: Random House, 1968).

[42] Several early essays are 'Dreaming and Depth Grammar', in R. J. Butler (ed.), *Analytical Philosophy: First Series* (New York: Barnes & Noble, 1960), 211–35, and 'Brains and Behaviour,' in R.J. Butler (ed.), *Analytical Philosophy, Second Series* (Oxford: Blackwell, 1965), 1–19.

[43] His best known essay is 'Sensations and Brain Processes', *Philosophical Review* 68 (1959), 141–56; cf. also 'Conflicting Views about Explanation,' in R.S. Cohen and M.W. Wartofsky (eds.), *Boston Studies in the Philosophy of Science*, vol. 2 (New York: Humanities Press, 1965), 157–69.

[44] David Armstrong, *A Materialist Theory of the Mind* (New York; The Humanities Press, 1968).

[45] Gabriele Amorth, the Roman Catholic's chief exorcist in Rome, makes reference to transfer cases involving animals, in , *An Exorcist Tells his Story*, Nicoletta V. MacKenzie (tr.) (San Francisco: Ignatius, 1999), 126–27.

[46] See Carl Goldberg, *Speaking with the Devil: Exploring Senseless Acts of Evil* (Harmondsworth, Middlesex: Penguin, 1996) for such an argument.

[47] Flavius Josephus, *Antiquities of the Jews*, bk. 8, ch. 2, para. 5.

the beings typically found in religious thought to be grounded in events belonging to the space-time-causal order. The Sadducees were known for repudiating claims about spirits, and can be viewed as the 'naturalists' in that culture.[48]

## Other transfer cases

The exorcism of the Gadarene demoniacs does not appear to be a *miracle* as this is commonly understood, for it does not appear to violate or be in conflict with well established natural laws, as would be levitation, say. This point becomes clearer when we consider a modern report of an exorcism that seemingly resulted in the 'same spirits' leaving one person and entering another. During my graduate studies in Adelaide, South Australia, I came to know a widely respected minister, Leo Harris, who, in addition to the duties that come with leading a movement of about sixty churches across Australia and New Zealand, also conducted exorcisms. In one of these events 'the voices' in an older man responded with the threat that if they (the plural form was used) were forced to leave, they would enter a certain young man, who was known to Leo. The young man also lived in Adelaide, which was a city of perhaps three-quarters of a million people at the time. Leo said that he ordered the spirits to leave the older man in spite of the threat, and also ordered them not to enter the young man. Within a half-hour or so of this exorcism, however, Leo received a telephone call from the mother of the young man who had been named. She begged Leo to come to the house immediately because 'something strange had come over her son.' When Leo arrived at the house he was ushered into the room where the young man was resting, and upon shutting the door behind him, Leo heard the threatening voice that he had heard a short while ago say, 'We told you we would get him, didn't we?' Leo construed the fact that the events were in close spatio-temporal succession, and that no apparent contact between the two had occurred, as evidence that the exorcised spirits had indeed entered the young man. Leo explained, with profound regret, that his authority to control the activity of evil spirits was limited, for reasons that were unclear to him.

A defender of a naturalistic explanation for these events might suggest that the speech and other behaviours of the two men can be

---

[48] Jesus evidently engaged them on matters of ontology; cf. Matt. 22:23f for his comments on the resurrection of the dead.

explained by the fact that both of them had DID. However, this explanation could only be viewed as adequate if we ignored the content of
what was said, the sequence of the reported events, and the apparent
link between them. We cannot be expected to ignore the content of the
statements, however, for such contents are typically used in psychotherapy in order to correlate psychological disorders with specific
events in a client's past. The individual behaviours of these two men
are not obvious violations of or conflicts with natural laws (miracles),
so the primary inexplicable feature of this case is that the remarks coming from each make sense only in the light of the remarks coming from
both of them. Although psychiatric sciences might deal with separate
events such as the two instances of peculiar, but intelligible, speech,
and might offer assessments of those who exhibit such behaviour,[49] no
exact inquiry appears to make *related* events of this kind the object of
scrutiny. In this 'accident' of the development of scientific inquiry, phenomena that have the capacity to render plausible existential claims
about a largely unobservable domain in religion have disappeared
from view.

Several other friends of mine tell of events that appear to involve the
transfer of 'spirits'. John[50] tells of an experience involving a woman,
Alice, from the church of which he was the pastor – the story has several parts. Alice was a well known member of the church community
that John led, and well thought of, but she began to exhibit strange
behaviours one day at the end of a service – groaning and grunting in
a loud manner, and kicking anyone within reach of her feet. John, his
wife, and several other women from the church went over to Alice to
find out what was troubling her. As they prayed with her these strange
behaviours became more intense, and Alice's eyes rolled back and the
blood-vessels in her eyelids burst. John and the women who were with
him were startled by this turn of physical events, but they still thought
her problem was spiritual in nature. John knew Alice well enough to
think that she did not have unconfessed sin in her life, but he wondered if Alice might be harboring unforgiveness toward someone.
When John suggested this possibility to her an alternate personality
seemed to take over, her face became contorted, and a voice came from
her that did not sound like her, which said, 'I will never forgive.' At

---

[49] See the discussion on 'Psychiatry and Possession' (ch. 7) in I.M. Lewis,
*Ecstatic Possession, A Study of Shamanism and Spirit Possession,* 3rd ed. (London and New York: Routledge, 2003), on this point.
[50] The names in this account are fictitious.

this outburst, the chair on which Alice was sitting moved more than six feet backward of its own accord, which those who prayed for her interpreted as evidence that some malevolent force was present. John then suggested to Alice that she might ask Jesus to help her forgive, and when Alice did so a sense of calm came over her. John again went to pray for her, and as soon as he did so Alice lost consciousness. Her face was still contorted, but after a short time a change came over her. John observed, as did the others who were present, that 'bubbles of air' seemed to come out of her mouth, and when she gained consciousness she began to laugh, as though she was experiencing great relief over something that had troubled her for a long time. She laughed for an hour or so, and later reported that she had awoken in the middle of the night and done the same. Alice later told John's wife that she had been sexually assaulted as a child, which was the matter that she could not forgive. John reported that soon after this event in Alice's life, the face of her adolescent daughter began to be contorted in a way that resembled that which Alice had exhibited during her deliverance. Some years later the daughter also underwent deliverance, which made John wonder whether something was passed from mother to daughter.

Alice came for healing prayer some years later for a sinus infection. She was in a standing position as several people, including John, prayed for her. They observed her take many deep breaths as they prayed, and with each breath she stooped over more and more, until she was in a position that seemed physically incapable of being maintained. This was interpreted as suggesting superhuman forces at work. When prayers for her were completed, she announced that she had been healed. Events immediately afterward confirmed her statement, for instead of requiring 25–30 doses of Claritin each week, she needed only two or three. However, John woke up the day after Alice had received prayer, and found that he had just acquired allergies, whose symptoms resembled those that Alice had exhibited.[51] John wondered if the ailment from which Alice had been healed had been passed on to him, so he rebuked the infirmity in his body, on the authority of Jesus Christ, and was finally freed from it after a month or so of this regimen. John wonders whether demonic powers were behind Alice's sinus infection, and whether these powers somehow latched onto him. Another question lurking here is whether the allergy-attack on John was reprisal for Alice's deliverance some years earlier? These are

---

[51] Amorth makes reference to comparable phenomena, *Exorcist*, 138–39, and to a 'transfer case' involving two girls, 74–75.

difficult to answer, but those who are involved in exorcism seem to encounter many mysteries associated with a largely invisible order. Much of science consists of manipulating observable objects and monitoring their effects on other objects, thereby building up knowledge of the natural domain. Obvious (and pressing) moral constraints fortunately prevent most people from 'experimenting' with the realm of the demonic, and so gaining more knowledge of it.

Another account of what sounds like the transfer comes from a friend, Walter Rusnell, who is best known in North America for his seminars on Spiritual Growth. This is his account:

> From my recollection [the event] happened in the summer of 1976 at the Grenfell Bible camp in Saskatchewan. I was one of the sponsoring pastors. It occurred during a Sunday afternoon baptismal service. We were baptising by full immersion in a baptismal tank at the front of the auditorium. There were about 400 people present. I was helping just outside the tank, and together the pastors prayed for a woman whom I did not know. As she stood in the water, she prayed out loud that she wanted to leave everything behind in the waters of baptism that was not of God. None of us expected what would happen next. She was immersed, and the moment she came out of the water she let out a momentary loud shrill noise similar to the noise Middle Eastern women make when grieving during mourning, which was then followed by expressions of joy and release. Moments later, our attention was turned toward the audience. In about the middle of one section of the auditorium, when the woman being baptised came out of the water with a shriek, another woman was thrown to the ground and began writhing on the floor. It was similar to an epileptic seizure, with this difference – blasphemous words began to come from her lips, which we recognized as a case of demonic activity. Several people around her quickly went to her side to both assist and pray for her, but to no avail. Eventually an ambulance was called, and she was taken to the hospital. I did not know this woman, and I do not know what happened to her in the days following. We did not expect this kind of activity, although some kinds of demon activity, although rare, were known to many of us. There had been no teaching or 'priming' to develop an expectation of the possibility of the transference of a demon from one individual to another, and I have never seen this kind of incident since.

Although the small number of instances I have advanced here of possible instances of evil spirits passing from one to another is not likely to silence sceptics about the reality of demonization,[52] these cases suggest that grounds exist for considering the phenomenon to be real.[53] These cases render the claims of demonization more probable than they are without (or prior to) their consideration, just as the claim concerning baryon-II is more probable after the reported experimental result than before.

## External and internal perspectives

A conspicuous feature of the Gadarene exorcism case is that nothing of what was phenomenologically experienced by the demoniacs is included in the account. In fact, no biblical accounts of exorcism describe events from the standpoint of those afflicted, or even from that of the one performing the exorcism. Auguste Poulain (1836–1919), a prominent Jesuit theologian of the Catholic Church, says that loss of consciousness usually occurs in a person undergoing exorcism,[54] which might partially account for incomplete information about the phenomenological aspects of possession and exorcism. A modern case from the Alister Hardy files, however, combines phenomenological and intersubjective elements in an important way. The event took place in the Rhineland, Germany, in 1947, and comes from an Anglican priest whom I will identify as William. I will refer to the person who underwent what appears to have been exorcism as Nathan, and the witness to the event as Thomas.[55]

> On the last evening of the Rhineland Keswick Convention three of us set out, at about 10:15 p.m. for a walk through a small wood which led to a village on the other side. Nathan, one of the party, started to tell the story of his life, and when we came to a clearing in the wood Thomas

---

[52] Amorth asserts that 'rationalism and materialism have polluted a segment of theologians, and their influence on both bishops and priests has been profound', in *An Exorcist*, 173.

[53] Oesterreich dismisses out of hand that portion of the Gadarene exorcism that speaks of evil spirits passing from the men to the swine, *Possession*, 4–5.

[54] Auguste Poulain, *The Graces of Interior Prayer: A Treatise on Mystical Theology*, Leonara L. Yorke Smith (tr.), (London: Routledge & Kegan Paul, 1956), 63–66.

[55] Religious Experience and Research Centre, case, 248. All the names of people I have used here are pseudonyms. The Alister Hardy Research Centre guarantees anonymity to those who offer first-hand accounts.

suggested that we should sit down for awhile. Nathan continued to relate his story. On joining the Royal Air Force he had missed the influence of home, and fell into bad company, unable to resist temptation. As Nathan finished his story there was silence. I sat with my eyes closed, wondering how I, as one of the convention leaders, could help the young fellow. What happened next was over in a very short space of time. Breaking through the silence, and crashing through the darkness with tremendous power came my voice, 'In the name of the Lord Jesus Christ depart.' Immediately Nathan let out a half-shout, and fell towards me. He said afterwards, 'At those words I saw a black form appear from somewhere at my feet and vanish into the wood, and, at the same time, something indescribable left me.'

I felt an urgency for prayer, and if Nathan did not pray, something would happen to him. It was at this point an event occurred so dreadful that since I have prayed that it should never happen again. It seemed as if horrifying pandemonium had been let loose; as if all the powers of hell were concentrated in that spot in the wood. I saw numbers of black shapes, blacker than the night, moving about and seeking to come between myself and Nathan, whom I was gripping hard. I saw three demon spirits, perhaps more, between Nathan and myself. These shapes were intelligences. They were different from one another. Each had a personality of its own. They began to buffet me, not striking me physically, but thrusting me backwards in spirit away from Nathan so as to make me recoil, perhaps from fear, and so loose my hold. Two other demon spirits, about shoulder high, were just behind me, one on my right, the other on my left. These two were moving about with a swaying, menacing up-and-down motion, such as boxers use when seeking an opening for attack. Again I felt an intense urgency for prayer, particularly for Nathan. 'Pray Nathan,' I called to him, but the poor fellow could do nothing but sob. With my hands on his shoulders I cried, 'The blood of Jesus Christ cleanseth from all sin.' Again and again I repeated the phrase. I did not notice that Thomas was silent until he said, 'What a horrible atmosphere.' 'Pray Thomas,' I commanded. 'Pray for us.' Together we cried with a loud voice, 'The blood of Jesus Christ cleanseth from all sin.' Then, after a pause, in a colossal voice such as I have never heard before or since came a verse from Scripture through my lips in terrifying power. The words were forced out of my mouth, 'I give to my sheep eternal life; they shall never perish, neither shall any pluck them out of my hand.' I was left absolutely gasping after this. My mouth had been stretched open wider and wider, as if the words were too big for my lips to utter. I then led with the Lord's Prayer. For Thomas this was a real climax. He saw nothing, but again felt the atmosphere change. As we reached the words, 'Deliver us from evil, for thine is the kingdom, the power, and the glory,' the feeling of power was immense. The atmosphere was charged with a living presence, impossible to describe. Then everything grew quiet. The air seemed soft and pleasant, as if angel voices were singing, as if a battle had ended, or a great storm had blown itself out. Nathan whispered, 'Praise God, Oh what joy.'

We made our way back to the conference centre. Nathan could not wait until morning to share the news of his deliverance. Quite independently, Nathan told of how he had seen seven black forms emerge from the trees in the wood, and how he felt some power pushing him forward out of my grip.

The correspondence in the Alister Hardy Research Center files indicates that the Center wrote to Thomas, asking him to give further details of the event, but he declined to do so even though he had written a full account at the time it occurred. He said that it was perhaps the most terrifying experience he had ever had, and did not want to relive it in any way. Thomas evidently did not object to the account given above, and his silence can be cautiously interpreted as giving consent to the gist of what was reported.

This case is interesting for the detail it provides concerning phenomenological experience, and the correlation of this with the features of the case that are reported to have been intersubjectively observed. As William first rebuked what he sensed to be a dark aspect of Nathan's life, Nathan saw a black form disappear from him and had the phenomenological sense that 'something indescribable' had left him. William then had a phenomenological sense of 'horrifying pandemonium' involving the powers of hell, which was followed by his seeing black shapes come between him and Nathan – this corresponds to Nathan's experience (phenomenological and visual). Nathan later reported seeing seven black forms, all (or most) of which William also reported. At the climax of the deliverance William had an indescribably holy sense of having a verse of Scripture uttered in and through him, combined with the physical sensation of having his mouth stretched open wide and being physically exhausted. The overlap of this part of his experience with Nathan's deliverance is not merely coincidence, but arguably the human participation in delivering a man from evil on the authority of Christ through the power of the Holy Spirit. No biblical account describes what Jesus or his disciples might have *felt* as they administered deliverance. However, the tight correlation here of what was said, felt, collectively observed and variously experienced (even by Thomas, who was primarily a witness to the events), makes this an impressive addition to the transfer cases. These cases shed light on events in which nothing significant is observed, in the usual sense of this term, although a diabolical or a divine presence is 'felt' – and this is what comprises most religious experience.

The question of how we should interpret accounts of what is seen (or 'seen') in such experiences is difficult to resolve, as I have discussed concerning contemporary visions or apparitions of Jesus Christ.[56] We should be cautious, I think, in asserting that things are exactly as they appear, given what modern physics teaches about our world, although the symbolic significance of such experiences should not be overlooked. When much the same thing is simultaneously seen by several observers, the normal conditions for objective perception are met, and we have the epistemic right to claim that something independent of ourselves is encountered. This case, like the transfer cases, demonstrates that claims about demonic realities are not merely the imposition of an archaic theory on phenomena, but a complex form of theorizing that resembles some of the theories found in modern science. The reality of demonic agents is not to be lightly dismissed, but neither need we live in fear of their power, in view of the authority over them given by Jesus Christ to his Church.

## Concluding remarks

The discussion in the last two sections sketches an empirical argument for the existence of demonic powers, which is seemingly unnecessary for those for whom the Christian tradition or its scriptures have authority. Even Christians, however, can be encouraged by empirical support for their tradition, and some who wish to regain a 'lost' faith can perhaps be helped to understand that embracing it is not irrational.[57] It is a truism to say that the religious experience that one personally undergoes, as well as that reported by close family and trusted friends, carries significant epistemic weight in people's decisions about

---

[56] Phillip H. Wiebe, *Visions of Jesus: Direct Encounters from the New Testament to Today* (New York: Oxford University Press, 1997), esp. chs. 5, 6, and 7.

[57] In *God and Other Spirits* I address in more detail some of the methodological issues related to religious experience.

religious questions.[58] However, the close scrutiny of credible cases seems only to have begun, and I view the contribution I am making here to be very modest.

The experience of Raymond Moody in connection with near-death experiences (NDEs) is instructive on this point of how a religious phenomenon can become credible in a scientific age. Moody published his first book on NDEs, *Life After Life*, in 1975, offering more than 100 cases for consideration, all of which he collected personally. One might think that with his credentials – a doctorate in medicine and another in philosophy – and a significant number of people whose experiences he reported, his work would have been well received. However, in *Reflections on Life after Life*, published two years later, he reported that his professional colleagues did not give credence to his 'discovery.' This situation changed dramatically by the year 2000, however, for by that time so many reports of NDEs were advanced from different parts of the world that scepticism about them became irrational. The probability calculus illuminates what happened here: If a reported event A is given a probability of only 1/1000 of having occurred as reported, and reported event B is given the same probability value, the probability that *A or B* occurred as reported has risen to 2/1000. This describes the effect of accumulated evidence that has made the NDE respectable. Theorists are not agreed about an explanation for the NDE, naturally, for a predilection for or against naturalism is apt to shape the kinds of explanations a person is inclined to consider, but the occurrence of NDEs is no longer questioned.

Experiential claims that are few in number, that are often inadequately documented, and that go against the intellectual currents of our time, have little chance of being considered in 'serious' theorizing. This is evidently the situation with claims about a malevolent and destructive form of reality that we describe as demonic. Whether this kind of religious experience will ever be given the imprimatur by the scientific community is unclear at this point. On the other hand, perhaps the status of demonic experience is exactly as it should be – intriguing, mysterious, powerful, dangerous, terrifying, and difficult to explore? Perhaps religious experience is general is somehow controlled by unseen forces, so that their existence will never be so

---

[58] William James says that personal experience 'has more influence over the mind than the largest calculated numerical probability either for or against', in *Essays in Psychical Research* (Cambridge, MA: Harvard University Press, 1986; orig. 1895), 73.

secure that it will be received without objection by those who control cultural forces, but never be so unreachable that those who seek some kind of confirmation of its claims will be denied? This is the view of Blaise Pascal, who wrote: 'God has tempered the knowledge of himself by giving signs of himself that are visible to those who seek him, and not to those who seek him not.'[59]

---

[59] Blaise Pascal, *Pensées*, Roger Ariew (ed.), (Indianapolis, IN: Hackett Publishing, 2005) sec. 12, adapted.

# Chapter 9

# Deliverance and Exorcism in Pop Culture

## *Lucy Huskinson*

I agree, it's not a bright future I see
But then again, can you blame me?
I won't carry the weight of the world on my back
But when I see tomorrow it looks black
Eerie
I need an exorcism
Wash me clean from man's pollution
I need an exorcism
Wash me clean
I admit, it's a weak solution to quit
But then again, can you blame me?
I have visions of blood flowing free in the street
Too numb to care for those in need
Weary
I need an exorcism . . .

*Gorefest*[1]

**Abstract**
Popular depictions of demonic possession far outnumber those of exorcism (and its less sensational counterpart, deliverance, even more so). Further-more, when exorcism excites the popular imagination it does so insofar as it

---

[1] Frank Harthoorn, 'Exorcism', in *Gorefest, La Muerte* (Germany: Nuclear Blast 2005). *Gorefest* is a death metal band. I am grateful to guitarist Frank Harthoorn and the other members of *Gorefest* for kindly allowing me to cite their lyrics by email on 3 Nov. 2008.

provides a platform to incite demonic activity further. This chapter adopts the premise that popular portrayals of the demonic or monstrous embody the underlying fears and anxieties of the cultural imagination, and, correspondingly, depictions of exorcism represent their purgation. On this basis it argues that popular culture is preoccupied with anxiety and despair at the expense of their hoped-for release. This argument is developed within the context of the evolving reception of exorcism in popular culture: from 'horror' in the 1970s (as with the hugely influential film, *The Exorcist*) to its more ambivalent nature today. This chapter attempts to understand how and why exorcism and its possessing demon have evolved in this way, with reference to particular examples in popular films, novels, songs, and Internet websites.

## Introduction

A head twisting three hundred and sixty degrees and projectile vomit reminiscent of pea soup: these are probably the most common images brought forth in popular imagination by the term 'exorcism'. These startling images are of course the depicted behaviour of Regan MacNeil, the possessed girl of the hugely successful 1973 film *The Exorcist* (directed by William Friedkin and based on the 1971 book of the same name by William Peter Blatty).[2] Although the portrayal of exorcism has developed in popular culture somewhat beyond the theatrical thrills of *The Exorcist* the impressions of Regan's behaviour is engrained in popular consciousness and its influence can be traced in successive popular interpretations of exorcism. Many a dire film was cast in the mould of *The Exorcist* to cash in on its success, but none could emulate the extent to which the original fascinated and influenced its audience both in and beyond the movie auditorium. And not only films, but other aesthetic genres of popular culture were influenced by its imagery and underlying messages, including literature, music, and even the cyber world of computer gaming. In this chapter I shall ask why a film dealing with the exorcism of a girl possessed by demons resonated deeply in the popular mindset of 1970s western culture, and how our continued attraction to themes of exorcism and deliverance is expressed today.

---

[2] The film earned ten Academy Award nominations in 1973 (winning two: written adapted screenplay, sound); and is the highest grossing film of all time (when inflation is taken into consideration).

'Each era chooses the monster it deserves and projects,' observes Frank McConnel.[3] That is to say, the monster represents unwanted, repressed aspects of the self that have been projected out of the self and experienced by it as an autonomous, unwelcome presence. Proximity to the monster induces in the self an anxious brew of repulsion and fascination: we are appalled by its disgraces and marvel at – and perhaps unconsciously crave and identify with – its moral transgressions. C.G. Jung refers to such monsters as shadow-projections of the un-integrated ego.[4] The monster is thus a severed aspect of our self – an alter ego or personality – and, in psychological terms, our only healthy option is to engage with the monster and reclaim it as part of our self, and not run from it. Here we have the makings of a psychological critique of the ritual of exorcism, with the notable exception that the monstrous demon is not reintegrated into the self per se, but expelled from it (and sent back to Hell). In terms of popular culture, the successful monster is the one who horrifies and possesses our collective imagination: the one who embodies our cultural dislikes, fears, and anxieties.

An examination of popular depictions of monsters or demons reveals our collective fears, anxieties, and those aspects of ourselves we are not yet able to accept. The more a monster holds our attention, the more likely it embodies aspects of our selves that seek reintegration. The monsters of popular culture are therefore useful psychological measurements of our popular identity. *The Exorcist* captured the popular imagination of its time precisely because it presented the monster of 1970s western culture, and, to lesser effect, it also suggested the means by which the monstrous can be tamed or healed.

In recent times depictions of the monstrous have become more human. In horror films prior to 1960, the monster rarely resembled a human being. According to Tony Magistrale and Michael A. Morrison,

> There was always something to set [the monster] apart as Other: dress, body-distortion, or animal appearance. Since then, however, the monster has been transformed into a 'more human' representative; the tortured and torturing creatures of our time are less exotic than their predecessors.[5]

---

[3] McConnel Frank D., *The Spoken Seen: Film and the Romantic Imagination* (Baltimore: John Hopkins University Press, 1975), 137.

[4] See for example, C.G. Jung, 'Psychological Aspects of the Mother Archetype' in *The Archetypes and the Collective Unconscious*, Collected Works, Volume 9i (Princeton University Press, 1974), par. 187.

[5] Tony Magistrale and Michael M. Morrison (eds.) *A Dark Night's Dreaming.* Fiction (The University of South Carolina Press, 1966), 6.

Magistrale and Morrison uphold the criminal sociopath as the archetypal monster of our era, 'as establishing the closest affinity yet between audience and monster. Even as he preys upon us, he externalizes our awareness of imminent societal collapse, the demise of values, the illusoriness of security, and our rage at not being able to change any of this.'[6] This echoes the impressions of acclaimed horror writer Stephen King, who writes in *Danse Macabre* that by the early seventies the fears of popular Western culture were mostly 'sociopolitical'. A fact, King suggests, that gives films like *The Exorcist* a 'crazily convincing documentary feel'.[7] King further notes that when horror films wear their 'sociopolitical hats' they function as 'an extraordinarily accurate barometer' of the anxieties and fears of society as a whole.[8] One likely explanation for the huge success of *The Exorcist* in 1970s America was its capacity to reflect and contain anxieties arising from the social disorder of the time: the war in Vietnam and the increasing social and cultural division between young and old generations. On *The Exorcist*, King writes,

> It is a film about explosive social change, a finely honed focusing point for that entire youth explosion that took place in the late sixties and early seventies. It was a motive for all those parents who felt, in a kind of agony and terror, that they were losing their children and could not understand why or how it was happening.[9]

In addition to the collective apprehension of lost or wasted childhood, the possessing demon tapped into the common underlying anxiety that we are all unsafe, and easy targets for victimization. This monster can manifest itself in anybody, anywhere, and at any time, and in *The Exorcist* the demon's choice appears random: an apparently average, innocent child living in the anonymity of American suburbia. That anybody could fall victim to this monster and have it penetrate our bodies and very being, appearing indistinguishable to us, is what shocked and entranced its 1970s audience. Indeed, one of the several extraordinary affects of this film on its vulnerable audience was to facilitate the delusion that they themselves, or somebody they knew, were genuine victims of demonic possession. As we shall see later in

---

[6] Magistrale and Morrison, *Dreaming*, 7.
[7] Stephen King, *Danse Macabre (London: Hodder & Stoughton, 2006)*, 156.
[8] Stephen King, *Danse*, 156.
[9] Stephen King, *Danse*, 196–97

this chapter, demonic possession became a popular diagnosis and excuse for all kinds of social, mental, and organic disturbance. Thus, in support of King's quotation above, Magistrale and Morrison claim that when Chris, the mother of Regan shouts 'that thing upstairs is not my daughter', she 'echoes the sentiments of an entire generation of parents whose children grew their hair long, listened to loud rock-and-roll, and dabbled with drugs and revolution'.[10] *The Exorcist* was art imitating 1970s American life, albeit an inflated, hysterical imitation.

To support the claim that the possessing demon was an archetypal monster of 1970s American culture I cite the infamous 'Zodiac' serial killer, who terrorized San Francisco at the time. The Zodiac boasted about his crimes in cryptic letters, which he sent to *The Chronicle* newspaper. One of these – referred to as 'The Exorcist Letter' – simply states: 'I saw + think "The Exorcist" was the best saterical comidy [sic] that I have ever seen.'[11] That a real life American monster of the 1970s makes special reference to *The Exorcist* in order to substantiate his own perceived capacity for evil indicates that demonic possession was regarded at that time as the benchmark for the truly horrific. In order for the general public to perceive him as a man/monster to truly fear, the Zodiac killer sensed the need to downplay, and thus supersede, the current monster of the time: the possessing demon of *The Exorcist*.

In exorcism we find the binary pair of monster and its heroic defeat. If the possessing demon represents our fears and anxieties, exorcism represents their containment and expulsion. The presence of exorcism in popular culture symbolizes recognition of our need to counteract our shared demons. Thus, in addition to being a good horror film in its provision of an effective screen on which to project the fears of popular culture, *The Exorcist* attempts to communicate hope and relief. However, this latter aspect is often overlooked and eclipsed by its portrayal of the monstrous, as the 1970s audience testifies with its apparent preoccupation with the demon over and above its eradication. Thus the portrayal of the exorcism was enjoyed not for its capacity to heal the monstrous, but, on the contrary, in its capacity to intensify demonic activity and make it even more horrific. Indeed, Blatty openly condemned Friedkin, the director of his screenplay, for cutting those scenes that both reinforced the positive role of exorcism and downplayed the affective power of the demon. While Blatty, a devout Roman Catholic, wanted to

---

[10] Magistrale and Morrison, *Dreaming*, 90.
[11] Zodiac, 'The Exorcist Letter', written to *The Chronicle Newspaper*, San Francisco, Jan 29 1974.

portray a clear message of good prevailing over evil, Friedkin wanted
to give the audience the chance to reach its own conclusions. Friedkin
therefore cut the original ending of the film, which symbolised the
restoration of 'normal' life in Dyer and Kinderman's banal conversation
about arranging a social trip to the cinema. He also cut Merrin's pro-
nouncement that possession is the demon's attempt to make us lose our
faith in God's love; and he made Kurras' suicide, after he has sum-
moned the demon into him, seem like a victory for the demon rather
than a sacrifice of unconditional love. Blatty maintained the underlying
spiritual message of the film was lost in favour of the sensationalism of
the possession: 'There was no moral centre to the film without these
scenes . . . it went from shock to shock'.[12] Only after 26 years of cam-
paigning, was Blatty able to convince Friedkin that the restoration of the
cut scenes improved the film; and in 2000 the uncut version of The
Exorcist was released.

## Sympathy for the devil: demonic domination and dwindling exorcism

Popular culture seems to be interested in exorcism insofar as it is attracted to the monster it necessitates. Compared to the multitude of images
of demons and demonic possession freely available in popular culture
today, images and allusions to exorcism are scarce, and its less sensational affiliate, deliverance, even more so. While the devil enjoys extensive representation in films, music, and literature, images of exorcism
are relegated to a few films, songs, and novels. In this sense popular
culture affirms the devil more than its eradication. In psychological
terms, we may say popular culture is more concerned with projecting
its fears than trying to engage them effectively; and symbolically speaking, we may say its tendency is towards despair rather than hope.

However, it could be argued that the very depiction of the monstrous entails its placation and hope for the overcoming of despair, for
the containing image of the monster introduces familiarity and subsequently dilutes its monstrous effect. Thus, as a container of projected
anxiety, the monstrous image provides the audience with some respite
from their discomfort. When anxiety is channelled into an object it dis-
sipates and transforms into the more manageable emotion of fear; the

---

[12] 'Interview with Blatty' in *The Exorcist: The Complete Anthology* (New York:
Warner Brothers, 2005).

object then becomes the feared scapegoat upon which anxiety is projected. The monster is therefore an ambivalent representation: it embodies both our fears and the expulsion of our anxiety. Experiencing a good horror film is itself a ritual of purgation – an idea that finds its roots in ancient Greece, with Aristotle expounding the *kathartic* effect of tragic performance upon its audience.[13] In this sense, *The Exorcist* is a self-critique: a sensationalized self-representation of the soul purged of negative feeling.

It is, however, unrealistic to assume that preoccupation with themes of demonic possession presupposes interest in exorcism, or that popular culture is attracted to images of possession simply because we seek to unburden ourselves from anxiety. Indeed, as I claimed earlier, the inverse is more likely: the popular imagination is attracted to themes of exorcism principally because in exorcism we find the demon animated and its monstrous aspects intensified (as the demon retaliates to the threat of its expulsion). Thus, when exorcism is portrayed in popular culture it is usually as a means to glorify the demonic presence.

Far from representing the antidote to demonic possession, popular portrayals of exorcism tend to cultivate it in a variety of ways. While it could be argued that the popular imagination of 1970s Western culture was gripped by horrific portrayals of demonic power, the popular response since then – particularly from the 1990s onwards – is more ambiguous. While popular culture today still relishes the demonic, and is as dominated by demonic imagery as it was in the 1970s, we do not fear and tremble in response to them as we once did. Portrayals of demonic possession today tend to promote humour as much as they do horror. While depictions of exorcism still strongly emphasize demonic possession, they often do so by trivialising it, and by belittling the power of the demon.

I shall now turn to portrayals of exorcism in popular culture in our day to illustrate how they stress the ambiguous nature of demonic power: by either affirming it as horrific and overwhelming, or by negating and belittling it.

## Affirmation of demonic power

The horrific power of the demon is affirmed in popular portrayals of exorcism in three principal ways. First, exorcism is depicted as provoking and

---

[13] Aristotle, *Poetics*, D.W. Lucas (ed.) (Oxford: Clarendon, 1980).

tormenting the demon into even greater displays of evil. Second, the consequences of the exorcism are highlighted to emphasize the devastation left behind in the demon's wake. And, third, there is a tendency to make the rite of exorcism appear as horrific as the demon it seeks to expel.

The increasing popularity in demonic or satanic themes in western music, especially in the 1980s and 1990s is well documented.[14] Heavy metal music is the genre that springs to mind when portrayals of the devil are concerned. However, both metal and rap music have evolved quickly into a variety of sub-genres, some of which cater for the increasing demand for demonic representation by evoking even darker and more chaotic themes than their antecedents (including, death metal, doom metal, black metal, extreme metal, hardcore hip hop, horrorcore, and deathrap). A very small proportion of metal and rap music alludes to exorcism as the majority of songs prefer to give the devil free reign. And within that small proportion, the majority of 'songs' refer to exorcism in order to incite the demon into greater feats of evil. For instance, in the song 'Exorcism' (1997) death metal band *Sathanas* employs exorcism to mark the moment when the supposed victim accepts his demonic possession and wills its escalation, causing him to proclaim: 'Let the demons thrive!'[15] Another song called 'Exorcism' (1994), by industrial metal band *Killing Joke* depersonalizes the possessing demon and describes exorcism as the realization and release of loathsome feelings of evil intent, such as hatred, resentment, and guilt. A third example is *Necro's* lurid hip hop track 'Nirvana' (2004), which takes the depiction of exorcism a step further, transforming it into a satanic ritual that cleanses the soul with suffering and corruption. Here exorcism is no longer the means to intensify demonic expression; it is the unholy rite of demonic expression.[16]

The second way exorcism affirms demonic power in its popular depictions is its emphasis on the damage caused by the demon. It is not surprising that popular accounts of unsuccessful exorcism attempts speak of disaster, with malevolent forces surrounding the failed exorcist. We thus see John Constantine's (antihero of John Delano's graphic novel

---

[14] See, for instance, Kahn-Harris, *Extreme Metal: Music and Culture on the Edge* (Oxford and New York: Berg, 2007); and Moynihan and Soderlind, *The Bloody Rise of the Satanic Metal Underground* (California: Feral, 1998).

[15] I am grateful to Alex Kurtagic, founder and owner of *Supernal Music*, for permitting citation of *Sathanas'* lyrics by email on 11 Nov 2008. 'Exorcism', Sathanas, Supernal Music, Website: http://www.supernalmusic.com.

[16] *Necro's* next album was called *The Sexorcist* (2005), but its lyrics reveal the title's allusion to 'exorcist' is completely downplayed in favour of its sexual component.

*Hellblazer*, 1988–present) failed exorcism attempt lead to the deaths of four people, including a girl, whose soul was banished to hell,[17] and also to chronic feelings of guilt within John himself, which culminate in his nervous breakdown and committal to a secure mental institute. We also see the Deliverance Minister, Revd Merrily Watson (heroine of Phil Rickman's novels, 1998–present) besieged by the malevolent spiritual presence of the depraved man Denzil Joy – of his unwholesome stench and aura – after she failed to deliver his soul at his death.

Slightly more interesting, however, is the popular notion that the demon continues his destructive rampage even after a successful exorcism. That is to say, a successful exorcism is often represented alongside the damage caused by the demon: an enduring demonic imprint, shadow – or legacy even – left behind. In *The Exorcist* the victorious exorcism is marked by the respective deaths of the two exorcists. In the song lyrics of 'Exorcist' (1985) by death metal band *Possessed* we find details of the permanent scars of a victim post-exorcism, which include an incinerated and fragmented mind, disturbing and evil memories, sick thoughts, nightmares, sin, and fear of living in the shadows of hell.

And, the heavy metal album *Voodoo* (1998) by *King Diamond* envisages the leftover damage of the demonic spirit as a full-bloodied legacy, in the form of a newborn demonic baby. The demon's progeny is born after the then-pregnant mother undergoes an exorcism. (The lyrics do not reveal whether the foetus becomes possessed within the womb at the same time as its mother, or whether the same demon possesses it immediately after the demon is expelled from the mother. The latter would provide a rather quirky argument in support of the existence of the pre-natal soul!)

The exorcism rite itself is often perceived as a damaging ordeal for the possessed victim. The popularization of this perception could well be attributed to the poignant real life case of Anneliese Michel, whose death during her gruelling exorcism became the centre of a court-case of international media interest. (The autopsy of Anneliese states the cause of her death as malnutrition and dehydration: conditions acquired during her exorcism. The two priests responsible for her exorcism were charged, and later found guilty of negligent homicide.) The song lyrics of 'Exorcism' (2002) by black metal band *Theatre des Vampires* plays on the violent nature of exorcism in its description of the intentions of 'Holy Mary of God' towards an evil vampire. Thus, she plans first to stab the vampire with a knife and then an iron, before

---

[17] See issues 11 and 233.

throwing the vampire into the fire where it will burn to death. Similarly, in the track 'Diary of a Madman' (1994) by *Gravediggaz* we learn of the torturous methods of an exorcism – First the supposedly possessed person is handcuffed and left to starve for two weeks, before having his eyelid sewn wide open. When the person is on the edge of death from dehydration, a minister forces him to drink cold vinegar. Then, after salt has been rubbed into his wounds, his hands and feet are spread and nailed to form a cross.

## Trivialization of demonic possession

Popular portrayals of exorcism negate the horrific power of the demon by trivialising it. The trivialization of exorcism in general is clearly illustrated by its infiltration into colloquial American parlance, where the expression 'exorcism' bizarrely refers to something trendy or fashionable. When I was a teenager in England in the 90s, the term 'wicked' was adopted in similar way; now, at the end of the first decade of the twenty-first century, the term 'exorcism' can occasionally be heard alongside the more common expressions 'sick' and 'ill' to refer, ironically, to that which is admired and valued. Thus 'that's exorcism!' is synonymous with 'that's really cool!'

In popular narratives of exorcism, the trivialization of demonic possession is illustrated in three principal ways. First, in the transformation of the monster from an object of horror to an object of comedy. Second, in the portrayal of exorcism as one event or task among many in somebody's day-job. And third, in the shift in perception of the underlying context and interpretation of exorcism, from theology to science and psychology. This shift in emphasis effectively strips the demon of its autonomy and reinterprets the demonic presence as an absence of health or anomaly of nature.

### The tragic made comic

The film *The Exorcist* was banned in cinemas in the UK by local authorities and it was not until 1998 that the British Board of Film Censors allowed its video release. Although the re-released film generated interest, it did not excite the popular imagination of the British public to the same frenzied-degree as it had its American audience in the early 1970s. Perhaps the majority of those eager to see it had found a way to bypass the national censors and had already been party to the frenzy, or perhaps the popular imagination had simply moved on, seeking a different monster to contain and satisfy its needs. Whatever the scenario, *The Exorcist* seemed to have lost its capacity to enthral and shock; indeed, today's audience is more likely to giggle than gasp in response to Regan's possession.

Two scenes of the film in particular are recalled to popular memory and have come to represent or emblemize *The Exorcist* as a whole, and even 'exorcism' in general. These scenes are the depictions of Regan projectile-vomiting green bile and of her twisting her head 360 degrees (two scenes that popular memory tends to conflate into one; imagining these different actions happening at one and the same time or one immediately after the other). The scenes have been the brunt of many jokes, and have spawned several comedy spoofs and numerous references in other popular movies, television programmes, novels, and songs. For instance, in an early episode of the long-running supernatural television series *Buffy the Vampire Slayer* (1997–2003), Buffy describes Miss French, the 'insect–teacher', as having done a 'full-on-Exorcist-Twist';[18] and in an early episode of *Angel* (the spin-off television series of *Buffy*), when making preparations for an exorcism ritual, Cordelia says to Angel, 'Are you expecting any big vomiting here? Because I saw the movie.'[19] Horror films also make explicit and ironic allusion to these motifs,[20] as do supposedly dark and morbid lyrics of hip hop.[21] Similarly, the two prominent spoofs of *The Exorcist*: 'The Exorcist' (1990) *French & Saunders*, and the film *Re-possessed* (1990) (starring Linda Blair, who played the original Regan in *The Exorcist*) heavily invest in twisting heads, and 'pea soup' vomit. Interestingly, both spoofs comment on our tendency today to trivialize and reduce exorcism and demonic possession to ordinary, everyday phenomenon. While *Re-possessed* turns the spectacle of exorcism into a televised game-show, Jennifer Saunders, as Regan's mother appears both fed up with her daughter's 'attention seeking', 'selfish, childish behaviour', and vaguely concerned that her daughter may be coming down with a nasty cold; the mother's prescription for her daughter's possession is a bag of satsumas!

---

[18] *Buffy the Vampire Slayer*, 'Teacher's Pet', season one, episode 4.

[19] *Angel*, 'I've Got You Under My Skin', season one, episode 14.

[20] Such as *Children of the Corn IV: The Gathering*, directed by Greg Spence, and based on a short story by Stephen King.

[21] Such as *Sathanas'* reference to exorcism as an occasion to vomit on the priest ('Exorcism', from the album *Armies of Charon*, 1997); and *Killah Priest's* boast that 'I get 'em with the rhythm. Twist 'em, spit 'em like exorcism' ('Black August', from the album *Black August*, 2003).

The iconic head-twisting and green vomit are found in abundance not only in likely places, such as spoofs of *The Exorcist* or the 'dark' genres of horror and the supernatural, but in unlikely places too, such as comedy films that are otherwise completely unrelated to exorcism or demon possession.[22]

Our enduring enjoyment of the once-horrific scenes of Regan's rotating head and her green vomit has helped their consolidation within popular culture as the definitive way we think a demonically possessed person behaves. And because these images tap into our sense of humour, exorcism is generally regarded as amusing. Exorcism as a serious, bona fide ministry is somewhat lost on the popular imagination. Although deliverance ministry may be flourishing, particularly in America, such ministry (as I later argue) is commonly devalued and trivialized: perceived as an everyday, commercial business rather than sacred ritual. Jane, a headstrong character of Phil Rickman's series of novels (1998–present), sums this up nicely. Jane, daughter of the sensible deliverance Minister Merrily Watkins, says of her mother's recently acquired role

> She's been appointed Deliverance minister. You know – like used to be called exorcist? Like in the film where the kid's head does a complete circle while she is throwing up green bile and masturbating with a crucifix? Mum gets to deal with people like that. Only, of course, there aren't many people like that, not in these parts – which is why it's such a dodgy job.[23]

In addition to the two enduring images of rotating head and green vomit, Regan's sexually implicit actions and comments have helped colour the stereotypical behaviour of a possessed person. Most notable, is the scene that Jane alludes to above, where the possessed Regan masturbates with the crucifix, and also the occasion when Regan addresses Kurras, whose mother had recently died, with the words, 'Your mother sucks cocks in hell'. These words have been translated into a variety of humorous sentences; such as, 'Your mother sucks jelly babies in hell' (followed by the supposedly derogatory remark, 'Your mother is a biology teacher in Cheshire');[24] 'Your mother knits socks that

---

[22] Such as *The Great Outdoors* (directed by Howard Deutch, 1988) and *When Harry Met Sally* (directed by Rob Reiner, 1989).

[23] Rickman, *Minwinter of the Spirit* (Macmillan, 1999), 158.

[24] French & Saunders, 1990.

smell';[25] and 'Your mother flosses in hell'.[26] Regan's sexual allusions are obvious targets for satirical appraisal, and the porn films *The Sexorcist* (2000) and *The XXXorcist* (2006) take full advantage. The publicity synopsis of *The XXXorcist* reads:

> After all other exorcism methods fail, Father Merkin has no other option but to screw the hell (and the devil) out of a possessed woman, Regan Teresa MacFeel . . . Father Merkin is forced to fight for his life with his genitals . . . Besides copious amounts of demonic possession, green vomit, head-spinning and bed-floating, the film features unique religious sex toys from *Divine Interventions*

The film adaptation of *The Exorcist* finds itself referenced all over the place. It is one of Dana Scully (FBI agent of the *X-Files*, 1993–2002) favourite films; the two exorcists (Merrin and Kurras, who are not mentioned by name) are called upon to exorcize an over-active rotating chair in *Austin Powers: The Spy Who Shagged Me* (1999); and the statue of 'Pazuzu' (the demon who possessed Regan) is even found in the graveyard of *Wallace & Gromit: The Curse of the Were-Rabbit* (2005). Exorcism in general finds itself an easy target for humour: from subtle irony as we find in the thrash metal band *Exorcist* (a joke band comprising members from the successful band *Virgin Steele*, who produced one album, *Nightmare Theatre* (1986) in order to mimic the extreme metal of the early 1980s), to the slapstick of such productions as *Re-possessed* (1990) and *Southpark* (2002).[27]

I shall end this part of the discussion with an outline of the very latest fad to expound the humorous side of *The Exorcist*: the very simple but effective Internet programme, *The Exorcist-Maze game* (also known as *The Scary Maze Game*: http://www.maniacworld.com/maze_game). The stated object of the game is to carefully guide a dot through a maze without letting it touch the sides of the wall. The first two levels are very easy, and the third requires more concentration. At this stage, as the player focuses intently on the screen, the distorted demonic face of the possessed girl Regan suddenly fills the screen with her piercing screams. The programme then ends leaving the 'player' stunned. The 'game's' objective is therefore to humiliate the 'player' in front of those onlookers, who are already wise to the event. *The Exorcist Maze-Game* is advertised as 'a prank', and because hilarious results are almost guaranteed, the

---

[25] *The Making of '. . . And God Spoke'* (directed by Arthur Borman, 1993).
[26] *Mystery Science Theater 3000*, 'Moon Zero Two' season one, episode 11.
[27] See 'The Biggest Douche in the Universe' season six, episode 15.

popular website http://www.youtube.com has hundreds of video clips capturing people's reactions: mini films of horror/comedy/Reality-TV rolled into one.

### Just another day at the office

Popular culture trivializes exorcism by making it just one event among many. We have already seen how its misdiagnoses of common illness or ordinary antisocial behaviour have been portrayed to humorous effect, but in addition to this there is popular emphasis on exorcism as a habitual event in a person's day-job. Those heroes of television series who work with all things supernatural have, more often than not, been party to an exorcism or two alongside other ghouls, demons, spirits, slimy creatures, and general weirdness. It is part of the job remit of such people as Mulder and Scully;[28] Angel;[29] Buffy;[30] Dean and Sam Winchester (and Bobby Singer) in *Supernatural*;[31] John Constantine in *Constantine*[32] and the *Marvel* comic book antihero Gabriel the Demon Hunter.[33]

Although the day job in question is portrayed as an unusual one, the fact that we, the audience, are subject to episode after episode of a variety of supernatural encounters where sinister goings on are both subdued and resolved by the hero as a matter of course, trivializes demon possession and exorcism. Perhaps as an attempt to counteract the monotony that such long-running series inspire, many supernatural portrayals are given a twist to keep the audience interested. *Angel* does this well. Thus, the exorcism-themed episode 'I've Got You Under My Skin' (2000) begins as one would expect: an average dysfunctional family experience sinister goings on. It is decided that the young son is possessed by a particularly nasty demon (an 'Ethros'), and the only option is to expel the demon with a particularly complicated exorcism involving special hard-to-find equipment. Once the demon has been

---

[28] See, 'The Calusari', season two, episode 21.

[29] See, 'Skin', season one, episode 14

[30] See, 'I Only Have Eyes for You', season two, episode 19.

[31] See, 'Devil's Trap', season one, episode 22; and 'Jus in Bello', season three, episode 12.

[32] *Constantine* (2005) is the film adaptation of the graphic novel *Hellblazer* (New York: D.C. Comics, 1998–present), which sees the original character of John Constantine, the humanist magician, remodelled as a staunch Catholic exorcist.

[33] Gabriel is a professional exorcist, whose temporary retirement was spent performing 'mock exorcisms' for people interested in the occult.

expelled from the boy, we realize that all is not what we had expected. We discover that it is not the boy who is possessed by an evil demon; rather, the demon is trapped within an evil, soulless boy.

### Autonomous demon demoted to absence of normality

A third sense in which exorcism is trivialized is in the popular tendency to conceive it as a phenomenon of natural science or psychiatry and psychotherapy rather than theology. Exorcism is trivialized because its appeal to divine authority is negated in its translation to rational terms. The demon's autonomous existence is made incoherent; the demon is instead understood as an absence of normality and lack of healthy functioning.

The move towards scientific explanation embodies our Zeitgeist. I have emphasized giggles and humour as today's typical response to *The Exorcist*, downplaying its capacity to shock us still. But there are moments when it still does leave us uncomfortable – yet, significantly, these do not occur in our relationship with the demonically possessed Regan, but with Regan the hospital patient. *The Exorcist* continues to incite horror today with its drawn-out scenes of Regan being subject to various harsh medical procedures that inevitably fail to diagnose or effectively treat her condition.

In addition to Regan's medical procedures, the novel version of *The Exorcist* portrays an intriguing conflict experienced by Kurras in his double role as priest and psychiatrist. Yet, many a poor film and novel attempting to cash in on the success of *The Exorcist* fail to emulate its underlying philosophical and social critique, choosing instead to emulate its superficial, sensational aspects. Their subsequent lack of depth contributes to their inability to engage their audience; they are not 'horror' films per se, but rather dull and occasionally comical.[34] The more successful ventures are those that explore and maintain the present-day tension between psychological and theological interpretations of demon possession and exorcism, rather than playing on the assumption that a definitive explanation or solution can be found in one camp rather than the other. The film *Stigmata* (1999) exemplifies both a success and failure in these terms. It thus captivated its audience in the first half when the protagonists are immersed in the confusion of why

---

[34] Truly atrocious recent examples, include *Demon Hunter* (2006), *Black Valley Water Exorcism* (2006); Jenna Black's novel *The Devil Inside* (2008); and *Exorcism* (2004).

a young atheist woman has stigmata, and whether a psychological or theological explanation should be sought. But as soon as the film commits itself to a theological explanation all tension and intrigue is lost, and the film quickly spirals into a farce (in both its special effects and its faulty theological premise that stigmata is a symptom of demonic possession). More successful attempts to portray the tensions between the different paradigmatic explanations for demon possession and exorcism are the films *The Exorcism of Emily Rose* (2005) and *Requiem* (2006). Both explore the conflict between theological and psychological explanations, as it was perceived to have arisen in the real life case of Anneliese Michel. While *The Exorcism of Emily Rose* presents the tension as a rational debate within a fictionalized court case and trial of a priest (the defendant for the theological explanation), who is accused of causing unlawful death to a girl during her exorcism, *Requiem* explores it in a more realistic portrayal of Anneliese's own life experiences: her ineffective treatments for epilepsy and her aggressive reactions towards her devout Catholic faith.

The focal point in popular portrayals of exorcism is the possessing demon – even in those portrayals that belittle the demon's capacity to incite horror. Exorcism is of secondary interest; it is simply a context or platform upon which the nature of demonic possession can be explored. Those contrasting depictions of demonic power that seek either to affirm or belittle it are not mutually exclusive. Indeed, the act of trivialising the horrific by turning an object of fear into an object of comedy is a proven method to manage discomfort. It is natural for us to try to explain or control what we fear or do not know, and comedy is one way of reducing the threat of the unknown and our fearful response to it. However, that we now tend to make jokes out of a monster that once terrified us almost forty years ago suggests there is something more significant going on. In other words, it would seem that our capacity to laugh and joke is not motivated by an unconscious need to deny our vulnerability in the face of the horrific, but, rather, by our discovery that a now-familiar monster is no longer horrific. The possessing demon (as it has come to be known through its stereotypical portrayal inspired by *The Exorcist*) is no longer an affective container for our collective anxieties, and the once frightful notion of a seemingly ordinary person besieged by malevolent spirits has been subdued and (controversially) explained away by psychological theories of dissociative identity disorder and schizophrenia. Indeed, the monster of our imagination has evolved into something else.

I shall conclude this chapter by outlining how the monster of our day has evolved from the possessing demon of the 1970s; and subsequently, how our perceptions and views on exorcism have also been revised.

### Conclusion: evolution of the monstrous and its exorcism

The popular demons we seek to expel today are not the evil autonomous influences of Catholic dogma; they are those experiences our parents helped to cultivate in childhood or the organic diseases that infect our bodies. If there is an effective possessing demon of our time it is the privation of health, and the exorcist is found at work in the hospital. That we tend to chuckle at ideas of autonomous possessing demons does not put us on par with the Zodiac killer, who also found *The Exorcist* amusing. The Zodiac was a sociopath, and thus represented the antithesis to social consensus and popular culture. Indeed, today's sociopath may well be conceived as the one who responds to the ideas of demonic possession with utmost seriousness!

The popularity of *The Exorcist* considered on its own could not maintain collective fascination for demonic possession and exorcism. Indeed, likely support for its continued celebration is found in the much publicized death of Anneliese Michel (1976) and in the general discomfort and anticipation of the end of the Millennium: two thousand years after Christ's death. The appearance of several novels, films, and music inspired by the film generated a snowball effect which guaranteed continued interest in exorcism and the installation of the possessing demon as an enduring monster of the time. One of these, the non-fiction work *Hostage to the Devil: The Possession and Exorcism of Five Contemporary Americans* (1987) by Martin Malachi, turned the snowball into an avalanche. According to the cultural historian, Michael W. Cuneo, if this book had not been published 'exorcism's popular celebrity might have run its course in late 1970s.[35] He further claims that this book caught the imagination of the general public because it argued for the reality of demonic possession using detailed real life case-studies; and it did so from a position of great authority, as Martin was a retired advisor and confident to the Pope. Its perceived mix of authority and sensationalism guaranteed to make this a best seller.

With an absence of other notable works together with the collective anticlimax experienced at the dawn of the new millennium (when the

---

[35] Michael W. Cuneo, *American Exorcism. Expelling Demons in the Land of Plenty* (New York: Doubleday, 2001), 15.

world continued just as it had done before with no dramatic divine intervention), the snowball effect inevitably dried itself out, and popular culture moved on. The relatively tired reception towards exorcism is symbolized by the general lack of interest in the recent prequels to *The Exorcist*,[36] and, more recently, by the rejection of the television series *Demons* (that documented the life and events of a fictional exorcist) by the American television corporation CBS, which scrapped it in 2008 before its pilot show was aired.[37]

The monsters of popular culture inevitably find themselves redundant by the popular imagination's ever-changing tastes for the horrific, and its persistent explorations and transgressions of taboo. Violent, 'slasher' films and reality-TV seem to satisfy today's popular palette. The film *The Blair Witch Project* (1999) was a successful diluted hybrid of the two; and I would not be surprised if the popular American imagination started to crave a more explicit hybrid (such as televised executions).

## Popular culture possessed by demonic nihilism

Because popular imagery focuses more on demons than it does exorcism, the monster of our day is imagined without antidote, and correspondingly, our popular cultural identity is one of despair without

---

[36] *Exorcist: The Beginning*, 2004; and *Dominion: Prequel to the Exorcist*, 2005.

[37] However, just before the completion of this chapter, it came to my attention that *Apparitions*, a television drama series, has been re-commissioned to appear on BBC from November 13, 2008. *Apparitions* was originally intended as a two-part programme for transmission at the beginning of 2008, but was redeveloped to form a longer series. The presence of this 'extended' series suggests potential revival of popular interest in the theme of exorcism. The drama features a Roman Catholic priest called Father Jacob, who must undertake a succession of exorcisms and prevent the End of Days. Although the drama is, in most part, theologically accurate and well-researched, its focus is nevertheless the possessing demon and demonic acts of physical and emotional violence (for instance, the pilot episode portrays a man skinned alive in a gay sauna, incestuous rape threats, and Mother Teresa fighting demons on her death bed). A spokesman for the Catholic Bishops' Conference says of *Apparitions*: 'I will not watch the drama myself, it is not tasteful. I haven't seen it but people might well be shocked. I have to stress, it is a work of fiction. The Catholic Church would not have chosen the drama form to explain the issue of exorcism.' (www.screenrush.co.uk/article: accessed 11/08).

hope. We could argue that popular culture is drawn to images of the devil precisely because they symbolize – thus both contain and represent – its prevailing sense of loss of hope. The demon or monster of our day is the embodiment of meaninglessness and nihilism. Indeed, popular culture is saturated with portrayals of despair either as a demonic source or autonomous agent that needs to be overcome. Thus, if we look more closely at those rock bands associated with satanic themes, we often find their demons are evocations of angst in response to a meaningless world. For example, Iron Maiden's celebrated song 'The Number of the Beast' (1982) describes a victim of recurrent evil dreams of a face which subsequently torments his mind and brings him to despair; and Marilyn Manson (who was 'ordained' a 'Reverend' by Anton LaVey, founder of the Church of Satan, and whose music was blamed for inciting the Columbine school shootings of 1999) has produced such titles as, 'I Want to Disappear' (1998), 'Disassociative' (1998), 'Dried Up, Tied and Dead to the World' (1996), and 'Posthuman' (1998). Likewise, popular depictions of exorcism also recognise the emptiness of life and a need to overcome it with the search for meaning. For instance, Jamie Delano reveals that he created *Hellblazer* and its magician-come-exorcist character John Constantine in order to comment openly on the depressing state of 1980s Britain: 'That was where I was living, it was shit, and I wanted to tell everybody.'[38] Similarly, music such as 'Empty Exorcism' by the 'Darkwave' project *Covenant of Thorns* (1998); *Evanescence's* alternative-rock song 'Bring Me to Life' (2003); and *Gorefest's* death metal song 'Exorcism' (2005), reflect upon the nihilism of our age.

Popular depictions of demonic possession and exorcism seem to fall into two categories. First, there are theological interpretations, of which my chapter has been principally concerned. In this category the focus falls heavily on the demonic (as autonomous demon) at the expense of the exorcism (as religious ritual). Second, there are secular interpretations, of which the focus is still very much on the demonic (as the embodiment of despair) with emphasis also placed on ways in which the demonic can be overcome.

'Secular exorcism' can never expel its demon successfully, because in denying God it denies the source of authentic transcendence and self-transformation. The secular world must therefore put its faith in the

---

[38] http://www.tabula-rasa.info/AusComics/Hellblazers.html (accessed 08/09).

rational discourses of science for the growth and healing of body and personality. But an overly rational grounding to life can generate the most intense desires for non-rational and irrational experience: a desire for something 'more', something 'Other', 'soul'. In the absence of God, the secular self can do nothing more than seek its own negation and escape from itself.

Secular exorcism is purgation by 'quick fix'. Thus, the self can experience temporary transcendence and escape through the obvious candidates of alcohol, drugs, and sex; and also through aesthetics, such as music, novel, and film. I mentioned earlier that horror films, such as *The Exorcist* facilitate catharsis and a containment of anxiety, and thus a way in which we can temporarily escape and relieve our troubled selves. However, Neil Strauss, a writer for *The New York Times* further suggests that nihilism is the basis for our dark fantasies, and therefore provides the means for temporary escape, from the emptiness of life,

> Death metal and death rap try to escape from reality, offering nihilism as a cure-all and suicide as an easy way out. But in doing so, both end up commenting on a reality so grim and alienating that the only direction its outcasts can turn is toward darkness. The fans of the two genres find comfort in fantasy, in finding a collective myth for their private pain.[39]

Secular remedies are ultimately unsatisfactory: the demon of despair and nihilism cannot be overcome. Indeed, quick fix remedies can turn easily into addictions, thereby feeding the sense of despair further and exacerbating the problem rather than providing a solution. Secular 'quick fix' remedies are the demon that needs exorcising.

Ironically, the theological category of demonic possession and exorcism has seeped into secular rituals of escapism in the form of 'deliverance therapy'. Deliverance, like its more sensational counterpart, exorcism, is trivialized in popular culture, as deliverance is reduced from theological rite to business transaction: a quick fix solution for a quick buck. Michael W. Cuneo (2001) writes lucidly on the rise in popularity of deliverance as a consumer product in contemporary America,

> Whatever one's personal problem – depression, anxiety, substance addiction, or even a runaway sexual appetite – there are exorcism

---

[39] Strauss, 'POP VIEW: When Rap Meets the Undead', *The New York Times*, Sept. 18, 1994, Arts Section.

ministries available today that will happily claim expertise for dealing with it. With the significant bonus, moreover, that one is not, for the most part, held personally responsible for the problem. Indwelling demons are mainly to blame, and getting rid of them is the key to moral and psychological redemption. Personal engineering through demon-expulsion: a bit messy perhaps, but relatively fast and cheap, and morally exculpatory. A thoroughly American arrangement . . . With its promises of therapeutic well-being and rapid-fire emotional gratification, exorcism is oddly at home in the shopping-mall culture, the purchase-of-happiness culture, of turn-of-the-century America.[40]

Deliverance therapy is seen as too good to be true, and as a consumer product, it works effectively only on those demons it manufactures. Phil Rickman's novels portray the deliverance ministry realistically and sympathetically, and yet the characters of his novels often allude to it as if it were an enforced government service, a 'local service you paid for in your council tax',[41] 'The Fourth Emergency Service',[42] and, 'The Soul Police'.[43] According to Jane (daughter of a deliverance minister), once this service is popularized and taken for granted it becomes dangerous:

It's like with these evangelical maniacs, where you like go along and you're looking a bit off-colour and in about three minutes flat they've discovered you're possessed by seventeen different demons and the next thing you're rolling around on the floor throwing up. You could really *damage* people.[44]

The demon of popular culture possesses us when we dislike ourselves, when life is found empty and meaningless, and when quick-fix solutions are sought to facilitate the delusion of self-escape (either with the promise of a 'better' identity external to us – such as we might find at the bottom of several bottles of alcohol – or by denying fundamental aspects of ourselves – such as our moral accountability, by selling ourselves to the business of deliverance therapy).

Just as this chapter began with an epigraph that calls for the exorcism of our contemporary demon of despair, it will end with words to

---

[40] Cuneo, *Exorcism*, xiii–xiv.
[41] Rickman, *Midwinter*, 328.
[42] Rickman, *Midwinter*, 184.
[43] Rickman, *Midwinter*, 37.
[44] Rickman, *Midwinter*, 135.

similar effect in Father Merrin's explanation for Regan's demonic possession,

> The demon's target is not the possessed; it is us . . . the observers . . . And I think the point is to make us despair; to reject our own humanity . . . to see ourselves as ultimately bestial . . . without dignity; ugly; unworthy. And there lies the heart of it, perhaps: in unworthiness. For I think belief in God is not a matter of reason at all; I think it finally is a matter of love; of accepting the possibility that God could love us.[45]

---

[45] William Peter Blatty, *The Exorcist (London: Corgi, 1974)*, 293.

# Chapter 10

# Deliverance and Exorcism in Theological Perspective 1: Is there any substance to evil?

## Nigel Wright

'The power against which faith is faith has its own reality, just as certainly as it does not have its own validity.'

*Otto Weber*

**Abstract**

This chapter advances a non-ontological, realist analysis of the devil and demons. Without seeking to reduce the reality of the powers of darkness, it nonetheless advances a position that denies them ontological substance. It begins by questioning the adequacy of traditional views that identify the devil as possessing personal existence. It also questions the idea of a fall of angels as insufficiently supported by Scripture. It then explores an alternative, non-ontological approach in dialogue with Karl Barth, Jürgen Moltmann, Walter Wink, Robert Cook, and Tom Noble. By means of this dialogue it concludes that evil should be seen as 'Godless emptiness' and that this perception is compatible both with Jesus' encounter with evil as recorded in the gospels and with a continuing, but chastened, approach to deliverance and exorcism. Crucial to this argument is the idea that evil as Godless emptiness nonetheless has ways of 'taking form', albeit it in complex ways, in the experience of societies and individuals.

In his book *After Our Likeness* Miroslav Volf makes reference to what he calls a 'sophisticated kind of obtuseness' which he finds to be 'so characteristic of second-rate intellectuals'.[1] By this he means, in context, the

---

[1] *After our Likeness: The Church as the Image of the Trinity* (Grand Rapids: Eerdmans, 1998), 7.

refusal of some theologians to give consideration to the transmission of the faith and the growth of the church. Such issues are beneath them and beneath the level of serious theology – an assumption that he is working to reverse. In a similar vein we could say that with some marked and honourable exceptions most theologians pass over the current topic swiftly. Talk of the devil and demons belongs to pre-critical and pre-theological reflection. Given that Christ was, among many other things, an exorcist, we are indeed entitled to see this neglect as a 'sophisticated kind of obtuseness'.

I have come to take a non-ontological view of the nature of the devil and demons. I do so not in any sense to deny the reality of powers of darkness but to explore their ultimate nature. A non-ontological position takes the view that finally evil is Godless emptiness. Concern was first raised in my mind by observing the tendency of some Christians to become excessively attracted to matters to do with the devil. In his remarkable novel *The Name of the Rose*, Umberto Eco paints a picture of a mediaeval monastery overtaken by demon-mindedness and consequently prey to all manner of delusions.[2] A more recent pagan publication captures the same danger in its title: *Lure of the Sinister*.[3] I believe this is a genuine problem. As a newspaper editorial once observed, a born-again army requires a born-again enemy, hence the rise in interest in the demonic. For too many Christians, especially on the 'enthusiastic' wing of the church, the idea of the devil is where they get their energy from. The antidote to this is to find better ways of thinking, ways which both take evil seriously and discount it.

In particular, the use of personal language about the devil is problematic. It personalises the devil and therefore gives a dignity he does not deserve. To refer to the devil as 'he' or 'him' (as I find it hard not to do in these reflections) confers upon the devil a form of language that properly refers to persons made in the image of God. It is only as a tentative and limited analogy that it is appropriate to use personal words of the devil. Nothing in the Bible suggests the devil is made in the image of God. Not even the angels are described as being in God's image. The term relates to human persons. Personhood is something into which we enter by means of relationships. The Christian vision of God is of One who is in eternal and essential relationship as Father, Son, and Spirit. Human beings bear the divine image as persons who

---

[2] U. Eco, *The Name of the Rose* (London: Picador, 1984).
[3] Gareth J. Medway, *Lure of the Sinister: The Unnatural History of Satanism* (New York and London: New York University Press, 2001).

are in embodied relationship with others.[4] This language is problematic in reference to the devil because it would require the devil to be in relationship in such a way as to constitute a personal identity. But it would be more accurate to think of the devil as a non-person, as sub-personal, or anti-personal, rather than personal.[5]

A further difficulty concerns *ontology*, the study of being. Talk of the devil creates the impression that in the order of being (God-angels-nature-humankind) there is a further way of being which also has its place – the devil and his angels. Jesus certainly used this language without embarrassment.[6] But it confers legitimacy upon the devil if he is thought to have an existence *of the same order* as that of God. The devil becomes respectable and acceptable by virtue of having place. We need to be able to assert with Otto Weber, 'The power against which faith is faith has its own reality, *just as certainly as it does not have its own validity.*'[7] The devil has no legitimacy. He does not have a place assigned to him by God. Evil is total and complete aberration, even if, as such, it does not fall outside of God's providential rule. Evil exists as chaos to order, as lie to truth, darkness to light, or death to life. For this reason the devil is not something, or someone to be believed in on a par with the creator. God is the Living God who possesses fullness of being and is Being Itself.[8] God and the devil stand in mutual contradiction.

Then there is the extremely important question of *biblical fidelity*. Not for a moment could we entertain the idea that the devil is unbiblical. But the assumption that the devil is a fallen angel is indeed, on close examination of the texts, highly debatable. The doctrine traditionally known as the 'fall of angels' occurs first in Tertullian (c.160/70–c.215/20)[9] and finds normative exposition in Augustine (354–430).[10] But

---

[4] Gen 1:28.

[5] Andrew Walker, *Enemy Territory: The Christian Struggle for the Modern World* (London: Hodder and Stoughton, 1987), 10.

[6] Matt 25:41.

[7] Otto Weber, *Foundations of Dogmatics* Volume I (Grand Rapids: Eerdmans, 1981), 489 (my emphasis).

[8] The term is Paul Tillich's.

[9] *Apology*, 22: 'We are instructed, moreover, by our sacred books how from certain angels, who fell of their own free-will, there sprang a more wicked demon-brood, condemned of God along with the authors of their race, and that chief we have referred to . . . Their great business is the ruin of mankind.'

[10] *City of God*, XI, 9, 11: 'But there were some angels who turned away from this illumination, and so did not attain to the excellence of a life of bliss and wisdom.'

if the Bible speaks of an angelic fall it is obliquely and on the margins. The texts concerned are problematic.[11] The OT passages appealed to, Ezekiel 28:1–17 and Isaiah 14:12–21, can only be cited indirectly since their direct reference is to identifiable human persons.[12] They prove what is required of them only if their meaning is assumed in advance on other grounds. It is more likely that they are heightened descriptions of historical persons rather than attempts to describe the origin of Satan.[13] It takes a major leap of biblical interpretation to refer them to a transcendental personage. The NT texts are more substantial, but even so are elusive. Jude 6 speaks of 'angels who did not keep their positions of authority but abandoned their own home'. 2 Peter 2:4 refers to the fact that, 'God did not spare angels when they sinned but sent them to hell (Gk, *Tartarus*).' If we accept Jude 6 as teaching an angelic fall are we also bound to accept the account in v. 9 about Michael disputing with the devil about the body of Moses, or v. 14 about Enoch's prophecies? Neither incident is found in the OT but belongs to Jewish extra-biblical literature. Jude is arguably using known Jewish traditions to illustrate his point rather than laying down authoritative teaching. 2 Peter 2:4 is also problematic. The 'angels that sinned' in 2 Peter as in Jude appear to be the heavenly beings in Genesis 6:1–4 who lusted after earthly women. The fate of these angels became a subject of speculation in Jewish thought.[14] If so, these angels fell *after* the creation of humankind and not before it. Additionally, the fallen angels of Jude and 2 Peter are *probably not demons*. In Jewish speculation of the time – see for instance 1 Enoch – these fallen angels did not become demons that wandered the earth afflicting people, but instead were bound in chains until the day of judgement. It may be that these are references to known traditions meant simply to illustrate the writers' theme of the danger of disobedience rather than disclose information concerning a fall of angels.

There are enough questions here to doubt whether the traditional notion of a fall of angels is an adequate interpretation of the biblical

---

[11] S.H.T. Page examines the relevant texts in *Powers of Evil: A Biblical Study of Satan and Demons*, Leicester: Apollos, 1995, and comes to similarly cautious conclusions as those that follow.

[12] Michael Green, *I Believe in Satan's Downfall* (London: Hodder and Stoughton, 1981), 33–42 makes far too much of these verses.

[13] See on this Walther Eichrodt, *Ezekiel* (London: SCM Press, 1970), 392; John Mauchline, *Isaiah 1–39* (London: SCM Press, 1962), 140.

[14] J.N.D. Kelly, *The Epistles of Peter and of Jude* (London: A.&C. Black, 1969), 331.

material. And there are sufficient theological questions about the ontology of evil to test out different ways of thinking. At this point we shall gather some alternative ways of thinking from Karl Barth, Jürgen Moltmann, Walter Wink, and then as we move towards a constructive statement from Robert Cook and Tom Noble.[15]

## Evil as 'Nothingness'

The notion of 'Nothingness' (*das Nichtige*)[16] is Barth's conception of a power in opposition to God that has a negatively dynamic character. He freely admits the term is one he has fashioned himself and is therefore to be taken with a grain of salt. But it does, in his belief, express briefly, tersely, and strongly insights that are truly biblical.[17] His intention is not to suggest that evil does not exist but that it exists in negativity, without any right to exist, without any value or positive strength. The translators of *Church Dogmatics* debated also whether to render *das Nichtige* as the *nihil*, the 'null', 'the negative', or the 'non-existent'.[18] Its existence is paradoxical and its nature is perversion.[19] The fact of Nothingness (that is to say of evil) is revealed through Christ in the sense that its hostility to God is revealed in its hostility to Christ.[20] At the same time Nothingness is under God's control and Christ's incarnation is God's answer to it. Nothingness takes form as real death, real devil, real hell, and the real sin of human beings.[21]

> In Him, i.e., in contradistinction to Him, Nothingness is exposed in its entirety as the adversary which can destroy both body and soul in hell, as the evil one which is also the destructive factor of evil and death that stands in sinister conflict against the creature and its creator, not merely

---

[15] For a fuller exposition see my, *A Theology of the Dark Side* (Carlisle: Paternoster, 2003).

[16] Barth's discussion of this theme can be found in *Church Dogmatics: The Doctrine of Creation* Volume III/3 (Edinburgh: T.&T. Clark, 1961), 289–368, 519–31. A useful summary may be found in John Hick, *Evil and the God of Love* (London: Macmillan, 1966), 132–204.

[17] CD IV/3/1, 178.

[18] CD III/3, 289. N.B. footnote 1.

[19] Barth asserts in a significant 'soundbite', *Das Nichtige ist nicht das Nichts* ('Nothingness is not nothing'), CD III/3, 349.

[20] CD III/3, 302.

[21] CD III/3, 305.

as an idea which man may conceive and to which he can give allegiance but as the power which invades and subjugates and carries him away captive, so that he is wholly and utterly lost in the face of it.[22]

Barth insists that our knowledge of this evil reality is not a matter of speculation but a clear deduction from the self-disclosure of God in Jesus Christ.[23] The term 'Nothingness' can be seen therefore to have value in that it attempts to describe the essence of evil. Evil is that about which nothing positive can be said or thought. It exists in negation and is itself wholly negative. This poses the question, how can such a power exist in a world that God has made? The concept of a premundane angelic fall is rejected scathingly as 'one of the bad dreams of the older dogmatics'.[24] In Barth's reckoning, angels do not and cannot fall. The devil was never an angel but a liar and a murderer from the beginning.[25] Verses in the Bible that point in the direction of an angelic fall are too uncertain and obscure to build upon.[26] Nothingness is an alien factor that can be attributed neither to the positive will and work of God nor to the activity of the creature.[27] Yet neither can it exist independently of the will of God since this would be to deny his Lordship.[28]

We are confronted with a genuine difficulty in understanding. Nothingness is real. It is not nothing and yet it has nothing in common with God or his creatures. It must therefore exist in a third way peculiar to itself. In this sense only, Nothingness 'is'.[29] Here Barth is keen to stress the invalid nature of evil. It has no right to exist as if it were a creature of God or on the same terms. Its existence is not a planned and willed existence as is that of humankind. We are faced with something that is real but has no right to be. Barth resents the equation of angels and demons. He sees the association of the two in much theology as 'primitive and fatal'.[30] He takes great delight in the subject of angels and seeks to restore their 'permanent residence visas' in Christian theology.[31] They are witnesses of God who precede, accompany, surround,

---

[22] CD III/3, 312.
[23] CD IV/3/1, 177.
[24] CD III/3, 531.
[25] CD III/3, 531.
[26] CD III/3, 530 with reference to Isa. 14:12; Gen. 6:1–14; Jude 6; 2 Pet. 2:4.
[27] CD III/3, 292.
[28] CD III/3, 292
[29] CD III/3, 349.
[30] CD III/3, 519.
[31] CD III/3, 416.

and follow the coming kingdom of God.[32] But angels 'slip between our fingers' because they are free from any personal desire for power or lordship. They belong fully to God and in no sense to themselves.[33] Because of this and unlike human beings angels cannot deviate and so cannot become fallen creatures.

In this context Barth turns his attention to the demons, the opponents of the ambassadors of God. He finds this subject distasteful and therefore is only willing to cast them 'a momentary glance'. Because demons thrive on attention and to contemplate them too intensely raises the danger that we too may become a little demonic – a quick, sharp glance is all that is necessary and legitimate.[34] The demons exist in a 'dreadful fifth or sixth dimension of existence' and are constantly active 'like the tentacles of an octopus'.[35] They exist as an army never in repose and always on the march invading and attacking, with falsehood as their manner of being.[36] God and the devil or angels and demons should not even be spoken of in the same breath.[37]

According to Barth, we cannot look for the origin of evil in a supposed fall of angels. Where then is such an origin to be found? Here he is at his most novel. Nothingness, he argues, has its origin in the 'No' of God which is implied by his original, creative 'Yes'. In other words, in saying 'Yes' to the creation and calling it into being, God uttered an implied 'No', a rejection of that which is evil, and this 'No', being also a powerful word of God, has created the realm of Nothingness. Nothingness is that which God rejects, opposes, negates and dismisses in the act of creation.[38] Exegetically, Barth roots his case in the chaos of Genesis 1:2. When it is affirmed here that 'the earth was a formless void and darkness covered the face of the waters', this is the chaos of Nothingness which God despised in his creative work, the lower sphere that God passed by without a halt. It is the sphere of chaos that behind God's back has assumed the self-contradictory character of reality.[39]

What are we to make of these remarkable mental gymnastics? The concept of evil as parasite and as non-being is deeply rooted in

---

[32] CD III/3, 457.
[33] CD III/3, 450.
[34] CD III/3, 579.
[35] CD III/3, 527–28.
[36] CD III/3, 525.
[37] CD III/3, 520.
[38] CD III/3, 351–52.
[39] CD III/1, 108.

Christian thought. Athanasius (c. 293–373) characterised sin as turning towards what does not exist, 'for what does not exist is evil, but what does exist is good since it has been created by the existent God'. Having come from non-existence, human beings surrendered themselves to corruption and death by espousing non-being.[40] Likewise Augustine (354–430) saw evil as *privatio boni*, an absence of goodness rather than a creature in its own right.[41] Barth however must be criticised for his exegesis of Scripture. His use of the chaos in Genesis 1:2 as proof of his theory is a classic *eisgesis* whereby he discovers his own theory of evil in the biblical account of creation.[42] On the face of it Genesis 1:1–2 is a bald suggestion that God made the world in two stages: bringing the chaos into being and then establishing order within it. It is not an explanation of evil.[43] His concept of the origin of Nothingness has more the character of a speculation than an exposition of firm biblical truth.[44] In fairness to him, the exegetical basis of an angelic fall is also problematic, as we have seen.

Barth's concept must also be faulted for its theological inadequacy. If God gives rise to Nothingness by virtue of the No! implied by his creative Yes!, we must ask the question, 'Was it God's will that his No! should have this effect, or was God powerless to prevent it happening?' Barth's concept does not stand up to scrutiny. At the same time he has given the analysis of evil some unusually valuable attention and the concept of Nothingness is well suited to a description of the essence of evil. The realism and yet contempt with which he casts his short, sharp glance at the demonic kingdom should be taken as a model for those who reflect on this subject. There are excellent theological and spiritual instincts at work here.

---

[40] *De Incarnatione*, 4.

[41] 'For evil is not a positive substance: the loss of good has been given the name of "evil".' *City of God*, 11.9; 'There is no such entity in nature as "evil"; "evil" is merely a name for the privation of good.' *City of God*, XI.22.

[42] Hick, *Evil and the God of Love*, 140 n. 2.

[43] Gerhard von Rad, *Genesis* (London: SCM, 1961), 51.

[44] G.C. Berkouwer, *The Triumph of Grace in the Theology of Karl Barth* (Grand Rapids: Eerdmans, 1956), 378.

## Evil and 'interiority'

Walter Wink's writing in this area is such that no future commentator will be able to ignore it.[45] Wink's work deserves a great deal of attention because of the insights that it offers into the nature of evil. He takes the biblical witness concerning the devil, demons, principalities and powers with the utmost seriousness and finds the language of spiritual power pervading the NT.[46] These concepts cannot be reduced to merely psychological or sociological entities, since to do this is to miss completely the spiritual dimension to reality.[47] Yet the mythological language of the Bible needs to be reinterpreted. As far as Wink is concerned the 'Powers' do not have a separate spiritual existence from the earthly reality through which they become manifest. The spiritual powers are to be understood as the 'innermost essence' of earthly realities. To illustrate:

> [A] 'mob spirit' does not hover in the sky waiting to leap down on an unruly crowd at a football match. It is the actual spirit constellated when the crowd reaches a certain critical flashpoint of excitement and frustration. It comes into existence in that moment, causes people to act in ways of which they would not have dreamed themselves capable, and then ceases to exist at the moment the crowd disperses.[48]

This innermost essence Wink proposes to call 'interiority'. It is necessary to explain the realities of human existence. His thesis is that 'the NT's "principalities and powers" is a generic category referring to the determining forces of physical, psychic, and social existence. These powers usually consist of an outer manifestation and an inner spirituality or interiority.'[49] In developing his thinking, Wink then goes on to apply his concept of 'interiority' to the specific features of the NT

---

[45] See his trilogy on The Powers, *Naming the Powers: The Language of Power in the New Testament* (Philadelphia: Fortress Press, 1984); *Unmasking the Powers: The Invisible Forces that Determine Human Existence* (Philadelphia: Fortress Press, 1986); *Engaging the Powers: Discernment and Resistance in a World of Domination* (Philadelphia: Fortress Press, 1992). These works are distilled in *The Powers that Be: Theology for a New Millennium* (New York: Doubleday, 1998).

[46] *Naming the Powers*, 99.

[47] *Naming the Powers*, 103

[48] *Naming the Powers*, 105.

[49] *Naming the Powers*, 105.

witness. Satan, for instance, 'did not begin life as an idea, but in experience'.[50] The context for Satan is that of an actual encounter with something or someone that leads to the positing of his existence. What is this encounter? Wink points here to an ambiguity in the Bible's witness. In the OT Satan especially is described as a servant of God and has the role of an *agent provocateur* or of a public prosecutor. He functions as an adversary, as 'that actual inner or collective voice of condemnation that any sensitive person hears tirelessly repeating accusations of guilt or inferiority'.[51] In sections of the NT Satan is portrayed as 'God's holy sifter' and sometimes as God's 'enforcer', called in to work us over when more gentle methods will not succeed.[52] How then does Satan, the servant of God, become the Evil One, the Enemy of God, the Father of Lies, the Archfiend of Christian theology? *Agents provocateurs* have a tendency to overstep their mandate and Satan appears to have 'evolved from a trustworthy intelligence-gatherer into a virtually autonomous and invisible suzerain within a world ruled by God'.[53] Wink however cannot mean this literally because Satan has no independent existence. Satan's fall, for him, did not take place in time or in the universe in any external sense but in the human psyche.[54] By human rejection of God, Satan has become 'the symbolic repository of the entire complex of evil existing in the present order'.[55] Because Wink defines the powers as interiority he must seek for a shift towards evil in this realm not in some fall of angels but in the interior life of humanity, that is in human sin. Satan is the expression of the corporate interiority of such a fallen race. 'Satan is the spirituality of an epoch, the peculiar constellation of alienation, greed, inhumanity, oppression and entropy that characterises a specific period of history as a consequence of human decisions to tolerate and even further such a state of affairs'.[56]

Wink offers a highly sophisticated analysis of evil which is credible both in terms of human experience and of the NT's concern with the power that opposes God. In particular, he illuminates the way in which evil is actually operative. He therefore moves away from an over-personalised portrayal of evil whereby evil spirits 'hover in the air'

---

[50] *Unmasking the Powers*, 4.
[51] *Unmasking the Powers*, 12: See 2 Sam. 24:1; 1 Chr. 21:1; Zech. 3:1–5.
[52] *Unmasking the Powers*, 12.
[53] *Unmasking the Powers*, 19.
[54] *Unmasking the Powers*, 23. See Matt. 10:25; 13:19; John 12:31; Eph. 2:2; 1 Cor. 10:10; 2 Cor. 4:4; 6:15.
[55] *Unmasking the Powers*, 24.
[56] *Unmasking the Powers*, 25.

without reference to the actual structures within which human beings fulfil their existence. Instead evil manifests itself in the realities of human life and society. More than this, he indicates that evil actually draws its negative strength and energy by preying upon the energy of sin which is to be found in humankind and human society. This is a highly significant insight.[57]

## Evil as God-forsaken space

Building on the Jewish thinker Isaac Luria's concept of the *zimzum*, which means 'concentration' and 'contraction', the German Reformed theologian Jürgen Moltmann advances the idea that since God is omnipotent and fills all things, he must first of all create a *nihil* (think of it as an empty space) within which to create a world outside of himself.[58] To create the space God must withdraw his presence and restrict his power (hence 'contraction') in an act of self-humbling and self-limitation. Creation can then be 'let be' within this space as something other than God but still embraced by God. However for God to withdraw from anywhere leaves that space as a literally God-forsaken space and therefore calls forth a Nothingness which is identified with hell and absolute death, the negation of God.[59] It is demonic. As creation is let-be within this space it exists under a constant threat of nonbeing, but the Nothingness that threatens it also threatens God and as such is a demonic power. By means of self-isolation from the divine being, otherwise known as sin and godlessness, creatures come under the threat of this *nihil*.[60] The humility and self-limitation of God which is displayed in the act of creation is continued in that act of God whereby in Christ God himself enters into creation, taking human destiny upon himself and enduring on the cross the demonic onslaught of the *nihil* in such a way as to overcome it.[61] Finally, as the outcome of this involvement with humankind in its suffering, God's purpose is to 'de-restrict' himself and so to transfigure creation in God's glorifying 'boundlessness'.[62]

---

[57] *Unmasking the Powers*, 21.
[58] *God in Creation: An Ecological Doctrine of Creation* (London: SCM Press, 1985), 86–87.
[59] *God in Creation*, 87.
[60] *God in Creation*, 88.
[61] *God in Creation*, 91.
[62] *God in Creation*, 89.

Moltmann's theology has been described as a 'Christian poetics' that oscillates between poetry and exegesis without sufficient rigour.[63] It is hard to see how biblical exegesis gives rise to this theory. It might well be argued that he is engaging in his own form of myth-making and is concocting, or adapting, a creation myth which introduces an alternative way of thinking about the origin of the world and of the evil that threatens it. It seems to me that Moltmann is 'playing' with ideas, but this is a legitimate thing to do. What his particular version has to commend it is an account of the way in which God's creative work gives rise *of necessity* to the threat to that creation we associate with the demonic. God does not create evil as such but it is a necessary consequence of his creative activity and this illuminates its origin while not directly implicating God in it.

### The origin of evil

In analysing the essence of evil in the previous section we found help from thinkers of the present and recent past. It was also necessary to question some of their perspectives. Now the task is to develop a coherent overall picture. This will involve asking what may be an unanswerable question: where did evil come from? By way of answer, Robert Cook has suggested that there can only be four possibilities within the framework of Christian theology: 'Logically its source must either be a created entity beyond our universe as traditional theology assumes, or in God himself, or in the structures of our created universe, or in the human race.'[64] This is a useful starting point and the options are worth reviewing in a preliminary way.

- Traditional opinion in the history of the church has favoured the idea of an angelic fall or catastrophe.
- A second option locates the origin of evil in some kind of 'dark side' in God. But this opens up fatal difficulties and assimilates evil into the divine existence. We share Cook's opinion that,

---

[63] A. Fierro, *The Militant Gospel: An Analysis of Contemporary Political Theologies* (London: SCM Press, 1977), 171–72.

[64] 'Devils and Manticores: Plundering Jung for a Plausible Demonology' in A.N.S. Lane (ed.), *The Unseen World: Christian Reflections on Angels, Demons and the Heavenly Realm* (Carlisle: Paternoster, 1996), 180.

'Neither a formerly evil God nor a formerly ignorant or immature one is worthy of Christian theology.'[65]

- A third option attributes the origin of evil to a kind of residual 'black noise' left over from creation out of the primordial chaos. This is Cook's preferred option (but only if pressed!).[66] In the biblical story the powers of negation and death at loose in the world are never quite overcome by Yahweh and exist to resist and nullify creation. The chaos makes incursions into creation, occasionally using historical agents to do so.[67]
- The fourth option locates the origin of evil on the level of humankind itself and in the human displacement of God which is called sin. This theme lies at the heart of the biblical story and in itself this suggests it is worth reconsidering.

Tom Noble builds upon Cook's framework. If we exclude the second option listed above, each of the three remaining options offers important insights.[68] But Noble in particular turns his analysis to the neglected fourth option. He draws attention to the fact that in Genesis, a book concerned with origins, the human fall is centre stage.[69] In redemption the Word of God assumes not an angelic nature but a human one, and that human nature itself recapitulates all the lower forms of life out of which it has developed. The incarnation is God's way of going to the heart of the problem, and it is a human one. Sin and death came into the world through the one man 'Adam' and not through an angelic fall.[70] 'Adam' therefore defines the human condition and history until it is redefined in a second Adam, Christ.[71] In the light of the weight given to the human fall Noble advances that supra-human evil be seen as both a projection and consequence of the human fall and not vice versa.[72] This, of course, is a reversal of the order suggested by a fall of angels.

Counting against this construct is the detail that in Genesis 3 the serpent acts as a tempter and therefore precedes human beings. However,

---

[65] 'Devils and Manticores', 181.
[66] 'Devils and Manticores', 182.
[67] Walter Brueggemann, *Theology of the Old Testament: Testimony, Dispute, Advocacy* (Minneapolis: Fortress Press, 1997), 528–49.
[68] 'The Spirit World: A Theological Approach', in A.N.S. Lane (ed.), *The Unseen World*, 220.
[69] 'The Spirit World', 205.
[70] Rom. 5:12–14.
[71] Rom. 5:15–21.
[72] 'The Spirit World', 215

Genesis itself does not identify the serpent as the devil, only as a wild animal. Is it possible that this could represent something else? We are helped here by Cook's third option concerning the structure of creation. God creates a chaos and then from the chaos establishes an ordered world. Yet the creation is pressured, according to Cook, by 'the urge back into formless, lifeless, meaningless chaos'.[73] This accords with the Hebrew tendency to see in the chaos of the sea the remnants of the still threatening primeval chaos and to depict this as a sea-serpent or a dragon.[74] In the light of this is not the symbol of the serpent in Genesis 3 significant in referring back to the threatening chaos? Humankind is born into a testing environment where the collapse back into chaos is a threat to the whole creation. This threat precedes humanity. Cook is inclined to see the chaos as itself evil, presumably precisely because it is chaotic. By distinct contrast my own inclination is to see it as the *occasion for evil rather than as evil in itself*. Of itself it is a stage in God's creative work.[75]

To develop this I draw attention to Reinhold Niebuhr's compelling analysis of temptation and sin. For Niebuhr the 'internal precondition' of sin is anxiety. Human beings come into the world as finite creatures who are capable of thoughts of infinity. This creates a state of anxiety as they are caught between finiteness and freedom. They fear the abyss of meaninglessness. This situation is not of itself evil because anxiety can be resolved through trust in God. Fearing insecurity however, and

---

[73] 'Devils and Manticores', 181.

[74] Job 26:12–13; Ps. 74:12–14; Isa. 27:1. See also Rev. 12:9.

[75] At this point my views appear to coincide with those of Paul Fiddes: '(T)his humility of God [in self-limitation] allows something strange and alien to emerge from God's own creation. There is something that God has not planned, something to be confronted, something therefore to be suffered. Since the thought of the early church fathers – Athanasius in the East and Augustine in the West – evil has been named "non-being". This is to assert that it has no real existence of its own. It is not an eternal reality alongside God who is Very Being, but is simply a turning away from the Good; it is a free turning from Something (God) to Nothing. Like the darkness which comes when the light is turned out, it is what happens when God's creation slips away from the divine aims. To call evil "non-being" or "the nothingness" (*nihil*) does not therefore deny that it is powerful, or pretend that it is some kind of illusion. It simply has no power of its own: it is a parasite, drawing its vitality from the life-giving trunk of a tree. Evil always perverts what is good, and twists what is full of life into what is destructive.' *Participating in God: A Pastoral Doctrine of the Trinity* (London: DLT, 2000), 166.

interpreting their situation falsely, human beings adopt another strategy. They find security in pride, in self-exaltation maintained by holding power over others. Alternatively they escape their insecurity though immersing themselves in sensuality. Sin comes into being therefore as a false response to the threat to their own security perceived in their finite existence.[76] The serpent represents this anxiety interpreted not as an occasion for trust in God but for the displacement of God. It is a temptation and a testing and perhaps for this reason merits the retrojective interpretation in Revelation 12:9 of the serpent in the Garden as 'that ancient serpent, who is called the Devil and Satan', although this reference could equally (or also) be to the image of the chaos as a sea-serpent. In this analysis it might also be possible to see the transition of the idea of Satan from 'holy sifter' to that of 'unholy adversary'.

*A crucial divergence of interpretation emerges at this point between seeing the devil as an ontological reality over and beyond humankind, preceding humanity in a fall, or as a construct or projection to emerge as a consequence of the human fall.* In exploring the second alternative Noble shows sympathy for Robert Cook's inclination 'to view Satan as the mythic personification of human society arising out of collective human evil, the supreme archetype from the collective unconscious of the wickedness of humanity'.[77] This corresponds with Wink's proposal.[78] In this way we can address the question of the ontological status of the devil. The devil has no ontology, but does have an ontological ground or a point at which he might emerge in the existence of humankind. He is the construct, albeit a real one, of fallen society. Without a created ontology he is nonetheless real, but in the same way that a vacuum or a black hole is real. A vacuum is intensely powerful even though it consists of sheer emptiness. A black hole is a collapsed star unobservable apart from its impact upon other stars and its capacity to suck matter into itself. Noble comments:

> (T)his speculation about supra-human evil is deficient if it understands Satan as merely a mythical projection or personification. Rather, we would have to conceive of a real and objective supreme power of evil

---

[76] Reinhold Niebuhr, *The Nature and Destiny of Man: Volume I, Human Nature* (New York: Charles Scribner's Sons, 1964), 178–244.

[77] 'The Spirit World', 214 citing Cook, 'Devils and Manticores', 182.

[78] *Unmasking the Powers*, 24–25.

which draws its reality and strength from the perverted corporate unconscious of humanity.[79]

To follow Barth, the devil is one of a number of ways in which Nothingness takes form. Satan language therefore is a 'mythic' personification of collective human evil *but it is the language alone that is mythic, not the reality.* Noble finds significant biblical support here in Paul's discussion of pagan gods in 1 Corinthians 8 and 10. They have no real existence (8:4) but there are many gods and many lords (8:5) in the sense that people believe in them and this investment of belief gives them a paradoxical but powerful reality.[80]

How does this approach impinge upon the discussion of a 'personal' devil? I have previously pointed to the difficulty of applying personal language to the devil. The issue recurs in thinking about redemption. If we are to believe that God's 'compassion is over all that he has made';[81] that in Christ 'all things in heaven and on earth were made, things visible and invisible' and that 'through him God was pleased to reconcile to himself all things, whether on earth or in heaven,'[82] must we not further conclude that it is at least possible for the devil to be redeemed if his existence is that of a rebellious creature? This exact conclusion was tentatively drawn first of all by Origen (c.185–c.254). Although the devil's purposes and hostile will would perish, his substance, which is God's creation, would be saved since there is nothing that cannot be healed by its creator.[83] Yet there is no suggestion in Scripture that the devil has such a future, in fact quite the reverse.[84] It could of course be objected this does not mean that the devil is beyond the possibility of salvation, simply that the possibility is not realized in his case, as Scripture foresees. But this issue is more adequately resolved if we follow Noble's construct since according to it there is no 'substance', no created ontology to be saved. If Satan exists as a

---

[79] 'The Spirit World', 215.

[80] 'The Spirit World', 216.

[81] Ps. 145:8.

[82] Col. 1:16, 20.

[83] Origen, *De Principiis*, III.vi.5: 'For the destruction of the last enemy must be understood in this way, not that its substance which was made by God shall perish, but that the hostile purpose and will which proceeded not from God but from itself will come to an end. It will be destroyed, therefore, not in the sense of ceasing to exist, but of being no longer an enemy and no longer death.'

[84] Rev. 20:10.

projection of the corporate spirit of fallen humanity and cannot exist apart from this, the day of redemption will spell the end of the devil and the demonic.

This need not however preclude the possibility of thinking of the devil as 'a malevolent intelligence, willing, acting, and knowing, but totally lacking in personal feeling or sympathy, and obsessed with self-aggrandisement'.[85] The devil, although a projection from fallen humanity, possesses a way of being, agency, even if this way of being is,

> inherently deception, falseness, delusion, vanity, emptiness and pre-tence. It appears to be what it is not. And this is not just what it does: it is what it is. Since it is inherently deceptive, and indeed self-deceptive, it is consequently quite impossible to give a structured, meaningful account of it. It is the surd element in creation. It cannot be analysed or accounted for in structured discourse, for it is the very opposite, the enemy and denial of the Logos of God. It can only be referred to by image and myth.[86]

Noble draws attention in the course of his discussion to the influential definition of the philosopher Boethius (c.480–c.524) of personhood as 'the individual substance of rational nature' and argues that while this falls woefully short of a trinitarian understanding of personhood, it is a minimalist definition that the devil might be able to fulfil in so far as he is 'an agent able to think, to know, to will and to act'.[87] Robert Jenson makes a similar point. Paraphrasing Boethius' definition as 'an individual entity endowed with intellect', he sees Satan fulfilling this minimalist definition: 'It is his ontological particularity to satisfy Boethius' definition and nevertheless lack personhood. There is doubtless some connection between the problem of demonology and the much-debated problem of machine intelligence – as much popular literature perceives'.[88]

This is no complete solution but it may offer a direction along which a solution might lie. There are difficulties with this perspective, but so there are with the more ontological alternatives, as I have sought to indicate. I am aware that it attracts the criticism of having one's cake

---

[85] 'The Spirit World', 217.
[86] 'The Spirit World', 219.
[87] 'The Spirit World', 217.
[88] R.W. Jenson, *Systematic Theology: Volume 1 The Triune God* (Oxford: Oxford University Press, 1997), 117 n.6.

and eating it. But since theology is the attempt to give a coherent account of diverse concerns, of holding together ideas that are in tension, this is not a fatal blow to it. Death itself, which is closely associated with the devil in the NT, is an example of a non-ontological reality which counts as a power in its own right and can even be personified, along with sin.[89] The devil possesses a much reduced and essentially malevolent way of being which to dignify as personhood would be vastly to overrate. The devil is not an individual being but a power, a dynamic which takes on the character of agency and intelligence and chaotically wars against God. It issues out of collective human resistance to God and holds in thrall the very beings on which it parasitically draws. It is immensely powerful but is at the same time a power that is negated and overcome in Jesus Christ.

## Engaging evil

What bearing might this analysis have on the actual practice of deliverance and exorcism? A non-ontological view does not deny that evil is able to take form in infesting and distorting people's lives. It sees it as a negative power not to be underestimated, just as death is such a power, even though there is no ontological substance to death. Death is the absence of life, not something in itself. For this reason this position is well described as non-ontological *realism*. To remove evil influences from people or places does not, of course, require that we first of all understand the full nature of those influences. But it will take greater account of those earthly, human and corporate media by means of which it does take form. Evil takes form as influences that afflict human beings in their spiritual vulnerability. Exorcism and deliverance are one remedy that can be applied to some of those forms. This is most particularly the case when they prove to have a dominating and intractable hold on people, depriving them of proper freedom.

All the ways in which human life is afflicted and wretched are in some sense the product of evil. But without trespassing too far into the realm of the psychiatrist, it may be possible to see in some cases of multiple personality disorder more obvious distortions of the evil one. And the phenomena of demonization can in part be understood as the manifestation of evil through unruly aspects of a person's personality that become split off from their conscious selves. In addition, far more needs

---

[89] Rom. 7:14–25; 8:37–39; 1 Cor. 15:55; Rev. 20:14.

to be understood about the ways in which groups or movements function at the unconscious or psychic levels and retain the ability to project negative energies into those they victimise. Non-ontological realism will apply to the healing of the human condition the full range of spiritual therapies. It will regard the healing work of Christ being realised in the church through word, sacrament, fellowship, and prayer as the primary way in which lives are recovered from the dominion of darkness. Within this framework deliverance has an occasional place in overcoming evil influences that prove to be persistent. None of the manifestations of evil in the gospels, against which Jesus laboured in the Spirit, need be called into question on a non-ontological view, and the means Jesus used to drive them out are the same means available to us in his name. Barth understood that evil can take form as what he described as 'hypostases of nothingness'. He was also strongly influenced, as were some other prominent theologians, by Johann Christoph Blumhardt and his son Christoph Friedrich and the account of the liberation of Gottliebin Dittus from demonic bondage that received widespread attention in the nineteenth century.[90] A non-ontological view need not lead to a narrow reductionism, since it is resolute in affirming that there is a spiritual dimension to reality, but it does seek to avoid an equally narrow naivety.

It is good practice when presented with apparent demonization to use all the resources of the cure of souls to bring peace to an afflicted person. But when faced with a clearly resistant power, expulsion in the name of Jesus in pastorally and ethically responsible surroundings is the appropriate response, and need not necessarily differ significantly from a more ontological approach. But non-ontological realism calls for more critical distance in the process and an unwillingness to draw too firm conclusions about what has been expelled. Certainly it is resistant to the constructing of demonic systems and kingdoms that have been an unfortunate feature of some modern demonology.[91] We return to the assertion that what is under discussion in this chapter is not the fact of evil, as though it could be taken less seriously, but its ultimate nature, what it finally is. And what it finally is, is Godless emptiness.

---

[90] See J.C. Blumhardt's account in F.S. Boshold, tr., *Blumhardt's Battle: A Conflict with Satan* (New York: Thomas E. Lowe Publishers, 1970). This event led to a renewal movement centred on Bad Boll, Germany.

[91] At this point I have in mind books like Bill Subritsky, *Demons Defeated* (Chichester: Sovereign World, 1986); Frank and Ida Mae Hammond, *Pigs in the Parlor* (Kirkwood: Impact, 1973) and Peter Horrobin, *Healing through Deliverance: The Biblical Basis* (Chichester: Sovereign World, 1991) and *Healing through Deliverance: The Practical Ministry* (Tonbridge: Sovereign World, 1995). See ch. 4.

Chapter 11

# Deliverance and Exorcism in Theological Perspective 2: Possession and Exorcism as New Testament Evidence for a Theology of Christ's Supremacy

*Kabiro Wa Gatumu*

**Abstract**

This chapter explores the New Testament teaching on demon/spirit possession and exorcism to assess whether those teachings may apply to modern
times. It is an attempt to outline a theology of demon/spirit possession and
exorcism relevant in the twenty-first century. Taking into account the theme of
Christ's triumph over the spiritual powers, the chapter concludes that emphasis on a theology of Christ's supremacy over spirits is the most germane way
of dealing with the same in the modern world.

## Introduction

Several monographs and journal articles on demon/spirit possession
and exorcism in the New Testament have been published in recent
years.[1] This indicates the growing interest that the subject of the

---

[1] Graham H. Twelftree, *In the Name of Jesus: Exorcism Among Early Christians*
(Grand Rapids, Michigan: Baker Academic, 2007); Todd E. Klutz, *The Exor-
cism Stories in Luke–Acts: A Sociostylistic Reading* (Cambridge: Cambridge
University Press, 2004); Clinton Wahlen, *Jesus and the Impurity of Spirits in
the Synoptic Gospel* (Tübingen: Mohr Siebeck, 2004); Peter G. Bolt, *Jesus'
Defeat of Death: Persuading Mark's Early Readers* (Cambridge/New York:
Cambridge University Press, 2003); Eric Eve, *The Jewish Context of Jesus'*

demonic is spawning. However, a problem encircles it: a controversy about the existence of evil spirits that can inhabit, control, and damage the health of a person. Suffice to say that the problems that modern scholars may have regarding demon/spirit possession and exorcism do not belong to the New Testament era. It is a problem for modern scholars who tend to anachronistically impose modern categories upon the New Testament.[2] There is also a trend to psychologise the New Testament view of demon/spirit possession and exorcism, referring to the phenomena as a problem of 'crowd psychology' and hence to place it 'off limits'.[3] However, as Twelftree notes, this 'is to miss what was, for most people, including early Christians, a significant aspect of their *Weltanschauung*'.[4] It is vital that we approach the study of demon/spirit possession and exorcism in the New Testament within the terms provided by its cultural milieu. This chapter seeks to do precisely that and then moves on to ask how this New Testamanet theology might be relevant today.

## The New Testament background to demon/spirit possession and exorcism

The New Testament cannot be detached from its historical, social, and cultural background. There can be no question that ancient Jewish beliefs about evil spirits influenced early Christianity. This section, therefore, briefly probes the Hebrew Bible and the literature of the Intertestamental period as the background for understanding possession and exorcism in the New Testament.

### The Hebrew Bible

There is no clear record of demon/spirit possession or exorcism in the Hebrew Bible though the reality and existence of demons is recognized

---

(cont.) *Miracles* (London/New York: Sheffield Academic Press, 2002); Eric Sorensen, *Possession and Exorcism in the New Testament and Early Christianity* (Tübingen: Mohr Siebeck, 2002); Ronald A. Piper 'Jesus and the Conflict of Powers in Q: Two Q Miracle Stories' in A. Lindermann (ed.) *The Saying Source Q and the Historical Jesus* (Lovain: Leuven University Press).

[2] See Walter Wink, *Naming the Powers: The Language of Power in the New Testament* (Philadelphia: Fortress Press, 1984), 4.

[3] See Peter Brown, *The Cult of the Saints: It Rise and Function in Latin Christianity* (London: SCM, 1982), 107–8.

[4] Twelftree, *In the Name of Jesus*, 26.

(see chapter 1). One possible instance of possession is the case of Saul (1 Sam. 16:14–16, 23; 18:10; 19:9). However, there are reasons for not accepting this as a genuine case of demon/spirit *possession*. Saul seems to have been sporadically under the influence of an evil spirit, but he was never *possessed* as the evil spirit came but also *went* after the playing of soothing and relaxing music. There is also the mention of evil spirits that oppressed Abimelech (Judg. 9:23). However, demons are only alluded to three times apart from the generic term 'evil spirits'. The Hebrew equivalent for demon is *shēd* and in the two texts it is used, their role is to promote idolatry and false religion (Deut. 32:16–17; Ps. 106:36–37). A second Hebrew term for demon (*sāʿir*) is used to refer to the goat demons worshipped by the pagan Gentiles surrounding Israel (Lev. 17:7). There can be no doubt that the interaction of the Jewish people with their ancient Near Eastern neighbours influenced their beliefs concerning demons. Even when the Jews were forbidden to sacrifice to the goat demons, some went ahead to do so and stirred Yahweh to jealousy when they sacrificed their children to them (Deut. 32:16–17; Ps. 106:37–38). However, whilst there are no clear-cut cases of full-blown demon *possession* in Old Testament literature, we can recognize the roots of later demonology and possession beliefs. And, of course, the lack of a straightforward demonology in the Old Testament does not mean that the Jewish people had no dealing with demons.[5]

### Jewish intertestamental literature

The Jewish literature during the intertestamental period has very elaborate indications that the Jews believed in demonic spirits which could possess and lead people astray. *The Martyrdom and Ascension of Isaiah* represents Beliar as the independent agent who influenced King Manasseh of Jerusalem to lead the Jewish nation to a reign of terror and evil.

> And Manasseh abandoned the service of the Lord of his father, and he served Satan and his angels, and his powers. And he turned his father's house, which had been in the presence of Hezekiah, away from the words of wisdom and the service of the Lord. Manasseh turned them away so that they served Beliar; for the angel of iniquity who rules this

---

[5] See a discussion on the Jewish belief as to evil spirits and demons in Kabiro Wa Gatumu, *The Pauline Concept of Supernatural Powers: A Reading from the African Worldview* (Milton Keynes: Paternoster, 2008), 97–100.

world is Beliar, whose name is Matanbukus. And he rejoiced over Jerusalem because of Manasseh, and he strengthened him in causing apostasy, and the iniquity that was disseminated in Jerusalem . . . Sorcery and magic, augury and divination, fornication and adultery, and the persecution of the righteous increased.[6]

This, of course, is a case of demonic *influence* rather than possession. Even so, the Jewish literature of the time provides evidence for elaborate views regarding demon-possession and exorcism some of which are reflected in the New Testament documents. As Eric Sorensen observes,

> Demonology and the practice of exorcism become more pronounced in content as well as in semantics in other Jewish intertestamental literature. Some of the documents among the Old Testament Pseudepigrapha and the scrolls from the Judean desert, especially in their testament and apocalypses, provide closer-to-contemporary and contemporary views of possession and exorcism as they occur in the New Testament, and serve as indicators that Near Eastern belief and practices had moved into some Palestinian environments from which the synoptic sources and other New Testament writings were to emerge[7]

The Jewish belief in demons during this period is clear in several texts, which are devoted to the origin of demons.[8] During this time the Jews believed in a complex world that had varied orders of demons that caused evil and misery as well as teaching unrighteousness.[9] They not only embodied resentment towards God but also caused physical suffering, sickness, and death.[10] Even so, the Jews held that when the demons caused problems to human existence, it was not because God had lost control of the world. Indeed, it was God who had allowed the

---

[6] *The Martyrdom and Ascension of Isaiah* 2:2–5.

[7] Sorensen, *Possession and Exorcism in the New Testament*, 59.

[8] See 1 En. 69:12; 3 Bar. 16:3: LAE 16:5; 17:4; 21:13; 39:1–3. It has been noted that some Jewish people identified demons with the progeny of the union between the 'sons of God' (held to be the fallen angels) and 'daughters of men' recorded in Genesis 6:1–4 (See 1 En. 11:15–16:1, Jub. 10:5. Also see Wa Gatumu *The Pauline Concept of Supernatural Powers*, 98).

[9] See 4Q 510 1:5; 4Q511 10:1–2; 11Q11 2:3–4; 1 En. 6:1–10:22; 11QT 26:3–13 (Cf. Lev. 16:7–10).

[10] See Josephus, *Antiquities* 8:46–47; *Assumption of Moses*; Geza Vermes, *Jesus the Jew* (New York: Macmillan, 1973), 61.

demons to have their way so that he can use them to punish his way-
ward people (even though he despised the darkness that the demons
epitomised). Since God alone had the power to remove demons, their
activity would go on unchallenged until the time of judgment. This
indicates that the Jews during this period held that it is only God who
could remove demons from the face of the earth.[11]

The evidence of exorcism is equally preserved in other Jewish texts
of this era.[12] For instance, in the Dead Sea Scrolls it is clear that the
Qumran community defended itself with a spiritual action consisting
of prayers and incantations to exorcise demons.[13] Philip Alexander
argues that 4Q510 and 4Q511 present a special liturgy recited by the
Maskil as the spiritual mentor and guardian of the community to keep
the demons at bay.[14] There is also a somewhat magical approach to
exorcism in the apocryphal book of Tobit. An angel gives instructions
to Tobias on how to drive away all kinds of devils by burning incense
made from the heart, gall and liver of a fish (Tob 6:7–8; 8:2–3). The texts
indicate that the Jews believed in demons and their evil activities – in
this case causing infertility (although it is not clear that we are dealing
with a case of demon *possession* in Tobit).

Some texts in the works of Josephus and in the Greek Magical Papyri
also provide some background from which we may grasp exorcism in
the New Testament. Josephus cites an incident concerning Solomon
and exorcism purported to belong to the Old Testament era. This incident provides some insights as to the Jewish belief in demon/spirit
possession. Josephus writes, 'God also enabled him to learn that skill
which expels demons, which is a science useful and sanative to men'.
He also notes that Solomon 'composed such incantations also by which
distempers are alleviated. And he left behind him a manner of using
exorcisms, by which they drive away demons so that they never
return'.[15] He writes about Eleazer who, although not called an exorcist,

---

[11] 1QS 3:15-26; 1Qap Gen^ar 20:8–32. See also 4Q213^a Levi.; Jub. 10:6–8; 1 En.
15:11–16:1. See also Wa Gatumu *The Pauline Concept of Supernatural Powers*, 99.

[12] See Apoc. Ab 14:5-8; Jub. 10:1–4.

[13] See 4Q370 1:3; 4Q381. Frags. 76–77:2; 4Q510 4–8; 1QS 3:17–21; 11QS
19:15–16; 11Q13.2.13, 25 (on possession) and 1Q20 28–29; 1QH^a 4:23; 13:28;
15:28–29; 11QS 27:9–10; CD–A 13:10 (on exorcism).

[14] Philip S. Alexander, 'Incarnations and Books of Magic' in E. Schürer, *The
History of the Jewish People in the Age of Jesus Christ* (Edinburgh: T&T Clark,
1987) 318–37, esp. 321.

[15] Josephus *Ant.* 8:45 (cited from William Whiston (tr.) *The Works of Josephus*
(Peabody, MA: Hendrickson Publishers, 1987)), 214.

exorcised a demon by putting 'a ring . . . to the nostrils of the demoniac, after which he drew out the demon through his nostrils; and when the man fell down immediately, he adjured him to return into him no more, making still mention of Solomon, and reciting the incantations which he composed.'[16] This text purports to be a case of actual demon-possession and exorcism. According to Josephus, this exorcism relied on tradition and methods which included adjuring the demon not to come back to the victim, mentioning the name of Solomon, and reciting the incantations. The Greek Magical Papyri (PGM) also offers a possible milieu for understanding exorcism in the New Testament.[17] In PGM V 1227–1264 exorcism is a power-encounter wherein the demon is expected to come out from its victim, having been driven away by the power of a god. So exorcists never acted on their own power; rather, it was the external power-authority they called upon that was seen to make the exorcism efficacious.[18]

So it appears that the early Christians inhabited a 'world' wherein belief in demons, possession, and exorcism were part of the fabric of reality. It is therefore crucial to look at the issue of spirit possession and exorcism in the New Testament against this background.

> Whatever the modern explanation might be and however much psychological or social factors might be involved, it must be stressed that Jesus and his contemporaries (along with people in most cultures) thought that people could be possessed or inhabited by a spirit or spirits from another plane. Their worldview took for granted the actual existence of such powers.[19]

### Demon/spirit possession and exorcism in the New Testament

The controversy regarding the reality of demon/spirit possession and exorcism does not belong to the New Testament era. It was not hard for

---

[16] Josephus *Ant.* 8:47 (cited from William, *The Works*, 214).

[17] See for instance PGM IV and V.

[18] This is very clear from PGM IV 11231–39, which reads 'Hail, God of Abraham; hail, God of Isaac; hail, God of Jacob; Jesus Chrestos, the Holy Spirit, the Son and the Father, who is above the Seven, who is within the Seven. Bring Iao Sabaoth; may your power issue forth from NN, until you drive away this unclean demon Satan, who is in him.'

[19] Borg, *Marcus Jesus: A New Vision* (San Francisco: Happer & Row, 1987), 63–67.

Jesus, his disciples, and other people to accept a diagnosis of demon/spirit possession (Matt. 10:1–5; 15:21–28; 17:14–21; Luke 10:17–20). Many people had the ability to recognize that the victims possessed by demon/spirits were non-functional people who were incapable of living ordinary lives (see Matt. 8:28; 17:14–15; Mark 5:1–5). It is also clear that those possessed by unclean spirits never sought healing for themselves but were brought by others who may have recognized that they were demon/spirit possessed (see Matt. 12:22; Luke 4:40–41). The possessing demon/spirits could also recognize the authority of Jesus – the supremacy of his name – and could discern the followers of Jesus (Matt. 8:29; Luke 4:33–34; cf. Acts 19:15). The gospels present the ministry of Jesus as a time of intense demonic activity.

The Holman Bible Dictionary states, 'The Jews of Jesus' time superstitiously believed that demons were lurking at every corner. They thought they could find them in rivers, seas, and on mountaintops. Demons were blamed for toothaches, headaches, broken bones, and outbursts of jealousy and anger.' However, calling the Jews' beliefs in demons 'superstitious' is, from a New Testament perspective, too simplistic.[20] On the one hand, we can say that New Testament teaching on demons and exorcism is far more restrained than that of certain other Second Temple Jewish texts. It is clear that in the New Testament exorcism does not belong to the realm of magic, though magical exorcism existed (as noted above). The sons of Sceva seem to have held the idea that the name of Jesus was another magical recital formula that could cast out demons.[21] The incident turned out to be direct rebuke to, and a denigration of magic. It is instantly recognizable that those who had trusted in magic were now convinced of its futility and so they burnt their magical books. The New Testament considers exorcism not as a matter of magic but of power-encounter and it is performed by a command and authority (Matt 17:18; Mark 3:23–27; Luke 4:35–36).[22] This is the power and authority, which is held directly by Christ or the power and authority of Jesus name, which Christ's authorized agents are empowered to use and exorcise

---

[20] Hans-Josef Klauck, *Magic and Paganism in Early Christianity: The World of the Acts of the Apostle* (Edinburgh: T&T Clark, 2000), 81; Hans-Josef Klauck, 'Religion without Fear: Plutarch, on Superstitions and Early Christian Literature' in *Skrif en Kerk* (1997), 111–26. See also Cicero *De Natura Deorum* 2:72.

[21] See Acts 19:13–20.

[22] See also Matt. 10:1 and Luke 10:17 where the disciples mandate to exorcise demons was an exercise based on power in Jesus' name.

demonic spirits. Conversely, the problem is that writing off the existence of spirits, with the Holman Bible Dictionary, as 'superstitious' is to dismiss what the synoptic gospels proclaim as the reality of wide-ranging demonic activity. They present many cases of demon possession overcome by Christ as an indication of his supremacy over them.

It is clear that the exorcisms of Jesus were understood as a direct attack on Satan and his demons. They were not only a reversal of satanic activity but also, and more importantly, a display of the arrival of the Kingdom of God. No wonder that the frequency of demon/spirit possession reached its peak during the time of Jesus' ministry on earth. Accounts of exorcism during the period covered by the Acts of the Apostles are less frequent than in Jesus' ministry and they do not feature in the epistles. Although less frequent, it should not be concluded that there are no cases of demonic possession or activity mentioned in the Acts and in the epistles. There is evidence of exorcism in Acts, for instance the episode of the sons of Sceva noted above and the story of Paul casting out a demon/spirit from a fortune-teller (Acts 16:16–18). There is also evidence of other forms of demonic activity. For instance, Paul warns the Corinthian Christians that they must not eat at the pagan altar since they cannot have fellowship both with God *and demons* (1 Cor. 10:21–22).[23] Paul also reminds the Galatians Christians that when they formerly did not know God, they were oppressed by beings that by nature were no gods. But since now they know God, or are known by God, they should not turn to the weak and beggarly elemental spirits, whose slaves they once were (Gal. 4:8–9). Paul and his partners also wanted to visit the Thessalonian Christians but Satan hindered them (1 Thess. 2:18). In his language of 'principalities and powers', Paul knew of spiritual beings which could influence people and the structures of human existence (including the social and political). Paul also links the destruction of evil powers with the coming of the Kingdom of God; although the destruction comes at the end of the time (1 Cor. 15:24–25). In the epistles, the focus has moved from demons *possessing* people to demons *oppressing* them, as the case in Gal. 4:8–9. Does this suggest that demonic activity shifted its focus from possession during the time of Jesus to other forms of tyranny afterwards? Could this point us to the idea that in the modern era demons may have changed tactics?

---

[23] Paul clearly sees pagan gods as, in reality, demons.

## The relevance of New Testament possession and exorcism for today

Some modern people, including Christians, would deny that demons exist and that possession is real.[24] They argue that demons are simply a way in which pre-modern people tried to explain various phenomena that we now know to have psychological causes.[25] The implication of this view is that New Testament authors and Jesus were mistaken in believing that demons exist. But we should hesitate before relegating belief in demons to pre-scientific societies. Possession and exorcism take place today not only in nations whose mind-set is shaped by primal religion and worldview but also in the most scientific and technologically advanced nations.[26]

Merrill Unger outlines three strategies, which are not mutually exclusive, used to oppose the idea that demon possession is a reality. He refers to them as the mythical, the accommodation, and the hallucination theories.

- The basic idea of the mythic theory is that the narratives concerning Jesus' expulsions of demons are merely symbolic and not to be taken literally. The theory says that the so-called demonic possession is but a vivid symbol of the presence of evil in the world and Jesus' expulsion of demons is the corresponding figure of triumph over evil through his life and teaching.
- The proponents of the accommodation theory, which might be seen as a subset of the mythic approach, suppose that when Jesus spoke of demon possession he just accommodated the prevalent

---

[24] See Joe Beam, *Seeing the Unseen: Preparing Yourself for Spiritual Warfare* (West Monroe, Louisiana: Howard Publishing, 2002), 110.

[25] See Tod K. Vogt 'Jesus and the Demons in the Gospel of Mark: Contrasting Secular and Animistic Interpretations', *Journal of Applied Missiology*, 7.2 (http://www.ovc.edu/missions/jam/markdmon.htm accessed on February 11th 2009).

[26] See Joel Frank, *Exorcism in Scripture and Today* (Nebraska: Southern Conference, 1973) in http://www2.mlc-wels.edu/schone/Frank-Exorcism.pdf. Accessed on February 4th 2009; Arthur Koepsell 'Exorcism in the Bible and Today' (Metro North: Pastoral Conference, 1974) in http://www.scribd.com/doc/3083524/KoepsellExorcism. Accessed on February 7th 2009; Edgar Lee 'Power over Demons' in *Pentecostal Evangel* (February 4th 1990) also available http://www.agts.edu/faculty/faculty_publications/articles/lee_demons.pdf. Accessed on February 7th 2009.

ignorance and superstitions of his audience without thereby affirming the literal truth of contemporary beliefs. Perhaps, they suggest, God chose to communicate his word through the mythology of the people to whom he was speaking and that for God-in-Christ to have explained possession in a more scientific way would have been fruitless in that ancient context. We have no reason at all to think that Jesus of Nazareth did not believe in literal demons, so presumably we must suppose that it was the divine Logos who accommodated to human myths and the human mind of Christ was unaware of this accommodation.

- The sponsors of the hallucination theory infer that demon possession is a mere psychological delusion of the victim who, diseased and distraught, becomes twisted to such high pitch of emotional fury or mental thrill that he imagines himself possessed or controlled by a more powerful being. The corresponding 'cure' for this strange illusion is understood to be the ejection from him of a demon.[27]

It was just such unease with a belief in literal spirits led some scholars to understand demonic phenomena as part of a now-obsolete mythology which has to be demythologised.[28] This view is found most famously in the work of Rudolph Bultmann. Bultmann rejected belief in evil spirits because he saw it as an element of a mythic worldview. For Bultmann 'myth' implied a primitive and pre-scientific way of interpreting the world. Modern scientific and technological advancement makes belief in spirits, whether good or evil, unbelievable.[29] He thus held that such beliefs must be demythologised and interpreted not cosmologically but rather anthropologically, or existentially.[30] He strongly resisted attaching the message of the Bible and of the church to what he saw as an obsolete worldview[31] since this was to accept 'a view of the world in our faith and religion which we should deny in our every day life'.[32] In Bultmann's view myths pictured spiritual

---

[27] Merrill F. Unger, *Biblical Demonology* (Wheaton, Illinois: Scripture Press Publication, 1953), 90–92.

[28] See a detailed discussion with regard to demythologisation and myth in Wa Gatumu, *The Pauline Concept of Supernatural Powers*, 168–208.

[29] Rudolf Bultmann, 'New Testament and Mythology' in H.W. Bartsch (ed.), *Kerygma and Myth*, vol.1 (London: SPCK, 1964), 5, 10.

[30] Bultmann, 'New Testament and Mythology', 10–11.

[31] Bultmann, *Jesus Christ and Mythology* (New York: Charles Scribner's Sons, 1958), 35–36.

[32] Bultmann, 'New Testament and Mythology', 10.

beings as intervening in the affairs of the world and of human existence. Myths are pre-scientific and, as such, no longer plausible for 'modern man'. Literally speaking they are false.

One problem with Bultmann is that he uses the word 'myth' to cover not simply talk of angels and demons but also talk of God. According to Bultmann, myth is just a way to express the otherworldly in terms of this world, and the divine in terms of human life. He ends up suggesting that speaking about *divine* action in the world is mythological and thus not literally believable today. Most Christians would feel very unhappy with that proposal.

It is vital to note that one problem with talk of 'myth' is that of definition. The word is used in some very different ways and can create more confusion than illumination. There can be different levels at which something may be seen as a 'myth' and Bultmann's understanding of it is arguably too narrow. The main failure of Bultmann's demythologization is that it works on one level of understanding myth, without realising that myth can move on several levels of definition.[33]

It may be less confusing if we move away from the question of myth to focus on the issue of metaphor. Now myth and metaphor are clearly different categories and we must acknowledge that the relationship between them is not uncontroversial. What Bultmann regards as mythical language is certainly metaphorical but shifting the focus towards regarding at it as metaphor allows us to set aside Bultmann's questionable assumptions about the impossibility of believing in demons today.[34] Metaphors are referential – they point to a reality beyond themselves – and so a focus on language about demons as metaphorical has some advantage over myth in the description and understanding of possession and exorcism.

Whilst the category of 'metaphor' has more potential than 'myth' as a way to take the discussion forward we must acknowledge that the definition and interpretation of metaphor, like myth, is disputed.

---

[33] See a detailed discussion on myth, its different level of definition, its indispensability and its problem with regard to the New Testament in Wa Gatumu *The Pauline Concept of Supernatural Powers*, 165–78. Bultmann sought to make the gospel relevant to his 'modern man'. The problem is that his 'modern man' is not universally representative. As Fee notes, the 'modern man' who cannot believe in such realities, is the true 'myth' and not the gospel that Bultmann set out to 'demythologise' (Fee, *The First Epistle to the Corinthians*, 472).

[34] See Dunn, 'Demythologizing', 297.

Nevertheless, *metaphors are referential* and they are a means of describing what is really there and what can be described only in the indirect manner of figurative language. The metaphorical 'is' at once signifies both 'is like' and 'is not like'.[35] Metaphor says that 'x *is* y' but whispers under its breath 'yet x *is not* y.' It refuses to allow us to either *collapse* x and y, or to *separate* them. In this tension between the 'is' and the 'is not' meaning is created. This opens up a way to see language about demons as true and as referential without needing to take it strictly literally, thereby preserving the mystery of evil. For instance, when we speak of a demon 'entering into' a person or 'possessing' them or being 'cast out' from them we are speaking metaphorically. Even the language of 'spirit' has metaphorical roots being linked to the movement of (invisible) air.

Some metaphors, according to Soskice, are ambiguous and irreducible. She notes three features of irreducible metaphors:

> The first is that irreducible metaphors are incorrigibles which are susceptible of no elaboration or explanation whatsoever; the second is that they can only be redescribed in terms of other metaphors; and the third is that they are metaphors which purport to be referential, but for which no ostensively identifiable referent [i.e., a referent that can be identified by pointed to it] is independently available.[36]

So if we suppose that language about demons falls in the category of irreducible metaphors, it 'must . . . only be redescribed by other metaphors and/or those which lack identifiable referents.'[37] The darkness of the demonic realm cannot be spoken of literally but must only be considered indirectly as a Gorgon in a mirror.[38] But, unlike Bultmann's category of 'myth', such language points to real spirit-activity that cannot be simply translated without remainder into anthropology.

The metaphorical understanding of demon possession is therefore to point to the demonic activity which upset human efforts to attain the fullness of life, while exorcism is the divinely authorized and empowered human effort to reverse the negative effects of spirit

---

[35] Paul Ricoeur, *The Rule of Metaphor: Multi-Disciplinary Studies of the Creation of Meaning in Language* (London/Henley: Routledge & Kegan Paul, 1977), 7, 247.

[36] Janet Martin Soskice, *Metaphor and Religious Language* (Oxford: Oxford University Press, 1987), 94.

[37] Soskice, *Metaphor*, 94.

[38] In Greek Mythology a Gorgon could not be looked at directly lest one be turned to stone. Instead it must be viewed indirectly in a reflection.

possession. Neither can be adequately explained except in tropes and figures. It is possible to understand talk of the demonic realistically but in an appropriately indirect manner.[39] This seems to make metaphor a more useful tool in dealing with the subject of demon possession and exorcism than myth.[40] Unlike demythologization it does not reduce and remove the activity of Satan or the working of God in human life.

## Excursus: Walter Wink

Where should we locate the influential work of Walter Wink in this discussion? He stands midway between Bultmann and traditionalists. With Bultmann he rejects the traditional belief in literal, personal spirit beings and yet with the traditionalists he repudiates Bultmann's attempt to reduce mythic notions to secular ideas. Wink considers Bultmann's demythologization as a move in the right direction but from a wrong foundation because Bultmann defines myth as a falsifying objectification of reality which he then sought to dispense with via an existentialist reading. Like Bultmann, he approaches the demonic from the side of myth, but against Bultmann he refuses to allow modern secular worldviews to dictate the terms. Of course, we modern people cannot take biblical mythology seriously 'as long as our very categories of thought are dictated by the myth of materialism' but the Bible draws us away from that modern 'myth'.[41] Wink believes that he is *not demythologising* the ancient myth but transposing it into a new key and juxtaposing it with the rising postmodern (mythic) worldview and asking how they may equally illuminate each other. He is *remythologizing* the Bible for the postmodern world.[42] He notes, 'The demonic is an inescapable fact of the twentieth century, perhaps its most characteristic trade mark and perverse attainment . . . No intelligent person wants to believe in demons, but the utter failure of our optimistic views of progress to account for escalating horrors of our time demands at least a fresh start at understanding the source of virulence of the evils that are submerging our age into night, leaving us filled with

---

[39] Colin Gunton, *The Actuality of Atonement* (Edinburgh: T&T Clark, 1988), 65–66.

[40] See a detailed discussion on understanding metaphor, its relation with myth, its problems of definition, distinction and interpretation and the referential problems of supernatural powers, which include demons in Wa Gatumu, *The Pauline Concept of Supernatural Powers*, 195–208.

[41] Wink, *Naming the Powers*, 4.

[42] Wink, *Naming the Powers*, 104.

a sense of helplessness to resist.'[43] So he holds that the atrocities perpetuated and sanctioned by political and religious authorities in human history have a demonic character and may warrant their being seen as demonic.[44] Whilst he wishes to retain the language of 'evil spirits' it is clear that he has, in his own words, a 'somewhat demythologized understanding of the demonic', which he hopes 'will counteract the tendency to personify demons'.[45]

So Wink highlights the impossibility of discarding myth and notes that whilst our *explanations of myths* are dispensable and time-bound, the myths themselves live on.[46] Nevertheless, he is still sometimes too close to Bultmann's program of demythologization for comfort. He notes that the reality of evil and suffering, which myth presents as attributable to powers such as demons, is now understood to be perpetuated by the structures of human existence. Those human structures may have spiritual depth-dimensions which can be 'demonic' but Wink cannot imagine the demonic apart from the structures and people who operate them and here I part ways with him. He is of the view that even though Paul himself believed in the reality of an invisible spirit world, he demythologised the powers such that their spiritual essence was no longer in his mind.[47] Wink therefore believes that we should think of demons as identical to the psychic or spiritual power emanated by organization or individuals whose energies are bent at overpowering others.[48] However, the problem as I see it is that his view of 'principalities and powers' is just too close to materialism redressed in the language of 'spiritual dimensions'.

That said, the main thrust of Wink's argument must be given the gravity it deserves and so it is important to give him credit where he excels.[49] His view that demonic activity is as real today as it was during the New Testament period suggests that the theology of the power of Jesus' name over demons and demonic activity is relevant today.

### Demons and exorcism today

The major point, which can be made from the above discussion, is that demythologizing demons is not the way to go. It is very

---

[43]  Walter Wink, *Unmasking the Power: The Invisible Forces that Determine Human Existence* (Philadelphia: Fortress Press, 1986), 41.

[44]  Walter Wink, *The Powers that Be: Theology for a New Millennium* (New York: Doubleday, 1998), 5–6; Wink, *Unmasking the Powers*, 42.

[45]  Wink, *Unmasking the Powers*, 68.

[46]  Wink, *Naming the Powers*, 142–43.

[47]  See Wink, *Naming the Powers*, 82–84.

[48]  Wink, *Naming the Powers*, 104.

[49]  Dunn, *The Theology of Paul*, 110, note 42.

possible that those who seek to demythologize may have thrown out the demonic baby with the proverbial bathwater and now lack adequate ways to make sense of various spirit phenomena.[50] The reality of demon/spirit possession in the New Testament cannot be denied casually or explained away in sociological, anthropological, or psychological terms. T.K. Oesterreich notes that a clear but puzzling 'residue remains, for which there is as yet no psychological explanation, and which continues to leave the question open as to whether certain happenings transcend nature.'[51] This means that 'psychologists are still faced with this unexplained residue in the interpretation of their fieldwork.' And 'while it is unhelpful to deny the medical, rational, and psychological perspectives regarding the unexplained residue the question of demonic influence remains open. Even if diseases have a natural or regular depiction, the demonic need not be ruled out.'[52] It is possible that demons oppress people physically and/or mentally without possessing them. Yet even if some psychological theories regarding spirit-possession may be credible, it is clear from a New Testament point of view that 'psychologising the phenomena too much robs it of its essential theological character.'[53]

If we accept the reality of demons then it is critical to develop a relevant theology for today regarding possession and exorcism. The heart of exorcism is that the encounter between demonic spirits and Jesus is a proclamation of the power of Jesus' name. The theology that emerges from spirit possession and exorcism is that of the supremacy of Christ over demonic and evil spirits. 'Failing to locate supernatural powers in proper perspective vis-à-vis Jesus Christ could be damaging for the theological and spiritual growth of the church.'[54] Cook rightly noted that 'a Christianity which refuses to acknowledge, confront and harness these chthonic powers will remain vulnerable to its young people leaving the church in favour

---

[50] See Wink, *Unmasking the Powers*, 4.

[51] Cited in my earlier study, Wa Gatumu, *The Pauline Concept of Supernatural Powers*, 84. See also T.K. Oesterreich, *Possession and Exorcism: Among Primitive Races, in Antiquity, the Middle Ages, and Modern Times* (London: Kegan Paul, Trench, Trubner & Co, 1930), 378.

[52] Wa Gatumu, *The Pauline Concept of Supernatural Powers*, 84–85. See also Twelftree, *Christ Triumphant*, 156.

[53] Laurenti Magesa, *African Religion: The Moral Traditions of Abundant Life* (Maryknoll, New York: Orbis Books 1997), 173–74.

[54] Wa Gatumu, *The Pauline Concept of Supernatural Powers*, 221.

of New Age spirituality.'[55] In fact, according to traditional Christian theology, demons are as real in our day as in Jesus' day and still desire to inhabit people. In that case, a theology of Christ's supremacy over demons is relevant in the modern world. Modern people can be truly demon possessed, oppressed, or afflicted. They may 'make friends with devils' even if they do not realise that this is what they are doing. And those who are demon oppressed or demon afflicted may be under the *influence* of demons even if it falls short of possession (Matt. 16:23; Acts 5:1–10, 2 Cor. 12:1–10). The point we are making is that people can be afflicted by demons without being controlled by them since people are ultimately the ones to make decision on their action. The demon-made-me-do-it era is over and people must take responsibility of their actions.

How do we explain the fact that exorcism seemed to receive different amounts of attention in different New Testament documents? And what are the implications of this for contemporary practise? Twelftree outlines four theories which are perhaps helpful for analysing the reasons why the question of ongoing manner of demonic influence remains open. The first theory that Twelftree considers, drawn from Wiles and Crossan, is that 'interest in exorcism, along with miracles in general, diminished over time.'[56] His second theory, based on Eric Sorensen's work, is that 'the variation we see in the interest in exorcism in the New Testament may be accounted for in terms of cultural variations across time and place.'[57] His third theory is that 'it could be that the diverse attitudes toward exorcism had theological roots that we might be able to detect and describe through a close examination of the New Testament documents.'[58] His fourth theory, based on two studies by Elizabeth Ann Leeper, is that exorcism came to have 'an association with baptism' and so it formed an essential part of the catechumenate and baptismal preparation. Baptism came to take, in fact, the place of other modes of exorcism.[59] The first and second hypotheses imply that exorcism may have no relevance for today if it has 'diminished over time' and can 'be accounted for in terms of cultural variation across

---

[55] Robert Cook, 'Devils & Manticores: Plundering Jung for a Plausible Demonology in A.N.S. Lane (ed.) *The Unseen World: Christian Reflection on Angels, Demons and the Heavenly Realm* (Carlisle, Cumbria: Paternoster Press, 1996), 183.

[56] Twelftree, *In the Name of Jesus*, 30.

[57] Twelftree, *In the Name of Jesus*, 30.

[58] Twelftree, *In the Name of Jesus*, 30.

[59] Twelftree, *In the Name of Jesus*, 30.

time and space'. As to the fourth theory, the link between exorcism and baptism may be clear but situating the whole phenomena within the context of baptism is too limiting. The third theory that variation in the emphasis on exorcism across the New Testament had a theological root appears to be the most plausible (see chapter 2). Another possibility is that the demons have changed tactics such that they do not possess people as often as they did during the ministry of Jesus. After the spiritual turmoil of that critical era, perhaps oppression became the main *modus operandi* of demons. That might explain why the number of cases of possession and exorcism recorded in the New Testament seems to have decreased after the Ascension. This does not mean that possession and exorcism would not occur today but it would suggest that they might not be as common as we find in Jesus' own ministry.

It has been noted above that attention to demon-possession was strong in the synoptic gospels, it somewhat decreased in the Acts of the Apostles, and was missing in the epistles. It has also been noted the exorcism that Jesus did was a unique act of authority demonstrating the power of his name (Matt. 9:33; Mark 1:27). The same authority was given to the twelve disciples (Luke 9:1–10) and to the seventy (Matt. 10:1; Luke 10:1–20) as evidence of their representative function in the proclamation of the Kingdom. This may suggest that exorcism may have not been intended to be an activity for *all* Christians. If that is the case it would place a question mark upon some deliverance ministries performed today, which may not be performed in line with the patterns of the New Testament. Modern exorcists ought to exercise some caution given that demons are more powerful than people. The episode about the sons of Sceva, the itinerant Jewish exorcists, who took it upon themselves to invoke the name of Jesus over those who had evil spirits gives modern exorcists a good lesson not to take things into their own hands. The evil spirits noticing that these unauthorized people lacked authority leaped on them, wounded them, and chased them away (Acts 19:13–16). This event hints that the New Testament regards exorcism to have been the sole prerogative of Jesus and those to whom he had given authority. This should make us very cautious about assuming that every Christian is authorized by Christ to combat demons. Traditionally the mainstream churches have recognized this principle. Thus, for instance, exorcism in the Roman Catholic Church can only be done under the authority of a bishop and following strict rules.

The story of the sons of Sceva should also make modern-day exorcists careful about the way in which they engage demons. The

Archangel Michael when 'contending with the devil, disputed about the body of Moses, [but] he did not presume to pronounce a reviling judgment upon him, but said, "The Lord rebuke you"' (Jude 9). Contemporary Christians should not take deliverance ministry lightly and approach it with a triumphalist attitude.

We also need to be very cautious in our diagnosis of demonic influence given that the signs of demonic activity are often ambiguous. We need to consider the real possibility that some of the people who may be 'delivered' through modern day exorcists may not have been demon-possessed at all, but simply have been people with physical or mental sicknesses which were mistakenly perceived by others or themselves as caused by demons.[60] It is true in some cases that evil spirits cause sicknesses but they do not cause *all* diseases. The New Testament distinguishes natural illnesses from those with demonic causes (Matt. 4:24; Mark 1:32, Luke 7:21; 9:1; Acts 5:16). So there is no simple link from the observation that someone is ill to the conclusion that a demon is responsible. In fact, some people could be afflicted with mental sicknesses which are easily confused with demon possession since the symptoms of spirit-possession are very similar to those of mental illness. The official Roman Catholic doctrine affirms that demonic oppression can occur and can be distinguished from mental illness, but emphasizes that great care must be taken to ensure that cases of mental illness are not misdiagnosed as demonic influence. Any person therefore called to investigate a claim of possession, as Richard J. Woods insists, 'Should not believe too readily that a person is possessed by an evil spirit; but he ought to ascertain the signs[61] by which a person possessed can be distinguished from one

---

[60] Due to the high expectation of faith in the deliverance ministry some people may be healed psychosomatically and believe that demons have left them. Yet, as sadly happens in many cases, the sicknesses tend to recur.

[61] According to the Roman Catholic Church the signs of possession include displaying superhuman strength frequently accompanied by fits and convulsions, changes in personality, having knowledge of the future or other secret information; and being able to understand and converse in languages not previously known to the victim. Other signs of demonic possession include the practice of lewd and obscene acts, or even sexual thoughts; horrible smells of bodily odours or of sulphur, associated with hell; distended stomachs; rapid weight loss where death seems inevitable; changes in the voice to a deep, rasping, menacing, guttural croak. The problem however is that many of these signs or symptoms can have non-demonic causes. Seizures and convulsions are symptoms of epilepsy. Personality changes can indicate hysteria, or schizophrenia, or other

suffering from melancholy or some other illness.'[62] So given the fact that one of the key problems in identifying possession is its similarity to mental illness, the final diagnosis must be made with expert consultation, which would necessarily include medical, psychiatric, and psychological tests. A diagnosis of demon possession must only be made after guardedly considering the evidence as a whole. It is judicious to be cautious to investigate the medical and psychological aspects of the person before performing the rite of exorcism.

Many psychologists would recognize that there is often more to illness than the simple mechanical failure of the body; that illness can have a spiritual dimension and that consequently healing must also integrate a spiritual dimension. In my book *The Pauline Concept of Supernatural Powers* I noted that mental illness can have a spiritual cause and so treatment must operate at all levels of illness. It was also noted that treating a spiritual problem as a mere physical or mental illness is unhelpful. And conversely, treating an illness that could be mental as demon possession is potentially harmful. It was noted that spirit-possession is a complex religious experience and that those who recognize its reality should have autonomy to develop their own diagnostic models which refuse to reduce the phenomena to nothing more than experiences that can be explained away in anthropological or psychological categories.[63]

The problem is that 'imprudent exorcism' in every historical epoch, 'increases rather than decreases the spiritual and mental damage of

---

(cont.) psychological malfunctions. Lewd and obscene acts can indicate mental disorders. Having sexual thoughts, if taken seriously as a sign of demonic possession, would indicate nearly all people are possessed, especially the men. Distended stomachs can indicate malnutrition and other medical disorders. Also, having knowledge of future events or information is known as clairvoyance by many occultists and Neo-pagan witches which they consider a special spiritual gift. In light of such evidence it seems that there are grounds for considerable caution when diagnosing demonic possession (see 'Demon Possession' in http://www.themystica.com/mystica/articles/d/demonic_possession.htm accessed March 18th 2009). Others include changes in attitude and behaviour (usually becoming hostile), changes in personality for instance an affable person suddenly becomes extremely quiet and cursing and which was not part of that person's character. Also included are changes in the way the person dresses and personal hygiene (see T. Cooney 'Warning Signs of Demonic Possession' 2005 in http://fspp.net/warn%20poss.htm accessed March 18th 2009).

[62] Richard J. Woods, *The Possession Problem* (Chicago Studies, 1973), 96.

[63] Wa Gatumu, *The Pauline Concept of Supernatural Powers*, 85.

*daimonomania'.*[64] It is awfully wrong for modern exorcist to move from place to place *actively looking* for cases of demon/spirit possession, rather than dealing with them if they come along. Even if the task of Jesus' followers in all periods of history is to redeem souls from Satan's spiritual grip, it is idiotic to lead people into a demon-phobia finding monsters lurking in every corner. Ironically then, deliverance ministry itself can inadvertently function as a *demonic* activity by leading people to become so focused on the devil that they take their eyes off Jesus Christ. The greatest task of every Christian is to remind people that Jesus has won the victory over the battle with Satan and his minions. For that reason, people must not be led to focus too much on the demonic activity but to realise that the name of Jesus is more powerful than any other name that is named under the world, in the world and above the world. The point is that exorcism proclaims the supremacy of Christ over and above the powers of darkness.

## Conclusion

According to the New Testament evidence, demons are real and active in all historical epochs. Paul's warning to the Christians of Ephesus that, 'we do not wrestle against flesh and blood, but against the rulers, against the authorities, against the cosmic powers over this present darkness, against the spiritual forces of evil in the heavenly places' (Eph. 6:12), is as relevant today as it was then. However, the presence of demons then and now must not lead believers to the kind of fear of the demonic that undermines faith in Christ's triumph. The victory that Jesus had over the demonic activity is, by extension, for those who trust in the power of his name. So even though demonic possession is an act of power and where power aggressively takes over a human being, Jesus has 'disarmed the principalities and powers and made a public example of them, triumphing over them in him' (Col. 2:15). It must be emphasized therefore that all New Testament passages on possession and exorcism display the power of Jesus' name over demons that tormented people during the first century and which might oppress people in the modern era. The point is that just as demons were real in the New Testament, so they are today. Yet it is vital to adorn modern views on the demonic with a right biblical view of the same. This would help Christians to avoid on the one hand an obsession with demonism

---

[64] Woods, *The Possession Problem*, 100.

that stresses exorcism for every sin or illness, and, on the other, an attitude of indifference or unbelief in what Scripture and experience teach to be a reality.

Jesus' exorcisms were an assertion that the Kingdom of God is in the midst of God's people. However, according to the New Testament, the Kingdom of God is both now and not-yet. So If Jesus' exorcisms were a proclamation of the presence of the Kingdom of God among his people, and if the Kingdom of God will climax in the future, then demonic activity will continue until the final coming of the kingdom. Until that moment, even though the decisive battle over the forces of evil and the powers of darkness has been won on the cross, the battle against demonic forces continues. The call for the church now, as the army of God, is to resist Satan and all his demonic forces. Yet in the modern time, as it ought to have been in all times, Christians must be careful not to give Satan and his demons too much attention. This can lead to a phobic allegiance or to an overestimation of his power, to a fascination with evil or even a kind of satanic worship.

> There are two equal and opposite errors into which our race can fall about the devils. One is to disbelieve in their existence. The other is to believe, and to feel an excessive interest in them. They themselves are equally pleased by both errors and hail a materialist or a magician with the same delight.[65]

All in all, it is crucial for Christians today, and in the days to come, to recognize the power and supremacy of Jesus and of his name over demons and their activities.

---

[65] C.S. Lewis, *The Screwtape Letters* (London: Harper Collins Publishers, 1942), ix.

## Chapter 12

# Demonology and Deliverance:
# A Practical-Theological Case Study

*Mark J. Cartledge*

**Abstract**

This chapter aims to bring together the different contributions contained in the volume. It does so by means of a practical-theological methodology that uses a case study as a focus for reflection. For this purpose, the demonology of John Wimber is considered in relation to his guidelines for deliverance. The different perspectives from the previous chapters are used as theoretical dialogue partners in order to critique and illuminate his theology and praxis. As a result of this critical engagement a number of suggestions are made in terms of theological understanding, as well as recommendations for renewed theological praxis.

## Introduction

We are all familiar with sensational stories in the media of appalling examples of deliverance ministry. For example, the report in 2007 of an Orthodox priest who conducted an exorcism that led to the death of a nun in a remote corner of north east Romania.[1] She had been chained to a cross and starved to death in a convent. Incredibly, he had acted with the assistance of four other nuns. It is stories like these that inevitably raise many questions and elicit very strong reactions. Therefore, the nature of demonology and the deliverance ministry of

---

[1] See http://news.bbc.co.uk/1/hi/world/europe/6376211.stm (accessed 28th January 2009).

the church is an important topic for contemporary discussion in theology. It is also essential that theology engages with other disciplines in its attempt to understand better the realities that this discussion represents. Therefore a multi-disciplinary approach is one that can be affirmed whole-heartedly from the perspective of practical theology. Practical theology pays particular attention to the contemporary practices of the church and brings those practices into critical dialogue with Scripture, history, and Christian doctrine. In the multi-disciplinary mode it allows theology to move beyond its internal dialogue between the sub-disciplines to one that critically embraces the insights of other disciplines, such as anthropology, psychology, philosophy, and cultural studies. However, in order to focus the discussion on contemporary practice, I have chosen a popular model espoused by the late John Wimber, founder of the Vineyard denomination. This model is regularly taught and practised within contemporary Charismatic Christianity and it is, therefore, a useful case study and a way of grounding more abstract discussions in relation to concrete practices. As in my previous contribution of this kind, I have followed the methodology based on the pastoral cycle within practical theology because it allows a specified case study to be engaged with a view to offering recommendations for a renewal of theological praxis.[2]

## A case study: John Wimber's demonology and guidelines for deliverance

John Wimber bases his cosmology on four basic premises concerning God and evil: (1) God does not directly will evil; (2) God does directly remove evil; (3) God sometimes overcomes evil not by removing it but by accomplishing his purposes through it; and (4) in practice this means that there are many kinds of evil we experience that we do not approach passively.[3] This active approach specifically informs his attitude towards demonology, which is further developed by his reading of the New Testament material. He understands the New Testament to teach that healing touches every aspect of life that is under the

---

[2] See Mark J. Cartledge, 'The Practice of Tongues Speech as a Case Study: A Practical-Theological Perspective', in Mark J. Cartledge (ed.), *Speaking in Tongues: Multi-disciplinary Perspectives* (Milton Keynes: Paternoster, 2006), 206–34.

[3] John Wimber with Kevin Springer, *Power Healing* (London: Hodder & Stoughton, 1986), 36.

influence of Satan, including: the forgiveness of sins, restoration from sickness, breaking the hold of poverty and oppressive social structures, deliverance from demonic power, and raising the dead.[4] Healing is linked with repentance for sin and conflict with Satan. '[W]hile sickness may be caused by our own sinfulness, not all sickness is caused by sin. Much sickness is caused by Satan.'[5] This means that healing is holistic, including: spiritual, emotional, mental, and physical aspects; and may even include the reversal of death itself.[6]

### Demonology and deliverance

For Wimber, the New Testament teaches the existence of both Satan and demons (Luke 10:17, 20; Rev. 12:7–10). Jesus confronted demons (Luke 4:31–37, 41; 6:18; 7:21; 8:2, 26–29; 9:37–43; 11:14–26) and gave authority to his disciples to cast them out of people (Luke 9:1, 49–50; 10:17–20; Mark 16:17). The New Testament contains teaching on the authority of Christians over demons (1 Cor. 2:6–8; 10:20–21; Eph. 6:10–18; Col. 1:13–16; 2:20) and examples of exorcisms (Acts 5:16; 8:6–8; 16:16–18; 19:11–12). This is because God the Father sent Jesus to destroy the works of Satan (John 12:31;1 John 3:8) and establish the kingdom of God. Four key points on the kingdom of God inform his theology: (1) God's reign came into the world in the person of Jesus (Matt. 12:28); (2) by repenting and believing in Jesus people are redeemed from the world, the flesh, and the devil and come under the reign of God (John 3:5); (3) the kingdom of God is destroying the kingdom of Satan (1 John 3:8); and (4) at the return of Christ, when he ushers in the fullness of the kingdom of God, Satan will be eternally destroyed (Matt. 13:36–43).[7] Therefore Jesus proclaimed the good news of the kingdom of God and demonstrated its power through the casting out of demons (Mark 1:24).

> We too have been commissioned to preach the kingdom of God and have been given authority to cast out demons. The nature of our authority over demons reflects the dilemma of living in the time before the return of Christ and the new age, the fullness of the kingdom. Jesus defeated Satan at the cross, and through his victory we have authority

---

[4] Wimber, *Power Healing*, 56.
[5] Wimber, *Power Healing*, 58.
[6] Wimber, *Power Healing*, 77–78.
[7] Wimber, *Power Healing*, 114–15.

over Satan. But we have yet to exercise that authority fully until Christ's return. So though the kingdom of Satan was decisively defeated through Jesus' death and resurrection, we do not yet enjoy the fullness of the kingdom of God. In other words, until Christ's return we are still in a battle with the world, the flesh, and the devil and his demons (John 16:33).[8]

In this interim period the whole world is under the control of the evil one (1 John 5:19) and he continues to war against the saints (Rev. 12:17). '[W]e live in a hostile environment, one ruled by Satan.'[9] Satan's open warfare and Christ's command to 'make disciples' mean we are 'locked in spiritual warfare' (1 Pet. 5:8–9; Eph. 6:10–12). 'What every Christian needs to know about spiritual warfare is that while Satan is strong, Christ is stronger. We have nothing to fear from Satan or demons, as long as we live faithfully and righteously, never backing down when challenged by evil.'[10]

Wimber maintains that Satan is a creature, the opposite not of God but of the archangel Michael. Christian tradition has interpreted Isa. 14:12–15 as a description of the fall of Satan from heaven for attempting to overthrow God. Paul refers to him as the 'ruler of the air' (Eph. 2:2), where he dwells awaiting his final state (Rev. 20:10). According to Wimber, the New Testament texts affirm that demons are angels cast down with Satan after his rebellion: 2 Pet. 2:4; Jude 6; Rev. 12:7–12. Two groups of demons exist: (1) those who have been placed in 'gloomy dungeons' and 'bound with everlasting chains' (cf. Col. 2:15; 1 Pet. 3:18–22); and (2) those who are free to roam about the earth and serve the purposes of Satan (Matt. 12:24–26; Rev. 9:1–11, 20:1), numerous and well-organised (Eph. 6:11–12). They are intelligent (Acts 16:16–18; 19:15–16) spirits (Matt. 8:16; 12:43–45; Luke 10:17–20; 24:39; Rev. 16:14) that manifest in different forms (Rev. 9:1–11; 16:13–14), being malevolent (Matt. 12:43–35; Mark 1:27; 3:11; Luke 4:36; Acts 8:7; Rev. 16:13), know-ledgable of their own end (Matt. 8:29; 25:41; Jas. 2:19), having supernatural strength (Matt. 12:29; Mark 5:4; Luke 8:29; Acts 19:13–16), even if they must bow to Jesus' name (Matt. 8:28–34; Mark 5:7; Luke 8:26–33).

In this model, Christians are a target for Satan and his demons because they have identified themselves with Christ, his prime target (1 Pet. 4:12–13). Satan attacks us in three main ways. First, through

---

[8] Wimber, *Power Healing*, 115.
[9] Wimber, *Power Healing*, 116.
[10] Wimber, *Power Healing*, 117.

*temptation* (1 Thess. 3:5), via the flesh (Gal. 5:17), although most temptations are the result of our own choices and the influence of the world. However, the Bible notes a second form of temptation that is direct (e.g., Christ, Matt. 4:1–11; Ananias, Acts 5:3; David, 1 Chr. 21:1). The world, the flesh, and the devil have a 'diabolical interrelationship' that can trap men and women. Temptations are testing and they only incur guilt when Christians succumb to them (Jas. 1:14–15). Second, by means of *opposition* to the preaching of the gospel or the influence of the kingdom of God, Satan can block the activity of Christians through accidents, events, and diversions (e.g., Elymas' opposition to Paul and Barnabas, Acts 13:6–10). Third, through *demonization*, Satan can obtain a grip on peoples' lives resulting in illness, habitual patterns of temptation and weakness (e.g., envy and selfish ambition, Jas. 3:15), sometimes accompanied by violence (Luke 8:26–29). But the gospels and Acts make a distinction between natural and demonic causes of physical and mental illness (Matt. 4:24; 8:16; 10:1, 8; Mark 1:32–34; 3:10–11; 6:13; 16:17–18; Luke 4:40–41; 6:18–19; 7:21; 8:2; 9:1; 13:32; Acts 5:16; 8:6–7; 19:11–12). Depending on the cause of sickness, Jesus and the disciples prayed differently (Matt. 8:1–4, 5–13; 9:1–8, 18–26; 20:29–34; Luke 17:11–19; John 5:1–15; 9:1–12; Acts 3:1–10; 14:8–10). Wimber maintains that the Greek word *daimonizomai* is best translated 'demonized' and means influence, affliction, or torment. Demonized people suffer differing degrees of influence, from mild to severe. For instance, the account of Jesus' healing of the Gerasene man suggests the latter was *severely* demonized (Luke 8:26–39).[11]

Wimber also believes that Christians can be influenced by the demonic, if not 'possessed' (he regards the demonic possession of Christians to be an unbiblical concept). However, if Christians walk in faith and righteousness, they are protected (1 John 4:4). If they live in unconfessed sin, then they open themselves up to demonic influence. He gives the example of Saul (1 Sam. 16:14), who was influenced after having been anointed with the Spirit (1 Sam. 10:1, 9–13) and of Peter, whom Satan wanted to sift as wheat (Luke 22:31–32). Satan was also the cause of Ananias and Sapphira's sin (Acts 5:3). He believes that the demonic can gain entry into people's lives through their own sin, such as anger, hatred, lust, sex, drugs, alcohol, and involvement in the occult; or through sin done to or against them, and perhaps passed on generationally. This is because 'until Christ's return we live in enemy territory, a sinful world that is in bondage to Satan's terror.'[12]

---

[11] Wimber, *Power Healing*, 120–26.
[12] Wimber, *Power Healing*, 132.

Nevertheless, Christ has equipped his people for the battle (Eph. 6:10–18): truth, righteousness, readiness to proclaim the gospel of peace, faith, salvation, the sword of the Spirit, which is the word of God, and prayer in the Spirit. Holy and righteous lives in the power of the Holy Spirit are the greatest safeguards against the influence of the demonic.

Wimber admits that, from his own experience, the majority of people who claim to be demonized are in fact *not* demonized.[13] By contrast, most people who are demonized are not aware of it. He suggests an incomplete list of symptoms that indicate the possibility that a person may be demonized. These include: contorted physical reactions, especially when the power of the Spirit is present in worship or prayer, addiction, compulsive behaviour, emotional problems, sinful attitudes, chronic physical sickness (especially generational), occult involvement and problematic family history.

### Guidelines for the practice of deliverance

To understand Wimber's guidance for deliverance we must appreciate that it falls within his general model of healing. This model is constructed from principles, values, and practices. He identifies six foundational *principles*: (1) God wants to heal the sick today; (2) healing is a corporate ministry; (3) our trust in God is demonstrated by action; (4) all Christians can pray because they are empowered by the Holy Spirit; (5) healing should be conducted in the context of loving relationships with our brothers and sisters; and (6) God wants to heal the whole person not just specific conditions.[14] He defines *values* as extensions of the basic principles, which determine the flow and direction of resources. These are: (1) the creation of a healing environment (the presence of the Holy Spirit and people full of faith); (2) ministry times, when teams pray for individuals; (3) the training of people to assist them in the healing ministry; and (4) the cultivation of a healing lifestyle, when prayer for healing becomes routine and a matter of fact. In order to engage in prayer ministry effectively, he advocates the following *practices*: (1) hearing what the Holy Spirit is saying via words of knowledge; (2) seeing via spiritual sight what God is doing in the healing process; (3) speaking words of love and encourgement, command, declaration, petition, advising a particular action or offering advice

---

[13] Wimber, *Power Healing*, 136.
[14] Wimber, *Power Healing*, 183–84.

and teaching, followed by follow-up instructions; and (4) using physical touch via the laying on of hands.[15]

Wimber identifies a five-step healing procedure, which begins with (1) the interview, during which the person is asked about the nature of the problem or condition; (2) the diagnostic decision, which discerns the cause of the problem; (3) the prayer selection, or decision about how best to pray; (4) the prayer engagement, when the Holy Spirit is invoked and the pray-er discerns what is happening to the person; and (5) post-prayer directions and advice.[16]

Wimber advises that prayer for the demonized is best done in a private setting, because it may take time and several follow-up sessions.[17] He recommends that prayer for the severely demonized is most appropriately done by a team of two to five people. There should be one leader and the others should be in support. He places people on either side of the person and tells them to pray, occasionally asking a person to record what happens, to write down the demons' 'functions and relationships' so that there is evaluation as to whether it/they have gone completely. If the session becomes protracted then he changes the roles of team members in order to maintain their concentration. He never calls anything demonic unless he has talked with the demon and used the following criteria. (1) Personality change occurs when the demon speaks through a person. (2) Their eyes roll back and flutter and whole pupil disappears, or they operate independently of one another or become very still, covered by what appears to be a film, or dilate to the extent that all that can be seen is the pupil. (3) Other common physical manifestations include: nostrils flaring, lips pursing, teeth appearing to grow, throat enlargement and the body puffing up. People have fallen to the floor, slithered and hissed like snakes, produced animal noises like barking, bellowing and roaring, and emitted foul-smelling fluids from body orifices.[18]

Once he is clear that there is a demonic presence he commands its attention by saying 'Look at me!' and then he commands the demon/s to tell him its/their name/s (Mark 5:9): 'in the name of Jesus, I command you, spirit, to tell me your name.' He observes that demons do not wish to do this and therefore will be evasive by asking why, or by saying that they do not have a name. He commands them to stop and

---

[15] Wimber, *Power Healing*, 191–97.
[16] Wimber, *Power Healing*, 208–44.
[17] Wimber, *Power Healing*, 240–44
[18] Wimber, *Power Healing*, 240–41.

reiterates the orginal command. If the name is given in a foreign language he commands the demon to tell him what it means in English. If more information is required, such as in relation to, say, fear, then he asks the demon what kind of fear. When demons start talking in order to avoid being cast out, he commands them to be silent (Mark 1:34). Most demonized people do not know that they are so influenced until prayer begins and then they often become frightened as the demon threatens them. If he suspects that this is happening he commands the demon to be silent and gains the attention of the person once again. When he is clear that he is talking with the person, he explains that there is nothing to fear and that Christ is stronger than the demon. The explusion comes about through commanding the demon to go: 'I command you in the name of Jesus to come out.' However, he notes that saying these words does not automatically ensure that the demon leaves. Some demons are more stubborn than others (Mark 9:29), requiring greater faith and prayer. Once the demon has left the person, there is often some form of reaction: falling down, crying out, moaning, deep exhaling, foul odours, followed by 'unusual peace' (Mark 9:26). If he is not sure that a demon has in fact left, he looks into the person's eyes and says: 'If there is a spirit in there, I command you to manifest.'[19]

He suggests that another way of identifying evil spirits is to pray for various parts of the body, asking for the Holy Spirit to consecrate them (Rom. 12:1–2). When there is some manifestation he stops this procedure and returns to the original one of: identify, silence, cast out. Occasionally when a stubborn demon refuses to leave, he says: 'Jesus, here is a demon of hell that is standing against you and your church. You take care of it.' Mild demonization is much easier to deal with and these demons normally leave with a simple command.

After he has expelled the demon, his goal is to see the person fully restored so that demons may not return (Mark 9:25; Matt. 12:43–45). Only Jesus fills the gap created by the departure of a demon. So he interviews the person and ensures that they have a sincere relationship with Christ. If they do not he explains the gospel message to them and invites them to receive Christ. He may lead people in prayer renouncing the occult or sinful practices and then he asks the Holy Spirit to come and fill them completely. When the Holy Spirit withdraws his

---

[19] This procedure is derived from a combination of three Markan texts: 5:1–20; 1:21–28; 9:14–29, which all have parallels in Matthew (8:28–34; 7:28–29; 17:14–21) and Luke (8:26–29; 4:31–37; 9:37–43a).

power, or the person indicates that it is complete, then Wimber knows that it is time to stop praying.

## Analysis of the case study

In order to analyse Wimber's model of deliverance, I shall use the perspectives from anthropology, psychology, philosophy, and cultural studies.

### Anthropology

Peter Versteeg's observation that anthropological research is largely concerned with the ideology of health, well-being, and a response to evil chimes in with Wimber's approach because he too places exorcism within a healing/health framework that is based upon presuppositions regarding God and evil. However, the anthropological 'normative indifference' to the phenomena it studies means that questions of ontology are insignificant, because it is interested in cultural practices and the meanings embedded in them, rather than any correspondence with external reality. The personification of evil is regarded as a way of controlling, containing, and combatting that which is feared and attributed to the 'spirit world'; although in many contexts the spirits are perceived as ambivalent and able to negotiate with the people seeking their expulsion. From an anthropological perspective this means that experience of the 'spirit world' is bound to specific social and cultural contexts.

Given the case study, the most useful approach identified by Versteeg is the hermeneutical work of Thomas Csordas, who, based on his work with American Roman Catholic Charismatics, aims to show that meanings are grounded in human embodied experience. He understands deliverance to be objectified within contemporary demonology that regards demons to be characterised by intelligence, agency, and powers of destruction. The influence of demons is seen in terms of agency from the outside of the person upon their thoughts, behaviour, and emotions. The healer in this context is a specialist in 'cultural objectification' and 'discerns' the origin of the problem and specifically whether it is demonic or not. Demonization occurs when the thought or emotion is considered as being 'out of bounds'. It is beyond the control of the person. In fact the person feels controlled externally and, therefore, deliverance is a release from this external control. The experience, diagnosis, and deliverance of demonization demonstrates the importance of control in North American and western culture. Furthermore, the dualism noted in non-western forms of Pentecostalism is also to be observed in contemporary Charismatic expressions of Christianity.

From this analysis, we can make a number of comments in relation to the case study. It would appear that evil is personified and this personification is certainly a means of control. This is obvious when Wimber requires the demon to identify itself by name, then he silences it at a command. He suggests that while the demon may wish to negotiate, he does not. It needs to be expelled and nothing more. Following the work of Csordas, we can see that Wimber's cosmology not only objectifies the demonic but it also classifes demonic entities as having intelligence, agency, and destructive powers. However, in the Wimber narrative the influence of the demonic upon a person is differentiated from mild to severe. I suspect the severe side of the demonic is not addressed by Csordas. The severe side not only demonstrates influence upon thoughts and emotions but also manifests itself physically and socially. This description would suggest that 'objectification' has greater power because of these added dimensions. It is certainly the case that 'control' is at the heart of the matter, but from Wimber's theology it is defined in terms of an ontologically understood cosmological dualism rather than North American cultural analysis. Wimber uses objectifying and personalising language because he assumes a particular ontological reality, which goes beyond anthropological discourse. Anthropologically, nothing more can be said about the dualism because of the discipline's 'normative indifference', but theologically it remains an important issue and will be considered later.

*Psychology and philosophy*

The contribution from William Kay raises the question as to how mental health issues intersect with the notion of the spirit world and the possible influence of that world upon the mental states of individuals. Clearly a materialist view of reality would require that all phenomena associated with so-called demonic influence within a spirit-orientated cosmology be reduced to psychological explanation. However, there are some themes emerging which are pertinent for an engagement with our case study material. The possibility of Dissociative Identity Disorder (hereafter: DID) suggests that there is a mental health condition that can show two or more identities or states within the one person. These different identities may influence certain types of behaviour and result in memory problems. It is interesting to note that sexual abuse is 'routinely' understood as a cause of multiple personalities and dissociative disorders, even if a small number of American psychiatrists throw a 'curve ball' by the introduction of extra terrestrials into the discussion, which I shall ignore completely for the purposes of this discussion!

When we attempt to ask mental health questions of Wimber's approach to delieverance we see that he clearly distinguishes between the two types of condition, so that he does not diagnose demonization, even though the 'patient' might, unless he has talked with the demon. However, given the nature of DID, would it not be possible to find oneself conversing with a person suffering from multiple personalities where these communicated in different voices? It is at this point that the first criterion mentioned by Wimber is potentially compromised. If this is supported by certain kinds of behaviour such as falling on the floor or acting strangely, then the third criterion is also compromised. This might be reinforced diagnostically when a sexual problem, such as abuse, is acknowledged by the person and this is both recorded as being associated with DID and with demonization by Wimber. After the deliverance has taken place, the person (in the Wimber paradigm) may not remember much of what has happened, and this corresponds with a feature of DID where there is memory loss; although this tends to be focused around childhood and adolescence rather than the immediate event surrounding a deliverance.

These features do not necessarily 'explain away' the Wimber model because it is based fundamentally on a Spirit-driven and Spirit-discerned practice that allows for the Holy Spirit to enable the people involved to assess the nature of the problem via revelation. Indeed, there are many mentally ill people who consider themselves to be demon-possessed, which would run counter to Wimber's basic thesis that most people who are demonized do not know that they are influenced in this way. It takes some form of 'power encounter' for the Spirit to reveal the true state of the condition. However, the possibility that there may be some confusion around whether it is DID rather than demonization that is being dealt with must remain; and this requires further consideration and reflection. The third option complicates the matter even more, namely: that there could, in fact, be a combination of both demonization and mental health issues.

Phillip Wiebe's discussion of deliverance in the context of philosophy of science also raises the question of DID, which he explores through analysis of the Gerasene demoniac and other more recent accounts. He suggests that while DID might explain the presence of different voices it does not explain the effect on the swine feeding nearby. It does not, therefore, explain the connected events within the overall scenario, even if the term 'spirit' may or may not be applied to '*something-we-know-not-what*'. The deliverance episodes that he later mentions reinforce his argument that DID cannot explain the whole event because other contextual information is ignored, such as: the content of what was said, the sequence of events, and the link between them. It is also intriguing to note that in his account of Alice's deliverance there is a striking resemblance to Wimber's description, fulfilling his criteria, even if the method of deliverance is different. It is also interesting that the cause of this demonization is related to sexual abuse. Therefore, at this stage it would appear that greater complexity is generated by these accounts in relation to the Wimber model and that there is likely to be some kind of *contextual information* available that supports a demonized interpretation over and against a solely DID one for those involved in deliverance ministry.

*Popular culture*

The chapter by Lucy Huskinson presents a fascinating account of how demon possession and exorcism have been portrayed within popular media. She argues that popular portrayals of the demonic are representative of societal anxiety and despair. This is traced from the (in)famous film, *The Exorcist*, first shown in 1973, to the present day. For the purposes of engaging with an American model of deliverance as represented by Wimber, we note the relevance of her discussion of the rite of exorcism as an accentuation of horror, the trivialisation of exorcism, and the scientific explanation of it as the prevailing *Zeitgeist*.

The first of these points suggests that the portrayal of deliverance in terms of a damaging ordeal for the person possessed heightens the sense of horror. This is accentuated by practices such as handcuffing, sowing eyelids wide open, and starving the person for a period before forcing him or her to drink cold vinegar and rubbing salt into wounds before nailing hands and feet to a cross. The second point of trivialisation is suggested by its humorous protrayal, especially in relation to the famous possession scene in *The Exorcist* (noted for a rotating head and green vomit), upon which subsequent films and portrayals make play. Trivialisation is also suggested by routinization, whereby deliverance becomes just another task in the rather boring working day.

Thirdly, the suggestion that deliverance can in fact be explained away by scientific rationality is a common one and this is noted by Huskinson as a significant problem because it resolves the tension between the theological and the psychological, rather than maintaining it. She suggests that this route is finally a failure because '[i]n the absence of God, the secular self can do nothing more than seek its own negation and escape from itself.'

When we relate these points to the model espoused by Wimber, we find that there is clearly a huge difference between entertainment culture and a popular Christian paperback book. In the latter, deliverance is not really sensationalised. Obviously Wimber discusses strange behaviour but this is done not to make the account horrifying. If anything the account attempts to 'normalise' the practice of deliverance, as part of the everyday life of a Christian, who might be asked to help his or her church leader engage in such activity. It is certainly not considered humorous in any sense. Wimber, no doubt would have concurred with Huskinson's third point, even if he might not have agreed with every aspect of the argument. He opposed the scientific *Zeitgeist* of the age and would have strenuously resisted any reductionist accounts. Nevertheless, the problem that is posed by Huskinson's contribution is the extent to which Wimber's model does represent, if you like, the anxiety of the Charismatic Evangelical church in the contemporary western world. To what extent does Wimber's approach to demonology and deliverance reflect this attitude as well as eschatological hope in the ministry of Jesus Christ? This is a question worth pondering.

## Theological reflection on the case study

Theology is mediated through a variety of different sub-disciplines, as illustrated by the chapters in this book. I shall select the most relevant features as they have been described in the essays in Biblical Studies, early Christian history, twentieth century Christianity, majority world Pentecostalism and a non-ontological realist account of demonology.

### Biblical studies and early church history

Wonsuk Ma reminds us that in the Old Testament the 'existence of good and evil . . . is under God's absolute control.' In the later period, Yahweh is portrayed as exclusively good, with the antagonist, Satan, appearing as a figure within Yahweh's overall sovereignty. This means that a full-blown dualism is missing from the Old Testament. The understanding that 'exorcism' is an expulsion of an evil spirit from a person appears not to be unequivocally represented in the material. This stands in contrast to the New Testament material.

Graham Twelftree's chapter gives an overview of deliverance and exorcism in the New Testament and argues that Jesus's ministry dominates the material on this theme because he is seen to be 'extraordinarily prolific and successful'. Jesus identifies himself with the power of God's Spirit and, rather than using incantations as other charismatic exorcists would have done, he simply orders the demons to depart. To understand the nature of deliverance in the New Testament, and especially in the gospels, one has to appreciate that exorcism is understood as a major assault on the kingdom of Satan and is a signifier of the arrival of the kingdom of God in and through the person of the Messiah, the anointed one of God: Jesus Christ. Thus Satan and demons are personified by the New Testament writers, even as there are differences of emphasis between them. For Mark, exorcism is of high importance, while for Luke it is part of a balance between word and deed against those oppressed by Satan, where healing and deliverance are not always easily distinguished. For the Johannine tradition the power of Satan is over those who do not believe but who are liberated as they embrace the salvation that Jesus brings. Paul assumes that Christians are in the Spirit and are freed from 'principalities and powers' through salvation in Christ. Even if there is still a battle to fight, they are no longer prisoners but are liberated through the cross of Christ (Col. 1:13–14; 2:15). Exorcism, although not a dominant theme in Paul, is illustrated in Acts, when Paul himself engages in deliverance ministry by speaking a word of dismissal to a demonic presence in a person (Acts 16:17). Indeed, Kabiro Wa Gatumu suggests that in the Pauline epistles there is a move away from *possession* to *oppression* of people by evil spirits.

Andrew Daunton-Fear's contribution builds nicely on the New Testament survey of Twelftree and key themes are repeated in the pre-Nicene and post-Nicene church. Importantly, the conversion of individuals is seen as the key means of delivering them from the influence of the demonic (and thus resonates with Paul), even if a lapse in discipleship can mean a new exposure to demonic influence (Tertullian). Again, exorcism in the name of Jesus Christ is the dominant method, repeated as necessary, and sometimes accompanied by credal statements (Justin, Origen), or the laying on of hands, or breathing upon the person

(Tertullian, Origen), or making the sign of the cross (Lactantius), or anointing with oil (Pachomius), or with water (Macarius), or simply protracted prayer (Palladius). Later church Fathers also believed that the use of holy relics had power to deliver the demonized (Augustine).

Twelftree's account is helpful in understanding how Wimber interprets the New Testament material. Wimber, as a popular preacher and writer, does not take a nuanced scholarly approach that distinguishes between the gospel writers, Paul, and other New Testament writers. Instead he blends material together thematically. He is also unfamiliar with the historical socio-religious context that would enable us to locate Jesus's praxis in the charismatic healer paradigm. However, he has correctly understood the New Testament dualism between the kingdom of God and the kingdom of Satan and placed his deliverance praxis within this framework. It becomes clear from Twelftree's description that Wimber would best fit into the Markan paradigm, giving healing and exorcism the highest priority. This becomes apparent when Wimber describes his practical steps for deliverance, matching a conflated Markan model step by step. Paul's perspective of seeing Christians as delivered from the domain of Satan by virtue of their salvation in Christ would, however, raise some questions against their potential demonization post-conversion. But as Daunton-Fear's contribution makes clear, the early church, while emphasising the power of conversion as deliverance, also noted the possibility of Christians being affected post-conversion if their discipleship lapsed. Wimber's understanding, therefore, resonates with this latter tradition. Luke's blurring, according to Twelftree, of the difference between healing and deliverance raises a question about their relationship, which is also noted by Wimber, and suggests that it is not always the case that a neat distinction can be made. Thus, in sum, it can be said that Wimber largely follows Mark, even if other New Testament influences can still be seen.

### *Twentieth century western Christianity and Majority World Pentecostalism*

James Collins offers a brief survey of twentieth century Christianity and covers Pentecostalism and the Charismatic Renewal as key movements through which deliverance ministry was brought to the attention of the church public. He notes the connection between healing and deliverance, the prevalent theological dualism, the high view of the spiritual protection that Spirit Baptism affords, and the discussion as to whether Christians could be influenced by the demonic (possessed or demonized). He observes how in the ministries of celebrated healing evangelists that deliverance took centre stage (e.g. A.A. Allen) and became a central feature of their work.[20] By legitimation through parachurch organisations, such as the Full Gospel Business Men's Fellowship International, deliverance became accepted in the emerging Charismatic Renewal, even as it had been part of classical Pentecostalism. It is here that we reach the work of John Wimber himself, the originator of the Third Wave movement.

Collins acknowledges that deliverance is one component in Wimber's theology, which is located in the 'power encounter' between the kingdom of God and the kingdom of Satan, and that Christ evicts demons. He asserts that Wimber did not prescribe a methodology. If he means by this an elaborate methodology, then I might agree. However, as Twelfree has described the New Testament material, it has become clear that Wimber bases his deliverance steps largely on Mark's gospel, and in this sense he could be said to have a methodology, that is, a procedure. Collins also notes that it is regarded as an 'essential element of church life', with which, no doubt, Wimber would agree; and I would add that Wimber would have also seen it as 'normal' not 'abnormal', and in this sense the routinization that Collins observes is correct. The use of Martyn Percy's critique, that Wimber's focus on the conflict with Satan means that he has a 'scapegoat for failure',[21] is perhaps an overstatement. This is because Wimber acknowledges that God might have purposes in suffering, all of which cannot be attributed solely to Satan (see his third basic premise).

Allan Anderson complements the survey of Collins by extending the discussion to Pentecostalism in the non-western world. He argues that in this context the ideas of the devil and demons are closely related to a shared worldview in which spirits predominate, a so-called 'enchanted universe', that is at odds with the western rationalistic worldview. In this form of Christianity, there is a very close affinity with the New Testament worldview, which provides the basis for the assumption regarding the ontological reality of Satan and demons. He observes how the language used to describe the influence of the demonic is varied (possession, oppression, demonization). Nevertheless, what is important for the movement is that, whatever it is called, the suffering

---

[20] Collins notes the well-known designation 'paranoid universe' for such demonic preoccupations, coined by Andrew Walker, 'The Devil You Think You Know: Demonology and the Charismatic Movement', in Tom Smail, Andrew Walker and Nigel Wright (eds.), *Charismatic Renewal: The Search for a Theology* (London: SPCK, 1993), 88–105, esp. 88.

[21] Martyn Percy, *Words, Wonders and Power* (London: SPCK, 1996), 55.

person is 'delivered' from demonic influence and set free, often through confrontational 'power encounters'. Ultimately the transformation of the person involves conversion to Christ as the means by which he or she is protected against malevolent spirits. In this ministry Pentecostals believe themselves to be acting in continuity with the New Testament ministry of Jesus and the apostles. This connection between the spirit world and the demonic is traced throughout Latin America, Africa, and Asia, although some local and contextual differences in Pentecostal deliverance methods are noted. There is a translation from existing spirit concepts and notional hierarchies, including the role of the ancestors, into biblical ones with some degree of carry-over from the indigenous meaning into the biblical concepts. But this high degree of connection in worldviews means that the Bible becomes utterly relevant to the church's life and message and provides a narrative from which to understand and participate in the deliverance ministry of the movement.

This is where John Wimber has much in common with global Pentecostalism. It is not so much to do with particular practices of deliverance because these vary across time and place; although, given the role of the Bible in the formation of practices, one would expect the influence of Mark's gospel and Paul's action in Acts 16:17 to be significant. Rather it has to do with the set of assumptions about the way the world is, what the problem is, and what the solution is, which are answers to worldview questions, and upon which there is a high degree of agreement. In the non-western world, the domain of evil spirits or demons is regarded as ontologically real and therefore any theology that aims to be inculturated will need to address this dimension at a primary rather than a secondary level. Wimber's theology does this and is similarly supported by the worldview of global Pentecostalism without necessarily realising that such a significant ally exists.

### Non-ontological realist theology

The chapter by Nigel Wright offers a critical theological reflection on the nature of evil, Satan, and demons, in the light of which suggestions for how evil is combatted are made. Wright argues for a non-ontological realist analysis of the devil and demons and advances a reading of Scripture that is allegedly consistent with this construct. He is especially concerned for those Christians who have been caught up in paranoia and overindulgence in these matters. Thus he argues that a personal designation for Satan and demons is inappropriate (even though Jesus used this language without embarrassment) and that they lack a place and any validity in the created order. He regards the attempt to locate the origin of evil in an angelic fall as sufficiently problematic, in terms of the intepretation of Scripture, as to cast doubt on the traditional Christian doctrine.[22] Therefore, he offers both a demythologising and a remythologising interpretation supported by various theological greats.

In his proposal evil is Nothingness, *das Nichtige* (Barth), or *privatio boni* (Augustine), which nevertheless has a dynamic negative character. But this is not a simple reductionist account (although it certainly contains some reductionism). It is a remythologisation using the theological speculations of Barth's (evil as God's 'No') and Moltmann (evil as *nihil* outside of God), the psychological constructs of Wink (evil as an expression of corporate interiority or human psyche) and Niebuhr (coporate anxiety or neurosis), as well as the odd scientific metaphor (black hole). It appears to be based on a classic dualism of form and substance: that is, evil has forms (devil and demons), but ultimately lacks proper substance, existing in a unique and peculiar manner (the reality of Nothingness). Using a particular ontology of personhood derived from Boethius ('individual substance of rational nature'), Satan is allowed to possess agency and intelligence for destruction but Wright sees this as less than full personhood, hence it is non-ontological. Therefore, Satan is a mythic projection, reflecting human destructive capacity, thereby expressing malevolence, intelligence, will, action and knowledge, even if other positive attributes are lacking (e.g., feeling and sympathy). Wright acknowledges that this proposal might be understood as wanting to have its cake and eat it: giving away demonic 'personhood' (defined in terms of *imago dei*) and ontology with one hand, whilst taking it back with the other (by use of Boethius' definition of 'personhood'). Perhaps we might call it a kind of ontologically non-ontological realism (which sounds more like Barth than Barth!).

So what does this mean for the practice of deliverance? On Wright's account, because evil is still real, exorcisms can still be applied in Christian ministry, although psychiatry can also be applied and perhaps should be dominant. However, the negative impact of social

---

[22] Interestingly, Walker's proposal, although somewhat similar in many respects to Wright, is more sympathetic to the traditional Christian interpretation of Scripture, see 'The Devil You Think You Know', esp. 96–99.

groups need to be analysed as having potential for victimisation and thereby expressing evil, and the healing work of Christ should be seen as appropriated through the usual means of grace (prayer, Scripture, sacraments, and fellowship). The gospels can still be interpreted as describing deliverance in the name of Jesus, but this proposal 'calls for more critical distance in the process and an unwillingness to draw too firm conclusions about what has been expelled'. So how can we relate this account to the Wimber model?

Clearly Wimber assumes the more traditional view of the origin of evil, the belief in a personal ontology of Satan and demons, and is far from embarrassed that Jesus Christ appears to have bought into the 'mythology' of his time. Had Wimber been alive today, no doubt, he would have rejected Wright's proposal as a modern western reductionist account, embarrassed by both the words and actions of Jesus in the gospels and by his fellow Christians who take the Markan model seriously today. Wright would appear to follow a more Pauline model, if we can say that, in terms of seeing deliverance as secondary to life in Christ as mediated by the church's means of grace (though I very much doubt that Paul would have been a non-ontological realist). Once again, we must mention the issue of worldview, which clearly influences the outcome of these kinds of discussions. Nevertheless, at the end of the day, one could adapt the Wimber model of deliverance to fit Wright's demonology. Two modifications would be most apparent: (1) a recognition that the conversation with the demon is more of a reflection of the evil in the person than outside of the person; and (2) a reservation in the personalisation of and the speculation about Satan and demons. However, for many Pentecostal and Charismatic Christians embedded in the Markan model, this adjustment would seem both false and unnecessary.

Alternatively, perhaps Wa Gatumu's contribution offers a middle way between Wright and Wimber. He makes the interesting suggestion that a metaphorical, rather than a mythical, interpretation of the demonic is a possible way foward. This is because metaphors are referential if ambiguous, thus realist, and yet non-literal thereby allowing something of the mystery of evil to be preserved. He suggests that the demonic be understood in terms of irreducible metaphorical language, requiring other metaphors to be used in order to describe the reality of evil but in an *indirect* manner. This fits with his preference for understanding demonic influence as *oppression*, with which he would part company with Wimber if not Wright. His suggestion that not everyone should be encouraged to engage in the ministry of deliverance and that it should be done in the context of a team, including mental health practitioners, appears sound advice.

## Conclusion

In the light of the above discussion, I shall conclude with four brief recommendations for renewed theological praxis in relation to the Wimber case study.

First, it would be useful to have a more rounded theological construct. It is understandable that Wimber based his approach on Mark (even if he has read Mark through other parallel gospel accounts), but the wider New Testament tradition would suggest that other emphases are possible as shown by Twelftree's chapter. The Vineyard and Third Wave movements would do well to integrate the insights from specialist New Testament discussions by Twelftree and others into their theology.[23] The effect might be to present a modified theoretical model to inform their deliverance practices.

Second, although Wimber mentions the issue of mental health, he does not really deal with the matter in sufficient depth and this is a central weakness of the model. The insights of psychology suggest that there are real concerns about the relationship between mental health and demonization that require a multi-disciplinary approach that is non-reductive. Therefore teams should include, as a matter of good practice, specialists in mental health care, who are also Christians and are able to use the spiritual gift of discernment as well as medical expertise.[24]

Third, Wimber does put the care of the individual person at the centre of his model and this feature should be commended. I would recommend building on this feature so that the pastoral care offered to an individual post-deliverance should be of the highest possible standard. This would ensure that, should further problems arise, there are the necessary support structures in place for the person concerned, so that they not only cope but flourish.

---

[23] See Graham H. Twelftree, *In the Name of Jesus: Exorcism among Early Christians* (Grand Rapids: Baker Academic, 2007); and John Christopher Thomas, *The Devil, Disease and Deliverance: Origins of Illness in New Testament Thought* (Sheffield: Sheffield Academic Press, 1998).

[24] This is similar to the recommendation made to the Church of England, see *A Time to Heal: A Report for the House of Bishops on the Healing Ministry* (London: Church House Publishing, 2000), 167–81.

Fourth, it has become clear from my analysis that there are real cultural differences between western and non-western expressions of Christianity (and perhaps between rationalist and experientialist ones), with Wimber and Charismatic Christianity being aligned with non-western worldviews. This must be a serious consideration for those engaged in pastoral practice in cross-cultural contexts. Ideally, teams should contain cultural diversity wherever it is likely that there will be individuals seeking this ministry for themselves and others from predominately non-western contexts.

# Index